Konrad Jünemann

Confidential Data-Outsourcing and Self-Optimizing P2P-Networks: Coping with the Challenges of Multi-Party Systems

Confidential Data-Outsourcing and Self-Optimizing P2P-Networks: Coping with the Challenges of Multi-Party Systems

by

Konrad Jünemann

KIT Scientific Publishing

Dissertation, Karlsruher Institut für Technologie (KIT)
Fakultät für Informatik, 2014

Tag der mündlichen Prüfung: 01. Dezember 2014
Referenten: Prof. Dr. rer. nat. Hannes Hartenstein
Prof. Dr. rer. nat. Ralf Reussner

Impressum

KIT Scientific Publishing

Karlsruher Institut für Technologie (KIT)
KIT Scientific Publishing
Straße am Forum 2
D-76131 Karlsruhe

KIT Scientific Publishing is a registered trademark of Karlsruhe Institute of Technology. Reprint using the book cover is not allowed.

www.ksp.kit.edu

Print on Demand 2015

ISBN 978-3-7315-0328-6
DOI 10.5445/KSP/1000045068

Confidential Data-Outsourcing and Self-Optimizing P2P-Networks:

Coping with the Challenges of Multi-Party Systems

zur Erlangung des akademischen Grades eines

Doktors der Ingenieurwissenschaften

von der Fakultät für Informatik
des Karlsruher Instituts für Technologie (KIT)

genehmigte

Dissertation

von

Konrad Jünemann

aus Wilhelmshaven

Tag der mündlichen Prüfung: 01. Dezember 2014

Erster Gutachter: Prof. Dr. rer. nat. Hannes Hartenstein
Karlsruhe Institute of Technology (KIT)

Zweiter Gutachter: Prof. Dr. rer. nat. Ralf Reussner
Karlsruhe Institute of Technology (KIT)

Zusammenfassung

Ein *Mehr-Parteien-System* ist ein verteiltes System in dem nicht alle Komponenten von derselben, sondern von mehreren verschiedenen Parteien kontrolliert werden, zum Beispiel von privaten Unternehmen oder Einzelanwendern. Mit der rasant gestiegenen Popularität des Cloud Computing Paradigmas werden heute viele wenn nicht sogar die meisten großen IT-Systeme als Mehr-Parteien-System entworfen. So ermöglicht etwa das Anmieten von Diensten sowie Rechen- und Speicherplatzkapazitäten nicht nur Kosten zu sparen, sondern es lässt sich gleichzeitig auch die Skalierbarkeit eines Systems erhöhen und der Betrieb vereinfachen. Im Ergebnis sind Firmen oft dazu gezwungen ihre IT auszulagern um kompetitiv zu bleiben. Auch komplett dezentralisierte Mehr-Parteien-Systeme beginnen mit Veröffentlichung von mehr und mehr kommerziellen Peer-to-Peer (P2P)-basierten Anwendungen ihre durchs File-Sharing getriebene Vergangenheit hinter sich zu lassen.

Trotz ihrer vielen Stärken werden Mehr-Parteien-Systeme von einer Vielzahl von Problemen betroffen die letztlich durch das Fehlen von *Kontrolle* und *Vertrauen* gegenüber einzelnen Komponenten hervorgerufen werden. Oft wiegen diese Probleme so schwer, dass sie beseitigt werden *müssen* um die inhärenten Vorteile der Mehr-Parteien-Systeme in Anspruch nehmen zu können. Deshalb ist es wesentlich zu verstehen, wie diesen Problemen begegnet werden kann. In dieser Arbeit beantworten wir diese Frage für zwei Klassen von Mehr-Parteien-Systemen.

Der erste Teil dieser Arbeit behandelt das „Database-as-a-Service" Szenario. Hierbei soll eine Datenbank, die vertrauliche Informationen enthält, zu einem externen, nicht komplett vertrauenswürdigen IT-Dienstleister ausgelagert werden. Dabei soll zum einen die Vertraulichkeit der ausgelagerten Daten gewährt bleiben, zum anderen soll dem Dienstleister aber auch ermöglicht werden, Anfragen über die Daten auszuwerten, also z.B. nach einem bestimmten Datensatz zu suchen. Hierfür wird der Ansatz *Securus* vorgestellt. Securus garantiert dem Nutzer ein bestimmtes Vertraulichkeitsniveau, das einem vom Nutzer in der domänenspezifischen Sprache Securus-Latin erstellten Profil von *Vertraulichkeits-* und *Zugriffanforderungen* entspricht. Hierfür wählt und verknüpft Securus einen passenden Satz von *Sicherheitsmechanismen*. Das hierfür zugrunde liegende Optimierungsproblem wird gelöst, indem es in ein ganzzahliges lineares Optimierungsproblem (engl.: Integer Linear Programming, ILP) transformiert wird. Dadurch, dass der Anwender die schlussendlich eingesetzten Sicherheitsmechanismen nicht kennen oder gar verstehen muss, gelingt es Securus, Sicherheitswissen zu externalisieren und auch für Domänen- anstatt Sicherheitsexperten anwendbar zu machen.

Der zweite Teil dieser Arbeit behandelt öffentliche Verteilte Hashtabellen (engl.: Distributed Hash Tables, DHTs). Eine DHT ist ein P2P-Netzwerk, das es erlaubt, Schlüssel/Wert-Paare zu speichern und wieder abzurufen. DHTs haben sich in letzter Zeit als attraktive Plattform für komplett dezentralisierte Systeme etabliert. Allerdings stehen Peers öffentlicher DHTs nicht unter zentraler Kontrolle und sind daher überaus unzuverlässig. Diese Unzuverlässigkeit hat das Potential, das Leistungsniveau der DHT empfindlich herabzusetzen. Der Fokus des zweiten Teils dieser Arbeit liegt deshalb darauf, dieses Problem zu charakterisieren und Gegenmaßnahmen zu entwickeln. In einem ersten Schritt wird hierfür der Aufbau und die Leistung der teilnehmerstärksten öffentlichen DHT – der BitTorrent Mainline DHT (MDHT) – im Detail analysiert. Insbesondere wird dabei auch die *Lookup* Operation betrachtet, die die wichtigste Funktionalität einer jeden DHT darstellt. Die Analyse beruht zu einem großen Teil auf einer mehr als vier Jahre umfassenden Messstudie. Als Kernergebnis ergab diese Studie insbesondere, dass die MDHT im Hinblick auf ihre Zusammensetzung nicht nur einer langsam aber kontinuierlich voranschreitenden Evolution, sondern auch drastischen, plötzlich auftretenden Veränderungen unterliegt, die auch von scheinbar unbedeutenden Problemen hervorgerufen werden können, wie zum Beispiel der Nichtverfügbarkeit eines einzelnen Servers. Mit Bezug auf diese Erkenntnis wird KadSim vorgestellt, ein Simulationsmodell der MDHT. Das Modell erlaubt es Entwicklern von dezentralisierten Anwendungen genauer zu untersuchen, welchen Einfluss Veränderungen innerhalb einer DHT auf die Leistung ihrer Anwendung haben könnten. Hierfür ermöglicht KadSim es, die MDHT in ihrer Gesamtheit von mehreren Millionen Peers zu simulieren. In einer Validierung konnte KadSim die Leistung von zwölf getesteten Lookup Algorithmen mit überzeugender Genauigkeit vorhersagen. Zuletzt wird ein Ansatz namens *Simulation-based Runtime Adaptation* (SRA) vorgestellt der es ermöglicht, auch auf unvorhergesehene, plötzlich auftretende Veränderungen in einer DHT adäquat reagieren zu können. Hierfür wird die Leistung einer großen Anzahl alternativer Konfigurationen des verwendeten Lookup Algorithmus in einem vollfaktoriellen Versuchsaufbau dynamisch zur Laufzeit gemessen und verglichen. Der durch diese Messungen hervorgerufene Mehraufwand konnte durch das Aufzeichnen und wiederholte „Abspielen" von mehrfach gleichartig initiierten Anfragen in einer Simulationsumgebung wesentlich reduziert werden. Eine abschließende Evaluation bestätigt die hohe Effektivität und Effizienz des Ansatzes.

Abstract

A *Multi-Party System* is a distributed system in which not all components are controlled by the same party. Instead, multiple independent parties are involved, such as private companies or individual persons. With the advent of the cloud computing paradigm, today many, if not most large-scale IT systems are designed as Multi-Party Systems. For instance, renting storage, computing capacity, or services allows to reduce costs, to increase scalability, or to make the system easier to manage. As a result, a company often has to outsource their IT in order to stay competitive. With the recent publication of more and more commercial Peer-to-Peer (P2P) based applications, fully decentralized Multi-Party Systems are furthermore starting to leave their "piracy-driven" past behind. Despite their great advantages, Multi-Party Systems are plagued by issues caused by the lack of *trust* and *control* over individual components. Often, these issues *have* to be resolved in order to leverage the inherent strengths of Multi-Party Systems. It is thus essential to understand how one can cope with the lack of trust and control in Multi-Party Systems. In this thesis, we cover this question for two classes of Multi-Party Systems.

The first part of this thesis covers a Database-as-a-Service scenario in which a database containing sensitive information should be outsourced to a not fully trusted storage provider while not only protecting data confidentiality but also allowing the storage provider to evaluate queries. To tackle this problem, the Securus approach is presented. Securus is able to provide hard confidentiality guarantees that match a profile of *confidentiality* and *access requirements* defined by the user in the domain specific language Securus-Latin. Securus satisfies this profile by selecting and combining a set of security mechanisms. To solve this optimization problem, it is transformed into an Integer Linear Programming (ILP) instance. As the user is not required to understand any of the eventually employed security mechanisms, Securus externalizes security knowledge and makes it applicable by non-security experts.

The second part of this thesis covers public Distributed Hash Tables (DHTs). A DHT is a P2P network that allows to store and retrieve key/value pairs. Recently, public DHTs have established themselves as attractive platforms for fully decentralized applications. However, as public peers are not centrally controlled they are notoriously unreliable and have the potential to severely affect the DHT's performance. The second part of this thesis focuses on characterizing and dealing with this problem. In a first step, an in-depth characterization of the largest public DHT, the BitTorrent Mainline DHT (MDHT) is provided, including an analysis of the DHT's key operation, the lookup. Our characterization is based on a long-term measurement study covering more than four years. As key findings we not only identify that most properties of the MDHT slowly change over time but also that the MDHT is subject to sudden, drastic shifts that can be caused by seemingly insignificant problems, such as the unavailability of a single server. In order to allow developers of decentralized applications to better assess the impact of changing DHT characteristics on their application's performance, we developed KadSim, a simulation model of the MDHT. KadSim is capable of simulating the MDHT in its entirety. In our validation, the performance of twelve tested lookup algorithm variants could be predicted with sound accuracy. In order to also allow clients to cope better with unforeseeable sudden shifts in the DHT, an approach called Simulation-based Runtime Adaptation (SRA) is presented. It optimizes lookup performance dynamically by measuring the performance of a large number of alternative lookup algorithm configurations directly at run-time, using a full-factorial experimental design. The overhead of the approach has been reduced drastically by "replaying" repeatedly initiated requests in a simulation environment. Our evaluation confirms that the approach is not only very effective but also comes at low costs.

Contents

List of Figures

List of Tables

1 Introduction

Today, basically all large IT systems are designed as *distributed systems*, i.e., they are composed of components[1] that communicate with each other by exchanging messages. Systems in which the system's components are not all operated and controlled by the same but by multiple independent parties such as, for instance, private companies, institutions, or even individual persons, constitute a subclass of distributed systems. In this thesis, we will refer to such systems as *Multi-Party Systems* (MPS).

In the form of the cloud computing paradigm, Multi-Party Systems have become a dictating topic not only for researchers and developers, but also for whole sectors of the IT industry. The reasons for this phenomenon are manifold: for instance, the "as-a-service" paradigm allows developers to rent storage, computing capacity, IT services, or entire application platforms on demand directly from specialized IT companies. This permits the developer to deploy and publish applications at reduced costs and without being concerned about how to operate an entire IT infrastructure that has to provide a high quality of service while also being resilient to external hazards and attacks. By leveraging economies of scale, specialization allows to decrease costs and improve overall quality of service. Service *elasticity* furthermore allows to drastically increase the throughput of rented services on demand, for example, in order to cope with peaks of incoming orders or in order to accelerate a specific task. As a result, companies often have no choice but to source out their IT, if they want to stay competitive.

Recently, it has also become more and more apparent that fully decentralized systems are starting to leave their "piracy-driven" past behind and mature at an increasing pace. This trend is witnessed by the recent publication of commercial Peer-to-Peer

[1] In [TVS07], Tanenbaum defines distributed systems to be composed of *computers*. However, in this thesis we will use the notion of (deployed) components.

(P2P)-based services such as the video streaming application *Tribler* [ZCBP11], the file synchronization service *BitTorrent Sync* [FSK14] (which already had 2 million registered users in December 2013), or the decentralized chat and voice over IP client *Bleep* [2]. With multiple millions of autonomic peers, public P2P networks constitute an extreme example for highly distributed Multi-Party Systems that allow to build and publish services at low costs.

However, the cooperation among multiple parties also introduces new challenges, typically caused by the (partial) lack of *control* or *trust* [AFG+10]. For instance, parties typically lack control over externally operated components but nevertheless depend on their reliability, robustness and performance. They hence either have to be able to predict the behavior of these components accurately or they have to be able to cope with fluctuations. This problem is especially apparent in public P2P networks, as it is typically impossible to control a peer's up-time, the technical infrastructure it is deployed on, or to predict its future behavior precisely. These uncertainties can easily affect the overall quality of service provided by the network.

Furthermore, individual parties involved in a Multi-Party System often trust each other only partially [GMR+12]. While they are likely to possess some level of trust (if not, they would most probably not be part of the Multi-Party System), they might not rule out the possibility that another party might try to seek a personal advantage. For instance, a customer might not trust the provider of a service not to analyze sensitive data for personal gain when receiving data from the customer for further processing. In this case data confidentiality would be at risk.

In many scenarios, these challenges lead to key issues that *have* to be resolved before an MPS-based architecture can even be considered viable. They thus constitute a barrier for harnessing the inherent strengths of Multi-Party Systems. For instance, if a company has to process sensitive data, outsourcing the data to an external storage provider might be out of discussion unless data confidentiality can be preserved reliably. Analogously, public P2P networks might not constitute a suitable platform for building a specific decentralized application unless their reliability and performance meet the application's demand.

We thus state the motivational question of this thesis as follows:

> *How can one deal with key challenges in Multi-Party Systems in order to leverage the inherent strengths of this class of systems?*

1.1 Objective

This thesis tries to answer the motivational question for two classes of Multi-Party Systems that are currently in the focus of both academic research and commercial applications: data outsourcing solutions following the *Database-as-a-Service (DaaS)* paradigm and public *Distributed Hash Tables (DHTs)*.

[2] http://blog.bittorrent.com/2014/07/30/bittorrents-chat-client-unveiled-bittorrent-bleep-now-in-invite-only-pre-alpha/, [last visited in October 2014]

Database-as-a-Service: The first part of this thesis targets the DaaS scenario. In a *DaaS* scenario, a database is outsourced to an external *storage provider*. The storage provider then accepts queries from its customer, evaluates them, and returns the results. The storage provider thus provides the service of hosting the database. With the advent of the cloud computing paradigm, DaaS solutions have become increasingly attractive, especially for companies that have to process a high amount of data but are not IT specialists themselves.

Often, the key issue in this scenario is that the confidentiality of the outsourced data has to be protected, because the storage provider is not considered trustworthy. While the customer might trust the storage provider not to sabotage its customers directly by tampering with the stored data, she might not trust the storage provider not to be "curious", i.e., try to extract information. This distrust could be caused by a number of reasons. For example, the storage provider could possess an economic interest in the stored data. The customer could also fear that the storage provider could be compromised by an external attacker. Lastly, the customer could simply be required by law to protect her data by technical means, because the data contains personally identifiable information, for instance, in an eHealth or eTraffic scenario.

A naïve approach to protect data confidentiality is to encrypt the entire database. Unfortunately, this approach would make it impossible for the storage provider to efficiently process incoming queries. Security techniques such as encryption thus have to be applied in a more efficient way. This is not a trivial task as any solution has to satisfy the customer's demands in terms of how she wants to access the outsourced data (*access requirements*) and in terms of the envisioned protection level (*confidentiality requirements*). We thus state the first research question of this thesis as follows:

> *How can confidential databases be sourced out to honest-but-curious storage providers while providing hard confidentiality guarantees?*

Public DHTs: The second part of this thesis targets public DHTs. A DHT is a P2P network that allows to store and retrieve key/value pairs. In *public* DHTs, peers are controlled by individual persons rather than by a company as it is the case for *private* DHTs such as employed by Amazon Dynamo [DHJ+07]. As a result, public DHTs are much harder to manage and maintain than private DHTs. Today, the most widely used public DHT, the BitTorrent Mainline DHT (MDHT), consists of millions of peers that participate at any time [JAH11]. While most public DHTs were formed in support of file-sharing applications, recently more and more commercial applications start to arise that provide DHT-based services outside the file-sharing scenario. For example, the services *Tribler*, *BitTorrent Sync*, and *Bleep* all leverage the MDHT.

However, this new class of DHT-based applications demands a far higher quality of service than file-sharing applications, as many applications are more sensitive to delays and the DHT typically has to be accessed more frequently. We thus state the second research question of this thesis as follows:

> *How can public DHTs provide the ongoing and reliable quality of service modern DHT-based applications demand?*

1.2 Contributions

In particular, this thesis presents the following contributions:

- **Confidential DaaS Approach**: This thesis presents a confidential DaaS approach called *Securus* that allows to satisfy hard confidentiality requirements of sensitive data while still permitting the storage provider to evaluate received queries. In order to do so, Securus combines various popular security techniques so that they satisfy individual *confidentiality* and *access requirements* specified by the user. Among others, Securus advances the research field in the following ways:
  - The user does not have to possess any cryptographic expert knowledge. This makes it possible for domain rather than security experts to maintain hard confidentiality requirements when outsourcing data.
  - Securus contains a meta model that allows to define access and confidentiality requirements while remaining cryptography-agnostic and still being specific enough to allow Securus to chose trade-offs appropriately.
  - Scenario-specific outsourcing solutions are generated by formulating the constraints between the confidentiality and access requirements as an Integer Linear Programming (ILP) problem. This way, a formal model of the underlying optimization problem exists which is furthermore easy to extend.
- **In-depth Characterization of the MDTH**: This thesis provides an in-depth analysis and understanding of the key operation of any DHT, the *lookup*. Besides presenting popular lookup algorithm variants and identifying important performance inhibitors, the thesis provides the tools required to further assess the performance of individual clients. Furthermore, results of a long-term measurement study of the MDHT, the most widely deployed public DHT, are presented. The measurements have been running continuously since August 2010 and are still ongoing. The results allow to characterize the MDTH with respect to various properties that may impair the DHT's overall performance. Among others, the number of participating peers, the peers' origin, the peers' session lengths, and the prevalence of NAT gateways within the MDHT are analyzed. To our knowledge, this makes our study the longest and most comprehensive study ever conducted on a public DHT. With the help of the collected data we do not only characterize the composition, popularity, long-term evolution, and stability of the MDHT, but are also able to quantify the impact of specific incidents such as natural disasters or the distribution of a malfunctioning DHT client version. In particular, our analysis shows that despite its remarkable stability and popularity in general, the MDHT is also subject to sudden, drastic shifts.
- **Simulation-based Model of a Multi-Million Peer DHT**: Based on the presented measurement results and other studies we built a model of the MDHT

for a discrete-event-based simulator. *KadSim* is designed to assess lookup performance within public DHTs and the impact of fluctuations within the DHT on lookup performance. *KadSim* models the MDHT at its real size of multiple millions of peers and also includes identified performance inhibitors often encountered in public DHTs such as the presence of NAT gateways. Our model is evaluated by predicting the performance of twelve alternative lookup algorithms and comparing key performance metrics to measured results. While this evaluation showed good results in most cases, we also identified cases in which the model is unable to predict lookup performance reliably. In order to further improve prediction quality in the future, possible extensions of our model are presented and discussed.

- **Self-Optimization of Lookup Algorithms**: Our measurement study showed that DHT clients have to cope with both long- and short-term fluctuations of key characteristics of the DHT. This thesis presents an approach that enables DHT clients to adapt dynamically to constantly changing conditions within the DHT. Due to its deployment in public DHTs, the approach is tailored towards being run automatically and unsupervised. It hence has been designed to be able to adapt even to unpredicted changes by making minimal assumptions about the state or behavior of the DHT. In an evaluation, it is shown that the approach is not only very effective at adapting to unforeseen changes but also that the approach comes at marginal costs.

Parts of the contributions presented in this thesis have been previously published in:

- Konrad Jünemann, Hannes Hartenstein; *Self-Optimization of DHT Lookups through Run-Time Performance Analysis*, In: Proceedings of the 2014 International Conference on High Performance Computing & Simulation (HPCS), IEEE, July 2014.
- Jens Köhler, Konrad Jünemann; *Securus: From Confidentiality and Access Requirements to Data Outsourcing Solutions*, In: Hansen, M., Hoepman, J.-H., Leenes, R., Whitehouse, D. (Editors), Privacy and Identity Management for Emerging Services and Technologies, Springer Berlin Heidelberg, pp. 139-149, 2014.
- Konrad Jünemann, Jens Köhler, Hannes Hartenstein; *Data Outsourcing Simplified: Generating Data Connectors from Confidentiality and Access Policies*, In: 12th IEEE/ACM International Symposium on Cluster, Cloud and Grid Computing (CCGrid), May 2012.
- Konrad Jünemann, Philipp Andelfinger, Hannes Hartenstein; *Towards a Basic DHT Service: Analyzing Network Characteristics of a Widely Deployed DHT*, In: Proceedings of the 20th International Conference on Computer Communications and Networks (ICCCN), July 2011.

- Konrad Jünemann, Philipp Andelfinger, Jochen Dinger, Hannes Hartenstein; *BitMON: A Tool for Automated Monitoring of the BitTorrent DHT*, In: Proceedings of the Tenth International Conference on Peer-to-Peer Computing (P2P), IEEE, August 2010.
- Jochen Dinger, Konrad Jünemann, Oliver Waldhorst, Michael Conrad; *Autonome Kommunikationsinfrastrukturen. Eine praxisnahe Betrachtung*, In: Praxis der Informationsverarbeitung und Kommunikation (PIK), K.G. Saur Verlag, Volume 31, Issue 2, pp. 69-75, 2008.

1.3 Thesis Outline

The structure of this thesis is illustrated in Figure 1.1. Following the thesis' introduction, Chapter 2 presents the scope and background of the thesis in greater detail. The chapter starts by presenting a definition of Multi-Party Systems and introducing the two key issues that this thesis is concerned with: the lack of control and trust in Multi-Party Systems. Then, it is demonstrated how these issues affect Multi-Party Systems by discussing exemplary challenges faced in the research projects *iZEUS* and *KAI*.

After Chapter 2, the thesis is split into two parts. The first part covers the Database-as-a-Service (DaaS) scenario under the assumption that the storage provider is not trusted completely. The second part covers public DHTs in their role as building blocks for fully decentralized applications. The focus lies on assessing and improving the DHT's reliability and performance under the challenge of uncontrollable peers.

Part I of this thesis starts with Chapter 3. In the beginning of this chapter, the challenge of ensuring data confidentiality in a DaaS scenario is motivated. The key concept of using confidentiality preserving indexes is identified in this process. Following this motivation, the main research questions that will be answered in the first part of the thesis are stated. The subsequent sections then introduce cryptographic concepts and other confidentiality preserving techniques that build the foundation of any confidential indexing approach.

Chapter 4 presents the main contribution of the first part of this thesis, the *Securus* approach. Securus is confidential DaaS framework that aims at satisfying a user's individual confidentiality and access requirements. It achieves this generating a custom-tailored software adapter for the user that serves as a proxy between the user and the storage provider and satisfies the user's specific requirements. After describing this concept in greater detail, Securus' technical architecture is presented. The remainder of the chapter focuses on the meta-model that is used to specify the user's requirements and on how software adapters can be generated that match such requirements.

Chapter 5 provides a concluding evaluation and discussion of the Securus approach. In particular, Securus' deployability, achieved level of protection, and performance are discussed. Then, future research opportunities are presented before the chapter is concluded.

Part II of this thesis is divided into five chapters and begins with Chapter 6. This chapter first motivates the vision of a public DHT playing the role of a *Basic DHT*

Service that can be used to build a diverse set of completely decentralized applications and shows that this vision has begun to become reality in recent years. It is furthermore motivated that DHTs have to provide a high quality of service reliably in order to constitute a viable foundation for more applications. Today, many characteristics of public DHTs are still poorly understood, in particular when considering their constant evolution.

Chapter 7 presents an in-depth analysis of lookup algorithms and their performance in the BitTorrent Mainline DHT. The chapter introduces the Kademlia protocol, surveys commonly proposed optimizations and motivates the MDHT's significance as an object of study. Furthermore, a unifying definition of lookup algorithms is given before the main inhibitors of lookup performance in public DHTs are introduced and discussed.

In Chapter 8, we assess and quantify the composition of the MDHT and its evolution with respect to the performance inhibitors identified in the previous chapter. The assessment is based on a long-term measurement study that is ongoing for more than 4 years. In particular, our analysis shows that despite its remarkable stability and popularity, the MDHT is subject to sudden, drastic shifts that can severely affect performance-critical properties of the MDHT.

Chapter 9 presents a model of the MDHT that allows to analyze the performance of lookup algorithms under the influence of specific DHT characteristics. After presenting the model in detail, the model is evaluated by comparing its performance predictions for twelve different lookup algorithm variants against measured values. While this evaluation showed good results in most cases, we also identified cases in which the model is unable to predict lookup performance reliably. In order to further improve prediction quality in the future, possible extensions of our model are presented and discussed.

In Chapter 10, an approach is presented that allows DHT clients to optimize the performance of their employed lookup algorithm on demand. This approach works by testing the performance of different configurations of the algorithm at run-time and choosing the configuration that provides the best performance, according to a specific metric. This approach allows DHT clients to cope even with unpredicted fluctuations in the DHT and thus constitutes an option for clients to provide more consistent lookup performance.

Finally, Chapter 11 concludes the two parts of this thesis, provides an unifying interpretation of the results presented so far and discusses directions for further research.

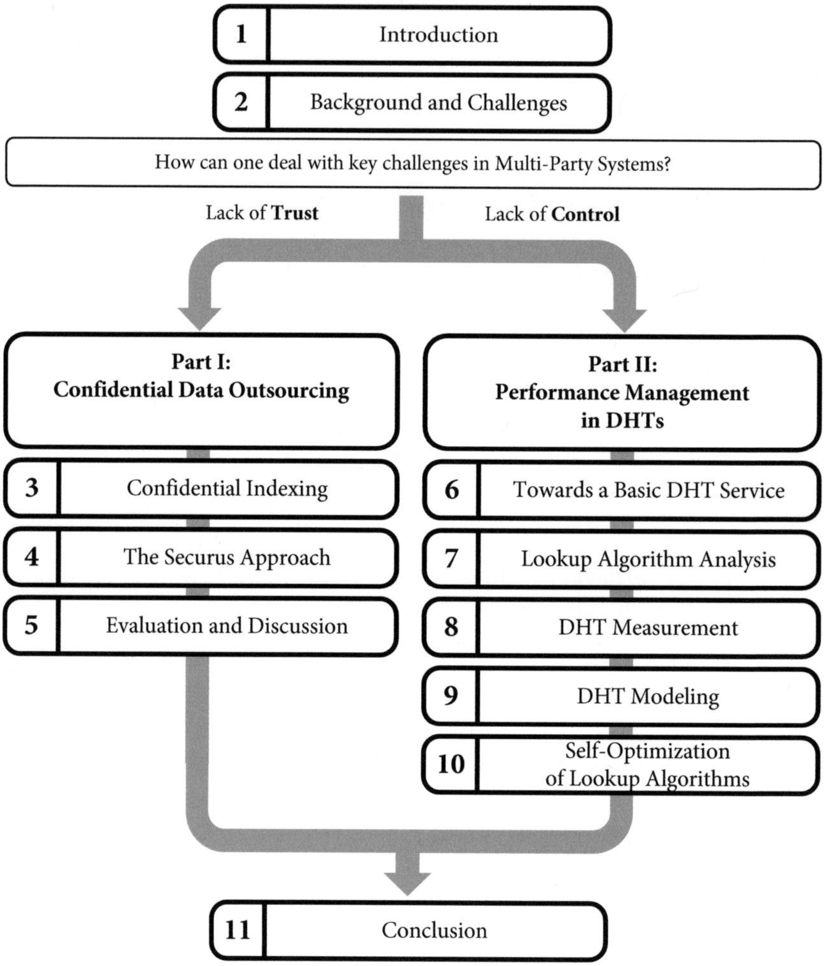

Figure 1.1: Structure of this thesis.

2 Background and Challenges

2.1 Distributed Systems and Multi-Party Systems

In [TVS07, p. 2], Tanenbaum and van Steen define *distributed system* loosely as follows:

Definition 1 (Distributed System [TVS07]) *A distributed system is a collection of independent computers that appears to its users as a single coherent system.*

While the definition is deliberately broad, it covers two important aspects: first that a distributed system is composed of independent components[1] and second that a distributed system acts as a single coherent system, i.e., it offers a cohesive service. In order to act as such a system, the components have to communicate with each other. Distributed systems thus have to employ some means of communication, primarily through computer networks.

The authors furthermore list some of the most important goals that distributed systems usually try to meet. In particular, a distributed system (1) should make remote resources accessible for the user, it should (2) hide specifics about how its components and resources are distributed, it should (3) be open to further extension, e.g., by using standardized interfaces, and it should (4) be scalable. Of course, not all distributed systems meet all of these goals to the same degree, but most cover each aspect at least to some extent.

The list of possible examples for distributed systems is long and diverse, including various grid and cloud computing systems, content delivery networks, sensor networks and other pervasive systems, as well as P2P networks, to name only a few. However,

[1]Although the authors use the term "computer", they later state that they are actually speaking about software components that are deployed on computers.

systems can roughly be categorized with the respect to the type of service they provide. For instance, Tanenbaum and van Steen propose the following three categories:

The first category includes systems that focus on providing access to a distributed set of resources. The emphasis of these systems typically lies on harmonizing the access to the provided resources rather than on locating the resources. Among others, this is achieved by providing a uniform interface to possibly heterogeneous resources, building a federation of resource providers, and handling the data transfer as well as exceptions. Not only raw storage or computing capacity but also IT services can play the role of the managed resource. Typically, goals 1 and 3 are especially important for this kind of systems. Examples include the grid computing sector, systems following the "X-as-a-Service" design, and distributed computing platforms such as BOINC [And04].

The second category includes systems that focus on managing the collaboration between autonomous components rather than on providing access to resources. In these systems, locating single components and routing information are typically complex issues, as components either exhibit a highly dynamic behavior or are not very reliable. Many of these systems are hence highly adaptive, for instance by employing mechanics that allow them to self-organize. Typically, goals 2 and 4 are most important for this category of systems. Examples for this category include P2P networks, sensor networks, and pervasive systems.

A third category is formed by systems that focus on the integration of other typically highly heterogeneous sets of services. These systems are typically designed with the help of frameworks that allow the user to chose from a wide array of services and combine the selected ones easily. Often, additional features are provided such as the support of transactional access or persistence. The emphasize of these systems hence lies on the composition of components. Typically, goal 3 is more important than the others. Examples for this category are common in the enterprise world and include systems based on the Service Oriented Architecture (SOA) model, workflow engines, and other popular middleware frameworks.

Orthogonal to this categorization, distributed systems can be distinguished by whether all components are managed by multiple different autonomous parties. We hence expand Definition 1 by the definition of *Multi-Party Systems*:

Definition 2 (Multi-Party System) *A Multi-Party System (MPS) is a* distributed system *whose components are not all operated by the same but by multiple independent parties. A* party *can be any organizationally independent entity such as a company, institution, or individual person.*

Multi-Party Systems thus present a subclass of distributed systems.

2.2 Issues in Multi-Party Systems

The separation of a system into distributed components leads to a number of unique issues. Among the most important ones are the following:

- The *unreliability* of the network or other components.
- The *untrustworthiness* of the network or other components.
- The *heterogeneity* of the network or other components.
- The *variability* of the network or other components over time.

While these issues may arise in almost every kind of distributed system, they typically are increasingly severe and more likely to appear in systems in which components are operated by multiple different autonomous parties (Multi-Party Systems). In the following, we illustrate the differences by analyzing exemplary pairs of Single- and Multi-Party Systems.

2.2.1 In-House Database vs. Data Outsourcing

As an example for centralized distributed systems, we compare two scenarios: in scenario A, a large company possesses offices in various areas of a country. The offices all have to access a database which is hosted by a central computing center operated by the company. As all components (the terminals located in the local offices and the central database) are operated by the same company, this scenario describes a Single-Party System.

In scenario B, the same company has decided to reduce maintenance costs by outsourcing the central data bases to an external service provider. As now the central database is operated by a different company, this scenario describes a Multi-Party System.

Although the technical architectures are almost identical, in scenario B the company has to cope with additional issues caused by the different trust relationship to the operator of the central computing center:

- The company might not trust the service provider to respect the confidentiality of sensitive data.
- The company is unable to control the security standards of the service provider.
- The company is unable to control how well the service provider maintains the computing center.

For this reasons, the company might want to additionally encrypt its data in scenario B in order to protect its confidentiality. However, encrypting the data might severely impact the system's performance, depending on factors such as the structure of the database. Depending on the quality of service promised by the contract with the service provider and the company's faith in its fulfillment, the company might also want to include additional mechanisms to improve or at least monitor the reliability and performance of the database.

2.2.2 Private vs. Public P2P networks

As a second example, we chose P2P networks. P2P networks constitute an example for massively distributed, decentralized, highly dynamic architectures that mainly fall into the second of our three categories of distributed systems. We compare *private* P2P networks, in which all peers are controlled by a single party (typically a company), to *public* P2P networks, in which peers are dynamically controlled by individual persons. Private P2P networks are commonly used to ease maintenance of highly distributed but centrally administered systems.

While both systems are equally decentralized, massively distributed and self-organized, it is for several reasons far harder to provide a constant quality of service in *public* P2P networks:

- In private P2P networks, peers typically all run the same code while in public P2P networks peers can usually choose from various compatible but different client implementations.
- In public P2P networks, peers typically exhibit a far more dynamic behavior than peers do in private P2P networks.
- In public P2P networks, peers are commonly deployed on unreliable or overloaded hardware.
- In public P2P networks, peers have to be expected to be egoistic, i.e., they might try to contribute as little as possible to the network while seeking a maximal personal benefit at the same time.
- The composition of a public P2P network can change significantly at any time without further notice.

In contrast, centrally maintained private P2P networks typically only have to deal with the occasional failing of individual peers. As a result, private P2P networks have reached maturity several years ago (for instance in Amazon Dynamo [DHJ+07] or Apache Cassandra [LM10]) while commercial applications that are based on public P2P networks have just recently began to arise.

2.3 Challenge

We have seen that Multi-Party Systems are typically more severely affected by classical issues of distributed systems than Single-Party Systems are. These additional issues are mainly caused by the lack of *control* and *trust* over externally operated components:

- Lack of *Control*: In a Multi-Party System, no party has direct control over any component maintained by another party. As a result, it may be way harder to predict how a component behaves and how it is maintained, depending on the relation between the two involved parties. In systems in which contracts provide long-term assurances, such a specific quality of service, components may be expected to be more reliable than in systems in which components enter the system ad hoc, e.g., in public P2P networks or pervasive systems. In a Single-Party System, the operator will typically be in a position to limit the heterogeneity of the components and to judge their reliability and variability over time as she is in control of all components.

- Lack of *Trust*: In a Multi-Party System, components controlled by other parties are typically not considered being as trustworthy as one's own components. For this reason, Multi-Party Systems often have to include security mechanisms to protect either components or the processed data from potentially malicious components. While in a Single-Party System the operator might still have to protect the security of her system from external attackers, she can furthermore typically consider all components being trustworthy.

The question now arises how one can deal with these issues. Unfortunately, no one-fits-all solution exists due to the high diversity of the class of Multi-Party Systems. Instead, systems have to be analyzed on a case by case basis. In this thesis, we will do so for two of the most popular classes of Multi-Party Systems: *trust issues* will be covered in a data outsourcing scenario while *control issues* will be covered in public DHTs, which are a special kind of P2P networks.

When dealing with trust issues, it is first key to understand and model the nature of the trust relations between the involved parties. Often, parties trust each other at least to some extent, i.e., it is reasonable to assume that a party does not take certain kinds of actions. This partial trust can often be leveraged to design a solution that is able to resolve the described issues more efficiently. We demonstrate this general approach with the description of the *iZEUS* project (see Section 2.4) and in Part I of this thesis, beginning in Chapter 3.

In order to deal with control issues, it is analogously very important to understand the behavior of the system's components and to be able to assess their impact on the system's overall performance. In many cases, the component's behavior – though uncontrolled – is either stable or predictable enough to adjust the system appropriately. Furthermore, the impact of the uncontrolled component's behavior on the system's overall performance could be negligible. In these cases, the issues could be resolved with minimal overhead. We demonstrate how distributed systems can be monitored and assessed with the description of the *KAI* project (see Section 2.5) and our measurement study and DHT assessment (see Chapters 7 and 8). We furthermore show how the behavior of a highly decentralized Multi-Party System can be modeled in Chapter 9. If the behavior of certain components cannot be controlled and is too unreliable to be neglected, the system has to be able to cope with unpredicted changes. We present an example of how a system can react even to unpredicted changes of the behavior of other components in Chapter 10.

2.4 Example: the iZEUS Project

The project *iZEUS*[2] aimed to develop and test novel approaches that help to further advance e-Mobility by integrating Smart Traffic with Smart Grid concepts. The project was supported by the German *Bundesministerium für Wirtschaft und Industrie* (BMWi) with almost 20 million Euro and lasted from January 2012 until June 2014. Multiple enterprises from the automotive, IT, and energy sectors participated as project partners. From the KIT, eleven research groups participated. The approach described in the following was developed in collaboration with the research groups for *Knowledge Management*, led by Prof. Studer, and *Software Design and Quality* (SDQ), led by Prof. Reussner.

2.4.1 Project Background and Requirements

One goal of the iZEUS project was to create a market for innovative IT services that target e-Mobility in Germany. For this purpose, a loosely coupled IT *service federation* should be created by developing a *platform* that eases cooperation between services, provides single-sign on functionality, and makes it easy for users to discover new services. In particular, the following requirements were defined for the platform to create:

1. *Data-centric e-Mobility Services:* The platform should target IT services from the e-Mobility sector. This in particular means that services could either be web applications, applications that are deployed on smart devices such as cell phones or cars, or even be run in the background on a server without requiring any user interaction. Services might furthermore *consume* or *produce* user-specific data, i.e., data that contains personally identifiable information. Services should be able to access user-specific data even if the user is currently unavailable. Such a service could for example be used to better control urban traffic by regularly retrieving the current position of a large number of cars and appropriately changing traffic lights. Other examples for personal e-Mobility services include personal routing applications, fuel monitoring and optimization apps, or services that allow customers to reserve parking spots in advance.

2. *Service Integration:* The platform should allow services to consume data produced by other services. E.g., if a certain service stores the energy consumption of the user's car, another service should theoretically be able access this data. We will describe below how data access is authorized.

3. *Registry and User Portal:* The platform should not only serve as a central registration point for services but also as a central service portal for users. The portal should allow users to conveniently browse and deploy available services.

4. *Open Platform:* The platform should be open to new service providers. It should be easy to add new services to the platform. In particular this also requires that

[2] http://www.izeus.de, [last visited in October 2014]

the scheme of the processed data is not fixed but extensible. In other words, it has to be possible for a service to produce data in a previously unknown format.

5. *Privacy Control:* At any time, the user should be able to easily monitor and control who has access to her data. It should be easy and convenient for her to grant services access to her data and revoke any previously granted permissions.

2.4.2 Problem Analysis

The service platform uses a centralized architecture. In the course of the project, all central elements of the platform were operated by the KIT. Connected services on the other hand could not only be deployed on servers provided by the KIT but also on user-controlled mobile devices or on servers run by external companies. The architecture hence describes a Multi-Party System. Figure 2.1 presents an overview over the system's components. Depending on whether we see the e-Mobility user or the service providers as the main user of the system, the system could be categorized in the first or the third category of distributed systems (systems that provide access to resources and systems that integrate services).

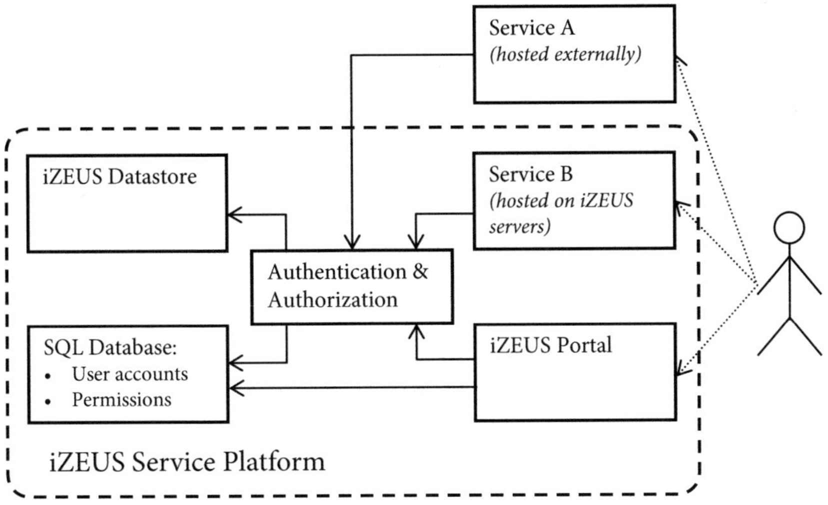

Figure 2.1: Components of the iZEUS service platform.

As a Multi-Party System, the iZEUS platform potentially has to cope with problems caused by the lack of trust or control between individual components. In the following, we will analyze the architecture for these kind of problems.

In our trust model, we assumed a worst case scenario. If component A distrusts component B, it is assumed that component B tries to gain access to A's data without A's consent. In order to achieve this behavior, B may even act maliciously, for instance by intercepting and modifying sent data packets. The system thus has to prevent these attacks from succeeding.

Figure 2.2 illustrates the assumed trust relations between the involved components. We assume both the users and service providers to trust the platform itself. The platform itself is thus not considered as an attacker in this model. However, users do not trust any service provider. That means that the platform has to protect the user's data from being accessed by the services without the user's consent. The service providers neither trust the users nor the other service providers. In particular, this means that the system furthermore has to enable service providers to forbid another service to access their data explicitly.

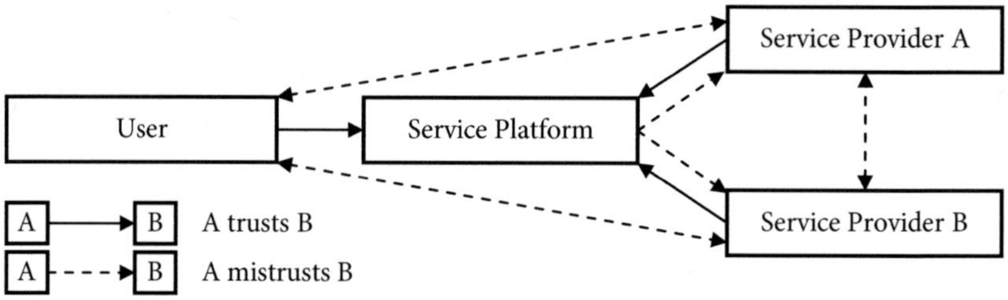

Figure 2.2: Trust model of the iZEUS service platform.

We identified only one occurrence at which the lack of control caused problems in this system, as the services do not directly depend on the performance of other services and we assumed the platform to be reasonable reliable. We hence found the lack of *trust* to be the main issue in this scenario. However, services might be hosted on mobile devices that are under direct control of the user. As from a service provider's perspective the user could potentially be malicious, the service provider could forward the received data to another, unauthorized service. The system thus has to allow service providers to forbid their data from being accessed from mobile devices.

2.4.3 Solution Outline

In the following, we will provide an outline of the architecture that we devised in order to deal with the lack of trust. As a complete description would go beyond the scope of this thesis, only important corner points will be provided. A more thorough description can be found in [WJL+12] and [JWHL13]. The platform was designed as follows:

- *Central Data Store:* The core of our platform is a centralized *Cassandra* database [LM10] that stores data items produced by the services. This allows services to access data even if the the service that originally produced the data is currently unavailable, for instance because if the data was produced by a mobile application and the user currently has no reception.
- Schema-less Data Model The data model is schema-less and based on the *Resource Description Framework* (RDF), which uses the approach to describe

relations of arbitrary data items. This scheme allows services to extend the data model flexibly. However, our data model defines some properties every data item has to possess: first, it must be specified which service produced the respective data item (the item's *source*) and it must be specified to which *user* (if any) the specific item belongs. This information is required when authorizing data access.

- *Service Model:* The system differentiates between three different kinds of services. Services are categorized based on how the deployed (as a web-application, as a non-web-based server-application, or as a mobile app). Each service furthermore has to specify which kinds of data it produces and which kinds of data it consumes.

- *User and Service Authentication:* The platform authenticates both users and services. For each class of service, a different authentication process has to be provided. The authentication method is based on the SAML standard **CITE**.

- *Authorization based on Data Source and Described User:* If a service wants to access any data item, it first has to be authorized by the platform. Authorization is based on the type of service, on the data item's source (the service that produced the item), and on the user the data item refers to. If the source service has forbidden that its data is accessed from mobile apps and the accessing service is a mobile app, access is not granted. Else access is only granted if both the source and the referred user granted their permission.

- *Web-Based Permission Management:* Permissions can be conveniently set and reviewed by service providers and users in a web-based user interface. A screenshot of the portal is depicted in Figure 2.3.

Figure 2.3: Screenshot of the iZEUS portal.

2.4.4 Summary

The iZEUS project demonstrates how issues caused by the lack of trust can manifest in centralized Multi-Party Systems. A thorough assessment of the trust relationship between the involved components allowed us to cope with these issues by authenticating and authorizing access between untrusted components.

However, our solution requires the data produced by external services to be stored on the service platform itself, as it constitutes the system's only universally trusted component. If a similar solution were to be deployed nationally, the operator might wish to delegate the hosting of the platform to a specialized storage provider. This is not possible without further protecting the data, as this storage provider would potentially not be completely trusted. This way, the iZEUS project also motivated our research towards providing a confidential DaaS solution, which will be presented in the next chapters.

2.5 Example: the KAI Project

The project *Kommunikation mittels autonomer Infrastrukturen* (KAI, English translation: *Communication by Autonomic Infrastructure*)[3] was funded by the German *Federal Office for Information Security* (BSI)[4] with the goal to develop an Internet-based system that allows a small, closed group of users to communicate securely, without requiring the help of any central services. The users should be free to use any available entry point to access the Internet and still be able to discover each other reliably. Once connected, the system should provide integrity and confidentiality for user communication.

2.5.1 Project Background and Requirements

The key problem in this project was to allow the KAI clients to locate each other, i.e., retrieve their IP addresses, without the help of any central components. This was achieved by letting the clients store their current IP addresses within an already existing public P2P network under a secret key. As all clients were aware of the secret key, they could look up the other client's IP addresses at any time.

In order to do so, the clients were required to "join" the P2P network. This is not a trivial task to achieve without the help of any central components as we will see in Part II of this thesis. For now it is sufficient to note that the probability for this task to succeed in a specific amount of time depends to a large extent on the size of the P2P network, i.e., the number of peers that are concurrently participating.

Furthermore, the system was designed to be used only in exceptional scenarios and remain dormant for the rest of the time. Still, it had to function reliably when activated. In its "dormant" state, each KAI client was maintained by one of its future users, which were assumed not to be IT experts.

[3] http://dsn.tm.kit.edu/english/projects_kai-project.php, [last visited in October 2014]
[4] https://www.bsi.bund.de, [last visited in October 2014]

2.5.2 Problem Analysis

The KAI system can be separated into two parts: the underlying public P2P network and the KAI clients. Figure 2.4 provides an overview over the composition of the KAI system. As not only the peers found within the P2P network is controlled by a different parties but also the KAI clients themselves, the KAI system is an example for a Multi-Party System.

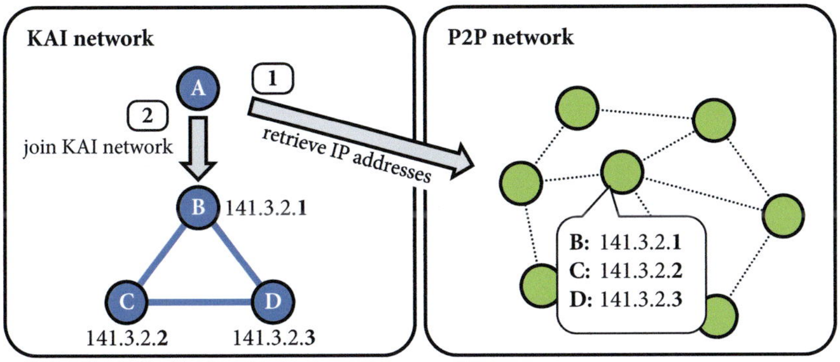

Figure 2.4: Components of the KAI system. The clients connected to the KAI network (blue) utilize a public P2P network (green) to locate each others. After retrieving the IP addresses of KAI clients B, C, and D (1), client A can join the encrypted KAI network.

When analyzing the system for trust issues, a clear line can be drawn between its two parts: the P2P network including all its peers had to be considered as untrustworthy while all KAI clients were trusted. Still, KAI clients were required to authenticate themselves in order to prevent impersonation attacks.

However, the key challenge was to deal with the unreliability of the involved components caused by the lack of control: as the P2P network consists of a multitude of autonomous and externally controlled peers, it had to be assumed to not only show unreliable performance but also had to be expected to change in the future. It could thus not be guaranteed that the P2P network still met the requirements of the KAI system when after a longer hibernation period. Furthermore, as the KAI clients were maintained by non IT experts, it could not be guaranteed that they remained operational during such periods.

2.5.3 Solution Outline

In order to solve these problems, another component was designed which was called the *KAI Management Console*. The Management Console was designed to monitor KAI's other components during hibernation periods. While the Management Console constituted a central component, it was not used when the KAI system becomes active an thus did not break any requirements. The Management Console fulfilled two tasks:

1. It monitored all KAI clients and verified that they were properly maintained. It was able to push updates to the client and report any encountered problems. It was also able to initiate tests on the remote clients.

2. It monitored the evolution of the underlying P2P network, in particular with respect to its size. The Management Console would report if the P2P networks shrank significantly or any other properties evolved in a negative direction. In that case, the clients could be patched, for example to use an modified method to join the P2P network. In extreme cases, the chosen P2P network could have been replaced by another. In Chapter 8, we will report in much greater detail on the measurements we conducted.

Due to space limitations, we abstain from going into more detail at this place. A more detailed description of the KAI system is provided in [DJWC08].

2.5.4 Summary

The KAI system illustrated how the lack of control can influence the design of a fully decentralized application. In fact, a large part of the KAI system was designed only to deal with the lack of control over the public P2P network and the KAI clients. This shows that similar problems should not be treated lightly.

In the KAI project, the main concept to solve the encountered problems was to monitor the P2P network and the KAI clients in order to gain a better understand of its behavior and to be able to react early to unexpected incidents. As we expect this approach to apply to most decentralized applications, we continued and further expanded our activities in this area of research. In the second part of this thesis, we will hence report more thoroughly on our measurement efforts.

Part I

Confidential Data Outsourcing

3 Confidential Indexing

With the advent of the cloud computing paradigm, data outsourcing has become increasingly popular, especially for companies that have to process large amounts of data but do not possess a substantial IT infrastructure themselves. Typical reasons for companies to outsource their data include the reduction of costs, the wish to achieve better robustness of central IT services or to adapt better to in- or decreasing workloads. In the database-as-a-service (DaaS) scenario, databases are outsourced to external *storage providers* which evaluate queries issued by the client in its stead and return the respective results.

One of the most important factors that inhibit the more widespread DaaS adoption is the risk of a confidentiality breach of the (potentially sensitive) outsourced data [AFG+10]. As the client looses direct control over the outsourced data, it has to trust the storage provider to respect its data's confidentiality. However, the storage provider is often not considered trustworthy by the client [GMR+12]. The storage provider (or one of its employees) might, for instance, have an economic interest in spying on its customers' data or might be required by law to provide access on demand. The storage provider might also get compromised by an external attacker in the future. Furthermore, the client might simply be required by law to protect its data by technical means, for instance in the eHealth or eTraffic domain. The confidentiality of the outsourced data thus has to be protected (for instance by encryption) in a way that still allows the storage provider to evaluate queries issued by the client efficiently.

In the first part of this thesis, we present *Securus* (**S**ecure **A**nd **E**fficient **C**loud **U**tilization **R**elying **U**pon **S**chemes), a confidential DaaS solution that targets this challenge.

Parts of the work presented in this part of the thesis has been published in [JKH12, KJH14, KJ14].

3.1 Structure

The first part of this thesis is structured as follows:

In Chapter 3, the problem of providing confidential indexing as a foundation for confidential DaaS scenarios is introduced and motivated. Furthermore, the necessary background for understanding the following chapters is established, in particular by providing a brief introduction into cryptographic key definitions and presenting a list of many popular security techniques.

Chapter 4 presents the Securus approach. Before diving into technical details, Securus' main concept and idea are introduced on a high level. Its usage workflow is also illustrated as it differs from conventional DaaS frameworks. Then, Securus' technical architecture is presented. Securus' two main contributions, the *policy profiles*, which are used to define the user's access and confidentiality requirements, and the transformation of these into *mediators*, which are software adapters that realize the corresponding requirements, are explained in the subsequent sections.

Chapter 5 concludes this part of the thesis by evaluating and discussing Securus' performance and deployability. An outlook of possible future additions to Securus is also given.

3.2 Introduction

Many approaches have been published that aim at allowing the storage provider to evaluate queries issued by the client efficiently. Most of them assume an *honest-but-curious* attacker model on which we also focus in this thesis. An honest-but-curious storage provider observes but does not modify the outsourced data. Typically, the storage provider is furthermore assumed not to monitor or alter queries. We will describe the assumptions made about the attacker more thoroughly in the beginning of the Chapter 4.

Most of these approaches use indexes that allow the storage provider to efficiently evaluate a certain kind of queries. The index itself typically contains encrypted data only. We call these approaches *confidentiality preserving indexing approaches* (CPIs). One example for a CPI is using deterministic encryption or hashing to build an index of a specific attribute, for instance the customers' names. In order to retrieve a customer with a specific name, the storage provider is asked to look for the respective name's ciphertext or hash. The customers' names are hence not revealed to the storage provider.

Another class of approaches is defined by the use of fragmentation in order to protect the confidentiality of attribute combinations rather than single attributes. If the combination of multiple attributes is considered sensitive, the relation can be split up into multiple, unlinkable fragments. For instance, the combination of the attributes *name* and *dateOfBirth* of a person could be considered sensitive as it allows to identify most people in a database. By storing the customers' names and dates of birth in different, unlinkable tables, the storage provider could be prevented from being able to identify any single person.

While each of these CPIs and fragmentation approaches solves a specific DaaS problem, they typically differ in the capabilities they assume the attacker to possess, in the confidentiality goal they target, and in the class of queries whose evaluation they support. Whether or not an approach fits the client's needs depends in particular (i) on how the data is going to be accessed (*access requirements*), and (ii) on the client's *confidentiality requirements*. In order to fully support its individual demands, the client thus has to assess its requirements, carefully study each available approach, and then select an appropriate set of CPIs. This task is complicated, error-prone, and can only be fulfilled by a combined domain and security expert.

A popular solution that targets the confidential DaaS domain is CryptDB [PZB11]. CryptDB avoids the problem of letting the user define her confidentiality and access requirements by applying and removing CPIs dynamically during normal operation: when a database is first outsourced, a high level of protection is applied. However, whenever a query is received that cannot be evaluated using the current level of protection, the protection level is lowered permanently. The protection level is thus incrementally relaxed. While this approach is very convenient to use, it does not provide hard security guarantees – depending on the initiated queries, the database might eventually be stored completely unprotected.

We thus state the motivational question for the first part this thesis as follows:

> *How can confidential databases be sourced out to honest-but-curious storage providers while providing hard confidentiality guarantees?*

3.3 Challenges and Research Questions

On the way towards tackling the motivational question, a couple of challenges arise. In particular, the fact that no combination of CPIs is able to satisfy all possible combinations of confidentiality and accessibility requirements ruins any hope to find a "universal" outsourcing scheme that can be applied directly to any scenario. Instead a different scheme has to be found each time that fits the specific scenario's access and confidentiality requirements. As very few people possess the required, very specific knowledge about a wide range of CPIs, data fragmentation approaches, and cryptography, this task cannot be fulfilled without external support in most cases. One challenge is thus to provide a tool that generates custom tailored outsourcing solutions based on the client's specifications. The generated solutions should provide hard security guarantees and still allow the client to access its data efficiently.

In order to allow the generation of a custom-tailored outsourcing solution, the client has to express its confidentiality and access requirements. One the one hand, this specification has to be specific enough to be used as a foundation for choosing appropriately between alternative security techniques. One the other hand, it should not be required to specify so many details that it becomes unrealistic to define real-world scenarios. Choosing an appropriate abstraction level is thus not a trivial task. As knowledge about the outsourced data's semantics is required in order to define one's confidentiality and access requirements, the specification has to be defined by a domain rather than an security expert. No expert knowledge about any involved security mechanics should hence be required during the specification process.

In summary, the following challenges prevent companies from outsourcing their data to external storage providers according to the DaaS paradigm:

- As the client company often does not trust the storage provider, often hard confidentiality guarantees are required when outsourcing a database. Current confidential DaaS frameworks are unable to satisfy these requirements.
- Confidentiality and access requirements vary on a case by case basis and are typically only understood by domain experts, which typically are not security experts at the same time.

In the first part of this thesis, we present *Securus*, an approach that aims to overcome these challenges. In order to do so, Securus in particular targets the following research questions:

- How can data outsourcing solutions be generated that meet specific confidentiality and access requirements?
- How can these requirements be defined by domain experts rather than security experts?

3.4 Cryptographic Fundamentals

In order to protect the confidentiality of outsourced data while still allowing the storage provider to evaluate received queries, most CPIs rely on cryptography. While the focus of this thesis is not the cryptographic analysis of these approaches, an understanding of some cryptographic concepts is required for being able to rank the level of confidentiality provided by alternative CPIs. In this section, cryptographic key concepts such as *ciphertext indistinguishability*, *deterministic* and *probabilistic encryption schemes*, and *keyed hash functions* are introduced. For a more formal and detailed introduction we refer to other publications such as [KL06].

3.4.1 Ciphertext Indistinguishability

Ciphertext indistinguishability is an important property of encryption schemes that allows to define security with respect to the confidentiality of the encrypted data. It states, "that for every two plaintexts m_0 and m_1, it should be hard to distinguish the case that a ciphertext c is an encryption of m_0 from the case that it is an encryption of m_1" [KL06, p. 42]. This definition is equivalent to stating that "a ciphertext reveals no information whatsoever about the plaintext." [KL06, p. 42] Due to this equivalency, ciphertext indistinguishability is of great importance for Securus, as it allows to judge whether or not a storage provider can reveal any information from outsourced ciphertexts.

A common definition is that an encryption scheme – such as the RSA cryptosystem – provides ciphertext indistinguishability if it is resilient to chosen plaintext attacks (IND-CPA). The cryptosystem is resilient to chosen plaintext attacks, if an adversary has only a negligible advantage over random guessing to win the game which is sketched as follows:

1. The adversary chooses two plaintexts and submits them to the challenger.
2. The challenger chooses one of both plaintexts at random, encrypts it, and sends the resulting ciphertext back to the attacker.
3. The adversary is free to perform a polynomially bounded number of computations. In particular, she may ask the challenger to encrypt any plaintext, even the ones she already submitted.
4. Eventually, the adversary has to guess which plaintext the ciphertext was generated from. She wins the game if and only if she picks the right one.

A more formal definition of IND-CPA can be found in [KL06, p. 241 f.]. While the IND-CPA model is defined only for asymmetric encryption schemes, equivalent definitions exist for symmetric schemes as well. An important implication of this definition is that an encryption scheme that satisfies it (almost always) has to produce different ciphertexts when encrypting two equal plaintexts. Furthermore, produced ciphertexts have to be indistinguishable from random data for the adversary.

A class of encryption schemes that provide ciphertext indistinguishability are *probabilistic* encryption schemes as opposed to *deterministic* encryption schemes, which do not. Probabilistic encryption schemes [GM84] use randomness to satisfy the indistinguishability requirement. Popular examples for probabilistic encryption schemes include public key encryption algorithms such as RSA-PSS [CJNP02], homomorphic encryption schemes [Pai99], and symmetric block ciphers in cipher block chaining (CBC) mode such as AES-CBC [FGK03] with random initialization vector.

Deterministic encryption schemes [BBO07] ensure that the ciphertext generated for two equal values is always the same. Popular examples include RSA when used without encryption padding and block ciphers in electronic codebook mode (ECB).

3.4.2 Keyed Hash Functions

Another important set of cryptographic tools are *cryptographic hash functions*. Cryptographic hash functions generate constant length "checksums" of plaintext data. For instance, these can later be used in an index as a substitute for the original value. This allows to hide the value from the storage provider.

Any cryptographic hash function has to meet the following requirements [Pre94]:

1. It must be a *one-way* function. It is thus "hard" to invert the function if the secret key is not known.
2. The function must produce *fixed length results*.
3. The function must be *collision resistant*, i.e., it is "hard" to find two distinct values that map to the same result.

Keyed hash functions are cryptographic hash functions that incorporate a secret key in the hashing algorithm. It should be hard for an adversary that does not have access to the secret key to determine the correct hash for a given plaintext.

Keyed hash functions and deterministic encryption schemes share the property that they always generate the same results for two equal input values, as long as the secret key remains fixed. Furthermore, they produce different results for equal inputs in at least almost all the cases if different keys are used. An adversary can thus only with a probability that is negligible higher than random guessing determine whether a given ciphertext was created from a specific plaintext value, provided she does not know the secret key. These properties are leveraged by many CPIs.

3.5 Confidentiality Preserving Indexing Approaches

This section introduces *Confidentiality Preserving Indexing Approaches* (CPIs), the building blocks Securus assembles outsourcing solutions from. First, a classification scheme is presented which will later be used to select CPIs that match specific requirements. This scheme is based on two dimensions: the *substitution category*, which describes how well a CPI protects its contained entries, and the *query category*, which specifies the queries that are supported by the CPI.

Following the classification scheme, popular CPIs are introduced. Each CPI is categorized according to out classification scheme and an outline of their general behavior is given. For completeness, CPIs that are promising candidates for future addition to Securus will also be introduced.

3.5.1 Classification

A CPI is an established data indexing technique that satisfies specific confidentiality requirements and permits specific kinds of queries to be evaluated by an untrusted storage provider. This is achieved by building an index for a specific attribute that needs to be accessed in order to evaluate the query. The index is created in a way that at least partly protects the confidentiality of the stored data. Typically, the index is either filled with plaintext values of the accessed attribute, or with *substitutes* created from the plaintext values by either a hash function or encryption scheme.

We categorize CPIs with respect to the following criteria:

1. The *substitution category*, which describes the kind of substitutes that are stored in the index (compare Section 3.5.2).

2. The *query category*, which describes the type of *queries* that can be evaluated with the help of the CPI (compare Section 3.5.3).

In the following two subsections, both categories will be explained in detail.

3.5.2 Substitution Categories

For our approach it is important to judge which kind of information can be deduced from the data stored in the indexes maintained by the storage provider. We call the entries stored in an index *substitutes* as they substitute the original values.

In particular, it is important to differentiate whether or not the substitutes of two equal values are equal as well or not. If they are equal, a storage provider could deduce information in case it possesses background knowledge: for instance, it could analyze which patients found in a database suffer from the same illness. We distinguish between the following three *substitution categories*:

- *Plaintext*: Values are not substituted.
- *Distinguishable Substitutes*: Values are substituted by ciphertexts or hashes that leak the information of whether or not two ciphertexts were created from the same value. In particular, distinguishable substitutes are produced by keyed hash functions and deterministic encryption schemes (compare Section 3.4).
- *Indistinguishable Substitutes*: Values are substituted by ciphertexts that leak no information about the original value whatsoever. In particular, an adversary cannot judge whether or not two ciphertexts were created from the same value. Indistinguishable substitutes are produced by probabilistic encryption schemes (compare Section 3.4).

Figure 3.1 illustrates the difference between the three substitution categories. The protection level increases from plaintext values, whose confidentiality is not protected from the storage provider in any way, over distinguishable substitutes, which leak some information that can be exploited by the storage provider under certain circumstances, to indistinguishable substitutes, which leak no information.

It should furthermore be noted that it is possible to extend this dimension by additional substitution categories to achieve an even more fine-grained differentiation of confidentiality protection. Order preserving encryption schemes [BCLO09] produce ciphertexts that could bridge the gap between plaintext values and distinguishable substitutes. We consider this and other extensions of Securus to constitute promising future work.

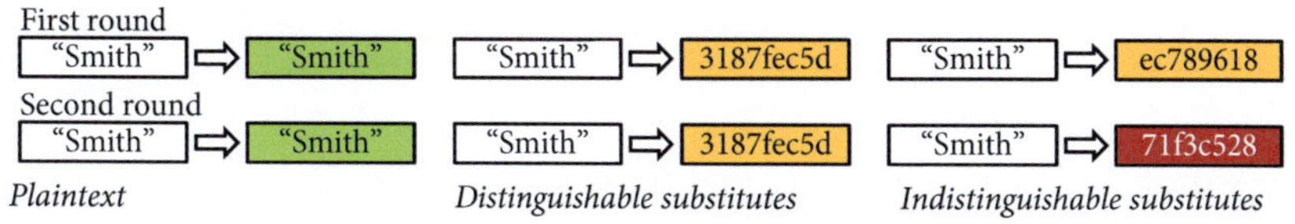

Figure 3.1: Substitution categories. The *plaintext* category means that values are not substituted at all. *Distinguishable substitutes* are equal for equal values while *indistinguishable substitutes* are almost always different, even if they were generated from equal values.

3.5.3 Query categories

Typically, a CPI allows only the evaluation of a specific kind of query as each kind of index only supports a limited set of operations to be performed. In Securus, we differentiate between three *query categories*: *equality selections*, *range selections*, and *aggregations*.

- **Equality selections**: If a CPI supports equality selections for a specific attribute, it enables the storage provider to select records based on whether or not the attribute's value is equal to a specific argument. An example for an equality selection is the query `SELECT ... WHERE name='Smith'`. In this case, the equality selection was defined for attribute *name*.

- **Range selections**: If a CPI supports range selections for a specific attribute, it enables the storage provider to select records based on whether or not the attribute's value lies within a specific value range. An example for an equality selection is the query `SELECT ... WHERE age < 30`. In this case, the equality selection was defined for attribute *age*.

- **Aggregations**: If a CPI supports range selections for a specific attribute, it enables the storage provider to perform some kind of operation on the values in order to compute a result, for instance the sum, average, or minimum of the values contained in a specific column. An example for an equality selection is the query `SELECT SUM(price) WHERE ...`.

Although all query categories accept only one attribute as an argument, more complex queries can be created by combining different query categories. If, for instance, a storage provider can evaluate equality selections for attribute *name* and range selections on attribute *age*, it can also evaluate queries that ask it to return all people that are named 'Smith' *and* younger than 30 years old. A query category thus simply describe the operations the storage provider can use to access the values of specific single attribute.

Similar to the substitution categories, this dimension, too, can be extended by additional query categories in the future. In Section 5.6, we will discuss this option in greater detail.

3.5.4 CPIs supported by Securus

In the following, a catalog of CPIs that are currently supported by Securus will be presented. Each CPI will be categorized according to the respective substitution and query category. Table 3.1 depicts the CPI catalog and lists the contained CPIs. The CPI catalog plays an important role for Securus' policy transformation process, as it constitutes the "library" of CPIs that can be used to satisfy the user's needs.

It can be seen that not for every combination of query type and substitution category suitable CPIs are available, as to our knowledge no CPIs exist yet that allow equality or range selections to be evaluated efficiently on indistinguishable substitutes. Because indistinguishable ciphertexts provide a higher level of protection than distinguishable ciphertexts, we furthermore consider homomorphic encryption schemes to "support" both substitution categories.

Query type	Plaintext	Distinguishable ciphertexts	Indistinguishable ciphertexts
Equality Selection	✓	Det. Encr. & Hash Indexes [DVJ+03, CDV+05]	×
Range Selection	✓	Bucket Hash Indexes [HILM02]	×
Aggregation	✓	Part. Homomorphic Encr. [HIM04, MT06]	Part. Homomorphic Encr. [HIM04, MT06]

Table 3.1: Catalog of CPIs that are supported by Securus. The ✓ symbol indicates that no CPIs need to be applied to support this category combination, whereas × indicates that Securus does not support any CPIs that fit the respective profile.

Hash Indexes

Substitution Category: Distinguishable ciphertexts
Query Category: Equality selections

One way to put the storage provider in a position to evaluate equality selections without storing plaintext values is the use of *hash indexes*. A hash index does not store the values in the clear but replaces them by a distinguishable ciphertext, which can either be generated by a deterministic encryption scheme or a keyed hash function. In order to select records based on whether or not the indexed attribute is equal to a specific value x, the query has to be rephrased to not look for x but its distinguishable ciphertext ξ.

Example: Table 3.2 shows how a hash index is added to a table for the attribute *name*. If the user wants to evaluate the query `SELECT ... WHERE name = 'Bush'`, the substitute α first has to be generated for name 'Bush'. In this example, she could use a keyed hash function together with her secret key, which the storage provider does not know. She then passes the query `SELECT ... WHERE name =` β to the storage provider which returns the record 2.

ID	name	age
1	Smith	46
2	Bush	60
3	Pitt	51
4	Smith	60

(a) Data to source out.

ID	name	age
1	α	46
2	β	60
3	γ	51
4	α	60

(b) Relation with hash index.

Table 3.2: Hash Index example: A relation is sourced out and a hash index in applied for attribute *name*. Names are stored as distinguishable ciphertexts, e.g., as keyed hashes.

Due to their reliance on distinguishable ciphertexts, hash indexes are vulnerable to attackers with background knowledge. If, e.g., the attacker knows that Smith is the most common name found in Table 3.2, she can infer that record 1 and 4 relate to represent people named "Smith". In [CDV+05], Ceselli et al. propose *flattened hash indexes* which aim at mitigating this issue. A flattened hash index maps different plaintext values to the same substitute so that each substitute occurs the same number of times. However, this approach still allows the storage provider to infer some information, as different substitutes can not have been created from the same plaintext. Records with different substitutes thus always contain different values. For this reason, Securus does not make use of flattened hash indexes.

Bucket Hash Indexes

Substitution Category: Distinguishable ciphertexts
Query Category: Range selections
Bucketization [HMCK12, HILM02] is an approach similar to hash indexes that allows to evaluate range selections on distinguishable ciphertexts. With bucketization, the substitute is not generated directly from a record's plaintext value. Instead, the values are sorted into "buckets" that cover a specific interval each. An ID is assigned to each bucket. The generated index contains distinguishable substitutes of the IDs of the buckets, the outsourced records belong to. In order to select records based on whether or not the indexed attribute falls into a specific value range, a query is started that asks the storage provider to return all records that cover parts of this range. The returned results then have to be filtered on the client side.

Example: Table 3.3 shows how a table is outsourced while applying the value bucketization approach to the attribute *age*. The bucket table contains the intervals the individual buckets span and the buckets' IDs. To evaluate the query `SELECT ... WHERE age < 49`, the user has to pass the query `SELECT ... WHERE bucket = encr(8) OR bucket = encr(6)` to the storage provider. The term *encr(x)* here means that a distinguishable substitute has to be generated for the value *x*.

Similar to hash indexes, the bucketization approach is vulnerable to attackers that possess background knowledge. Again, *flattened* bucket hash indexes [HMCK12] promise mitigation of the issue, but cannot prevent an information flow in all cases.

ID	name	age
1	Smith	46
2	Bush	60
3	Pitt	51
4	Smith	60

(a) Data to source out.

B-ID	range
8	31 - 40
6	41 - 50
3	51 - 60
5	61 - 70

Bucket Table

ID	name	bucket	age
1	Smith	*encr(6)*	α
2	Bush	*encr(3)*	β
3	Pitt	*encr(3)*	γ
4	Smith	*encr(3)*	δ

Main table (with index)

(b) Relation with bucketization.

Table 3.3: Bucketization example: A relation is sourced out and a bucket hash index is used to index attribute *age*. Distinguishable ciphertexts are used for the *bucket* column, indistinguishable ciphertexts for the *age* column.

Homomorphic Encryption

Substitution Category: Indistinguishable ciphertexts
Query Category: Aggregations

Homomorphic Encryption is a class of encryption schemes that allow a (limited) set of operations to be executed directly on ciphertexts without having access to the secret key [Pai99, OU98, RAD78]. Authors such as Hacıgümüş et al. [HIM04] or Mykletun and Tsudik [MT06] proposed to use these schemes to build indexes that store indistinguishable ciphertexts of the outsourced data but still allow the storage provider to perform additions or multiplications. This allows the storage provider to aggregate values stored in the index. For example, it could calculate the sum of the indexed values.

In Securus, we make use of *partially* homomorphic encryption schemes only. Partially homomorphic encryption is more efficient than fully homomorphic encryption, but does allow homomorphic computation of only one operation.

3.5.5 Candidates for Future Addition

For several reasons, Securus does not support all available CPIs.

First, a CPI was not considered for inclusion if it did not allow the storage provider to evaluate queries *efficiently*. As evaluation performance depends on a wide range of factors, ranging from the employed database system to the user's network connection, we assess performance on a high level only. In particular, we deem a CPI's being not efficient if the number of sequential communication rounds required to evaluate a query depends on the number of records stored in the data set. We furthermore rejected CPIs that require to touch $O(n)$ record in order to evaluate a query, where n is the number of records stored in the index.

Second, a CPI was rejected if the provided confidentiality level was lower than that of any other approach that supports the query category – i.e., if the index was more likely to leak information.

In the following, each CPI is presented and it is stated, why it is not yet included. It should be noted that some of these CPI may be promising candidates for future addition to Securus, for example together with a possible extension of the employed classification scheme (compare Section 5.6).

Order-preserving Encryption

Substitution Category: Distinguishable ciphertexts
Query Category: Range and Equality selections

Order-preserving encryption schemes [BCLO09, AKSX04] are a way to perform range selections directly on distinguishable ciphertexts. Therefore, these encryption schemes generate ciphertexts that maintain the order of the plaintext values. Compared to bucket hash indexes, order-preserving encryption has the advantage that no false positives are transferred to the user, i.e., the results returned by the storage provider do not have to be filtered on the client-side. However, as the ordering of the ciphertexts is not protected from the storage provider, the index is very susceptible to attackers that possess background knowledge, even if they do not have the capability to observe any data modifications or insert operations. Because range selections are already supported by bucket hash indexes, Securus does not include order-preserving encryption schemes.

Searchable Encryption

Substitution Category: Indistinguishable ciphertexts
Query Category: Range and Equality selections

Searchable encryption schemes generate indistinguishable ciphertexts that allow the storage provider to check directly whether or not the contained value matches a specific predicate [KV08, BBO07, LO05, SWP00]. Predicates can be used to perform equality and range selections. In order to do so, a *token* has to be generated on the client side from the secret key and the predicate the index should be checked for. When passed to the storage provider, the storage provider can use it to check which ciphertexts match the predicate. The predicate remains unknown to the storage provider.

Until recently, searchable encryption schemes came at high costs that prevented their use in production environments. Typical, these costs included large indexes, slow search performance, or the absence of support for adding items to the index [KPR12]. Searchable encryption still has the disadvantage of requiring to access every item contained in the index. Evaluation time thus scales linearly with the number of outsourced records. For this reasons, we did not include searchable encryption schemes.

3.6 Data Fragmentation

Often, only the combination of multiple values within a record is considered sensitive while any value alone is not. For instance, the combination of the *age* and *name* of a person could be considered sensitive, as it allows to identify most people in a database while either of the two attributes alone will not be enough in most cases. *Data fragmentation* is a technique that aims at preserving the confidentiality of a combination of attributes by splitting up a relation into two or more *unlinkable* fragments.

A key requirement of the data fragmentation approach is that the fragments are unlinkable, i.e., stored in a way that makes it impossible for the attacker to determine that two fragments belong to the same record. At the same time, the user has to remain able to link fragments, as she eventually has to reconstruct the record. To solve this problem, two different approaches exist that are also illustrated in Table 3.4:

1. Fragments can be stored on the same storage provider and linked by ID columns (see [For10, CDVF+07, MPP05]). The ID columns contain indistinguishable substitutes.

2. Fragments can be stored on different, non-colluding storage providers (see [ABG+05, GTF+11, HHK+10]). The ID columns do not have to be encrypted.

When storing all fragments on the same storage provider, an ID column has to be added to each fragment in order to allow the user to link fragments after retrieving

ID	name	age
1	Smith	46
2	Bush	60
3	Pitt	51
4	Smith	60

(a) Data to source out. The combination of a person's *name* and *age* is considered being sensitive.

ID	name
α	Smith
β	Bush
γ	Pitt
δ	Smith

ID	age
ε	46
ϕ	60
χ	51
η	60

(b) Option A: Fragments are stored on the same storage provider. The *ID* columns have be protected.

ID	name
1	Smith
2	Bush
3	Pitt
4	Smith

ID	age
1	46
2	50
3	51
4	50

(c) Option B: Fragments are stored on different storage providers. The records' *IDs* can be stored in the clear.

Table 3.4: Data fragmentation example: the confidentiality of the attribute combination *name* and *age* should be protected from the storage provider(s).

them. By encrypting all IDs deterministically (but using a different secret key for each fragment), the storage provider is prevented from linking the fragments on its own. It cannot infer any information even though deterministic encryption is used, as each ID is unique. In order to access data that spans multiple fragments, the user has to issue multiple sequential queries. If, for instance, the user wants to retrieve the age of a person named "Bush" in Table 3.4c, she has to first run the query `SELECT ID FROM fragment1 WHERE name='Bush'` to retrieve the ID of the corresponding record. She then has to decrypt the ciphertext with a secret key used for *fragment1* and encrypt it again using the secret key used for *fragment2* to compute ϕ. Then, she can retrieve the age by running the query `SELECT age FROM fragment2 WHERE ID=`ϕ.

Storing all fragments on the same storage provider has the main advantage of requiring one storage provider only. The option of using this approach is thus available in almost all DaaS scenarios. A disadvantage of storing all fragments on a single storage provider is that the approach is vulnerable under certain conditions. In particular, any attacker that is able to monitor a single query or data modification (i.e., an insert or update operation) that affects multiple fragments is able to link these fragments, thus breaking data confidentiality. If, for example, the storage provider monitors that fragments β, *'Bush'* and ϕ, *60* are added in short succession, it can assume that they belong to the same record. An attacker might furthermore be able to infer some information about the confidential attribute combination just by analyzing both fragments. For instance in Table 3.4, the attacker knows that "Pitt" is either 46, 51, or 60 years old, as these are the only values contained in the *age* column. These kinds of attacks would not be possible if at least one of the two attributes was encrypted.

We feel that these issues make it very hard to judge whether or not the confidentiality of an attribute combination is still protected appropriately when using this approach. We hence decided not to employ fragmentation on single storage providers in Securus.

As an alternative approach, fragments can be stored on multiple, non-colluding storage providers. To our knowledge, this idea has first been published by Aggarwal et al. in [ABG+05], but has been used by others as well [GTF+11, HHK+10]. The principle of this approach is to restrict access to at least one fragment for each storage provider, rather than just concealing the fragments' relation. As no storage provider knows the data contained by the other fragment, the ID columns can be stored in the clear. Furthermore, this approach is robust to both before-mentioned issues that occur when storing all fragments on one storage provider.

Securus makes extensive use of data fragmentation if multiple non-colluding storage providers are available.

4 The Securus Approach

In this chapter, the Securus approach is presented. First, Securus' main concept is introduced on an abstract level in Section 4.1. In the same section fundamental assumptions are presented and discussed. Securus is furthermore compared to other confidential DaaS solutions. Section 4.3, presents Securus' technical architecture. All main components are introduced and two key contributions – the definition of *policy profiles* and their transformation into *mediators* – are motivated. In Sections 4.4 and 4.5, these contributions are presented in detail.

The subsequent chapter covers Securus' evaluation, discussion, outlook, and conclusion.

4.1 Concept

With Securus, we present an approach that aims at satisfying a user's specific confidentiality and access requirements. In order to do so, the user has to define her requirements explicitly. Securus differs in this regard from conventional DaaS solutions. Before delving into technical details of our approach, we will in this section hence first provide a high level overview on Securus from a user's perspective in order to highlight fundamental assumptions Securus is based on and illustrate differences to other approaches. We start with listing the assumptions made about the attacker's and user's capabilities (*user* and *attacker model*). We then illustrate Securus' usage workflow from a user's perspective. After that, Securus is compared to other confidential DaaS solutions.

4.1.1 Attacker Model

We assume that the user does not only want to protect her data from the eyes of external attackers but also from the storage provider. There are multiple possible reasons for a user to have this demand:

1. First, the user might not trust the storage provider to not look into the outsourced data. The storage provider as a company might have an economic interest to spy on its customers or might even be required by law to provide access to its customer's data under some circumstances. Even if these possibilities can be ruled out, singular employees might develop a personal interest in the stored data. In particular, employees such as administrators that have to possess far-reaching rights to do their job pose a threat to data confidentiality. As it is typically hard or impossible for the user to check the storage provider's internal security policies, she might prefer to be safe instead of being sorry.

2. Second, the user could be required by law to take special care when handling its data, for example because the data contains sensitive information about the user's customers. This is especially important in eHealth, eTraffic, and Smart Grid scenarios, which often also constitute "data-heavy" examples. Consider for example a hospital that wants to source out their patients' medical histories or a car manufacturer that stores accurate movement profiles of its newest electric car to provide special services to its buyers. National law might require the user to protect its data by technical rather than contractual means.

3. Third, the storage provider could get compromised by an external attacker. As stated before, most of the time it is impossible for the user to rate the storage provider's security standard accurately and assess the likelihood of an attack to succeed.

By considering the storage provider as an attacker, we cover all of these demands. We hence assume the storage provider to be *honest-but-curious*. This means that the storage provider observes the outsourced data but does not manipulate any data, queries, or returned results. While protection against malicious adversaries, i.e., against storage providers that *do* manipulate data or queries, is surely an important topic, it is out of the scope of this thesis as we focus on preserving data confidentiality rather than integrity. The user can, however, apply her own integrity preserving techniques to her data prior to outsourcing it in order to discourage any tampering.

Like most other confidential DaaS frameworks, we furthermore assume that the storage provider does not actively monitor queries in order to analyze their access patterns, e.g., to derive which (encrypted) parts of a database were accessed. These access patterns can be exploited by an attacker that possesses background knowledge about the outsourced data. Most CPIs are unable to protect against this kind of attack[1].

[1]While approaches such as Oblivious RAM [ABG+05] target similar scenarios, they do not fit our performance requirements as the number of sequential communication rounds required to evaluate a query depends on the number of records stored in the database (compare Section 3.5.5).

We feel that this is a reasonable assumption especially in scenarios in which the storage provider is compromised by an external or internal attacker that only has access to the data for a short time and might thus not be able to actively monitor incoming queries for an extended time period. If, however, an storage provider with enough resources to actively monitor and analyze query patterns for a longer time period is considered (for instance the NSA), more advanced security techniques might be required.

We furthermore assume that one or more *non-colluding* storage providers are available to the user. Non-colluding storage providers do not exchange any information about outsourced data between each other. If more than one provider with this property are available, Securus can use data partitioning techniques to distribute the data among them and meet the user's confidentiality requirements more efficiently.

4.1.2 User Model

We will later see that it is not always possible to organize a database in a way that ensures the confidentiality of all contained information and also allows to execute every possible kind of query efficiently. In general, trade-offs have to be made, either by relaxing the envisioned confidentiality level for some parts of the data or by giving up support for some kinds of queries. In order to enable Securus to choose trade-offs appropriately, the user has to specify the requirements she has on the outsourced database. In particular, she has to specify confidentiality requirements (e.g., which parts of the data demand for protection), and access requirements (e.g., how she wants to access her data in the future). However, she does *not* need to possess any cryptographic expert knowledge or understand any of the various security techniques Securus employs. In fact, one of Securus' main strengths is to make this knowledge more available, manageable, and more easy to integrate, even for non-experts. We expect the user to fit the following profile:

- The user has to understand the structure and semantics of the outsourced data. If, for instance, the user wants to outsource a relational database, she has to know the schema of the database and understand the nature of the contained content. For example, she has to know whether a table contains natural persons, articles to be sold, or hashed user passwords. The more the user knows about the data, the better will the solution generated by Securus fit her needs. If, for instance, she knows that every value contained in specific column of a table is unique, Securus might be able to leverage this fact to execute queries over this attribute more efficiently without impairing the satisfied level of protection.

  This requirement makes Securus an suboptimal approach for users who manage the data of others and are agnostic of its meaning.

- The user has to know how she is going to access the outsourced database, i.e., which kinds of queries Securus needs to support. In particular, she needs to know by which attributes she is going to *select* individual entries. In SQL, this relates to the attributes referred to within the *WHERE* part of a *SELECT* statement. She furthermore needs to know whether she is going to use *equality selections* (...*WHERE attribute* == *'value'*), or *range selections* (...*WHERE attribute* >= *'value'*), and whether she wants to *aggregate* the return results (...*SELECT SUM(attribute)*). In general, the fewer kinds of queries need to be supported, the stronger can the confidentiality requirements be that Securus is able to satisfy.

In case the set of query types that need to be supported changes after the database has been sourced out, the whole database may have to be reorganized and re-encrypted from scratch. Furthermore, the achievable protection level might be lower in this case than it would be if all query types are known from the beginning. The reason for this is that it has to be assumed that the storage provider combines the information pieces it was able to infer from the first encryption scheme with the ones it can infer from the second. However, as the best-case scenario, it is also possible that the new query types can be supported without requiring any re-organization of the data at all.

- The user has to be able to state her confidentiality requirements. In particular, she has to know which information has to stay confidential and from which parts of her data this information can be inferred. While this requirement may seem hard to fulfill by a non-expert, the user is only required to specify her confidentiality demands on a high level using two elemental expressions: first, she can specify attributes whose values should remain hidden. The storage provider should thus be unable to decipher or infer the clear-text values of these attributes. These attributes will in the end often have to be encrypted. Second, the user can define sets of attributes that are considered sensitive. No storage provider should not be able to reveal all of these attributes' values for any data entry. For example, if the combination of the attributes *name* and *salary* of an employee are considered sensitive, the storage provider should not be able to determine both name and salary of any employee. The storage provider may, however, know all employees' names, as long as it cannot link them to their salary.

4.1.3 Usage Workflow: User perspective

Figure 4.1 depicts a workflow that illustrates how Securus is used. To initiate the data-outsourcing process, the user first has to define a *Policy Profile*, which specifies her individual confidentiality and access requirements (1). The policy profile is written in the domain specific language *Securus-Latin*. No cryptographic expert knowledge is necessary in order to create the document. Policy profiles will be explained in greater detail in Section 4.4.

Securus then computes which set of *Confidentiality Preserving Indexing Approaches* (CPIs) fits these requirements best (2). Securus contains a catalog that covers various popular CPIs (compare Section 3.5). The catalog can be extended in case new CPI's are published. To determine which set of CPIs fits best, the policy profile is internally translated into an *Integer Linear Programming* problem (ILP) which is then solved by a generic ILP solver.

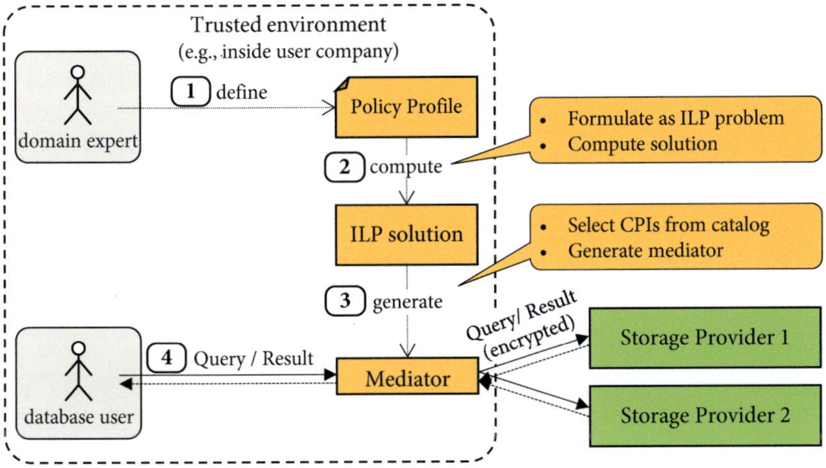

Figure 4.1: Securus' usage workflow from a user perspective.

Based on the ILP's result, a custom software adapter called *Mediator* is generated for the user (3). The mediator covers the user's requirements and implements the CPIs that were determined by the ILP. Depending on the specific scenario, it is also possible that the requirements defined in the policy profile cannot all be satisfied at the same time with the available CPIs. If this case occurs, the user is prompted that her requirements are too strict. She can then weaken either her confidentiality or access requirements. The transformation of the policy profile and the generation of the mediator is covered in Section 4.4.

From now on, the user accesses her data exclusively through the mediator (4). The mediator creates all required tables and indexes on the storage provider(s) for the user and handles all requests and cryptographic keys. For this reason, the mediator has to be run in a trusted environment in the user's domain of control and should not be outsourced as well. Its main task is to transform and encrypt queries specified by the user, forward the requests, and decrypt and restructure any received responses before handing them over to the user. In Chapter 5 we evaluate the performance of the mediator and discuss aspects related to the operation and deployability of the mediator and Securus in general.

4.2 Related Approaches

In recent years, much research has been done in the area of confidential query evaluation, and multiple systems have been proposed that aim at integrating different confidentiality preserving techniques. We categorize these systems in two classes: (i) systems that focus on applying CPIs without using fragmentation to a large extent, and (ii) systems that mainly rely on data fragmentation. The perhaps most popular member of the class of CPI-based approaches is *CryptDB* [PZB11], whereas a solution advanced by a group of Italian researchers [For10] probably constitutes the most popular example of an fragmentation-based approach. In the following, we will introduce and discuss representatives from both classes of systems and compare their strengths and weaknesses to those of Securus.

4.2.1 CryptDB

Similar to Securus, CryptDB [PZB11, PRZB11] aims at preserving data confidentiality in a DaaS scenario. CryptDB is a self-regulating approach that selects a mix of CPIs adaptively at run-time to preserve confidentiality. With CryptDB, the user does not have to specify her requirements before outsourcing her data. Instead, the complete data set is encrypted before it is transmitted to the storage provider. Multiple encryption layers are used in this initial encryption process. The strength of the layers increases from the inner to the outer layers. Whenever the user starts a query that cannot be evaluated by the storage provider with the current encryption scheme used, CryptDB removes one layer from the corresponding attributes by given the storage provider access to the key. The protection level is thus incrementally relaxed with each new currently unsupported type of query. The preserved confidentiality level of the outsourced data depends directly on the processed queries. It can thus be hard to judge at any given time whether or not the confidentiality of the data is still unbroken.

In contrast, Securus provides strong confidentiality guarantees but requires the user to define a policy profile. We argue that this is the better trade in scenarios in which data confidentiality is a must rather than an optional feature. As another difference, CryptDB cannot leverage multiple SPs to improve query execution performance or satisfy more advanced confidentiality requirements.

4.2.2 Fragmentation-based Approaches

Another approach has been proposed by Foresti et al. [For10, CVF+10]. Similar to Securus, this approach combines fragmentation with encryption in order to preserve data confidentiality. However, different from Securus, the system does not make use of multiple non-colluding storage providers, should they be available, but stores fragments on a single storage provider exclusively. As was already explained in Section 3.6, it is key in this setting to prevent the storage provider from linking data fragments. For this reason, each outsourced attribute must only be contained in exactly one fragment. If it was contained in two fragments, the storage provider could link the fragments based on identity of the values stored in the respective columns. In Securus, an attribute can be contained in multiple fragments if they are stored on different storage providers.

The fact that attributes cannot be stored in multiple fragments can impede evaluation performance. If, for instance, an attribute has to be accessed for evaluating two different kinds of queries, it cannot be part of both indexes. That means that one type of query cannot be evaluated on the server-side alone. Instead, the results returned by one sub-query have to be transferred to the client. The client can has to process the second sub-query himself. This query evaluation process can introduce considerable overhead, as (depending on the respective sub-queries) a high number of false positive results have to be transferred to the client. This problem does not exist in Securus.

From a security point of view, the proposed solution and Securus differ in the assumptions made about the storage providers: in Securus, it is assumed that all fragments stored on the same storage provider can be linked, as the attacker only needs to observe one INSERT operation in order to be able to link two fragments. In contrast, the Italian approach does not make this assumption. Instead, it is considered an unrealistic assumption that multiple external storage providers do not collude [For10, p. 87]. Which of both proposed approaches provides the higher protection level hence depends to a large degree on which of these two assumptions is deemed to be more realistic.

With *MimoSecco*, another fragmentation-based approach has been proposed by Achenbach et al. and Gabel et al. [AGH11, GH14]. Similar to the approach presented by Foresti et al., MimoSecco fragments tables in order to hide attribute relations of the original data. For each attribute exactly one fragment is created, which then serves as an index for efficient execution of equality selections. Within these indexes, values are stored in the clear. In [GH14], the authors state that in the future MimoSecco will furthermore support hashed or encrypted indexes. The inclusion of these types of CPIs would allow MimoSecco to evaluate equality selections efficiently without storing them as plaintexts. The MimoSecco project furthermore presents an architectural blueprint for incorporating trusted hardware into the data-outsourcing environment.

The *Cumulus4J* abstraction layer proposed by Huber et al./ [HGSB13] constitutes another technique targeting secure database outsourcing. With some of the original MimoSecco authors coauthoring the Cumulus4J publication, both projects employ very similar data outsourcing and fragmentation concepts. Cumulus4J, however, is more focused on performance than MimoSecco (cmp. [GH14]) and furthermore introduces the security notion *Ind-ICP*, which provides a formal description of the security property that a specific (fragmentation) approach hides attribute relations. This notion is not only used to formalize the security guarantees made by Cumulus4J, but also those made by MimoSecco.

Both MimoSecco and Cumulus4J differ from Securus in that they are vulnerable to attackers who are able to observe single INSERT or UPDATE operations. They share this property with the Italian fragmentation approach discussed earlier. As neither homomorphic encryption nor bucket hash indexes are supported, it is furthermore not possible to efficiently process range selections or aggregations without storing the outsourced data in the clear. Due to this simplicity the user, however, has to specify her individual scenario in much lesser detail than she would have when using Securus. Compared to Securus, MimoSecco and Cumulus4J this way achieve a distinct improvement in usability by lowering the maximum security level that can be achieved and limiting the range of operations that can be executed efficiently.

4.2.3 Summary

To conclude this section, we summarize Securus' strengths in comparison to the previously mentioned approaches as follows. To our knowledge, Securus is the only approach that combines all of the following strengths:

- *Strong confidentiality guarantees*: Securus allows the user to express her confidentiality requirements. If these requirements can be satisfied by data fragmentation and the available set of CPIs, Securus guarantees that they are satisfied and stay satisfied in the future.
- *Multiple storage providers supported*: Securus is able to leverage more than one storage provider in its generated solutions in case multiple non-colluding storage providers are available.
- *Combines fragmentation and CPIs*: Securus incorporates both data fragmentation and CPIs in its problem finding algorithms. This gives Securus a broader set of tools than it is available to approaches that only use one of both.

4.3 Architecture

In this section Securus' technical architecture is introduced. Each of Securus' main components will be discussed briefly and put into Securus' context. A detailed description of Securus' two main novel concepts, namely the policy profile and its transformation to the mediator, follows in the next two sections.

4.3.1 Components

Figure 4.2 depicts on a high level how Securus is deployed. Securus' main components are the *registry* and one or more *mediators*. The registry is a management component that contains the logic for parsing policy profiles and generating mediators. Usually, only one registry instance should exist per deployment. For each independent database that has to be sourced out, one mediator is generated by the registry.

In the following, the behavior of each component will be illustrated in greater detail.

Registry

The registry is Securus' central management component. It is the only component that exists when Securus is initially deployed. The registry contains Securus' core routines and is responsible for storing policy profiles and generating mediators. For being able to do so, the registry also contains a catalog of CPIs that Securus supports. Policy profiles are submitted by a domain expert that understands the semantics and confidentiality requirements of the data (compare Section 4.1). They are stored in order to allow to link to data structures that were defined in previously submitted policy profiles.

When a new policy profile is submitted, the document is first checked for errors. Then, it is checked whether or not the policy profile can be *satisfied*. A policy profile

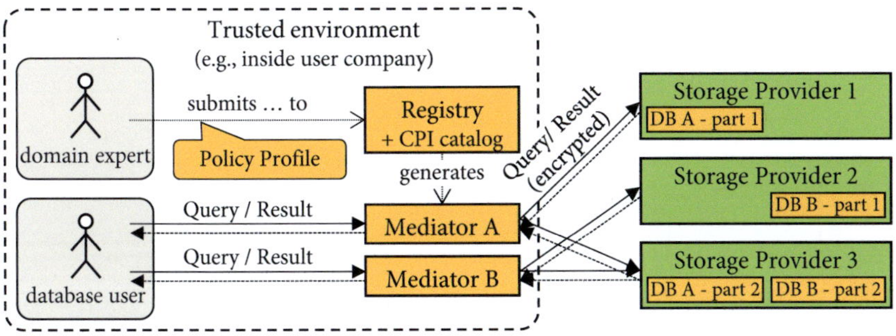

Figure 4.2: Illustration of Securus' high-level architecture. Components that belong to Securus are colored yellow while components that are outside the user's direct control are colored green.

can be satisfied, if all access requirements can be fulfilled without breaking any confidentiality requirements. This process will be explained thoroughly in Section 4.5. If the policy profile can be satisfied, the registry generates a new mediator that matches this profile. The mediator generation process can be influenced by configuring the registry. For instance, it has to be defined which storage providers are available.

Mediator

A mediator is a software component that implements a set of CPIs that are required to satisfy a specific policy profile. For each outsourced database, one mediator is generated. However, multiple instances of the same mediator can be deployed, if necessary. A mediator provides an interface that allows database users to initiate only those requests they specified in the corresponding policy profile. Whenever a query is initiated, the mediator transforms it to one or more queries to the storage providers. How exactly the query is transformed depends on the specific CPIs that are used for this type of query. Typically, some arguments of the query will have to be encrypted before transmitting them to the storage providers. For being able to do so, the mediator also has to store the required cryptographic keys.

Often, results received from the storage provider will have to be reordered or filtered to match the query issued by the user. This is also the mediator's responsibility.

Storage Providers

Each mediator communicates with a specific set of storage providers. Multiple mediators can use the same storage provider, if this does not break any confidentiality constraints. Each storage provider has to provide a suitable interface to which Securus can connect. Our approach is agnostic of the type of data-base used. In our prototypical implementation, we support relational MySQL databases [Sue02], column-oriented HBase databases [Whi09], and the document-oriented MongoDB [Cho13].

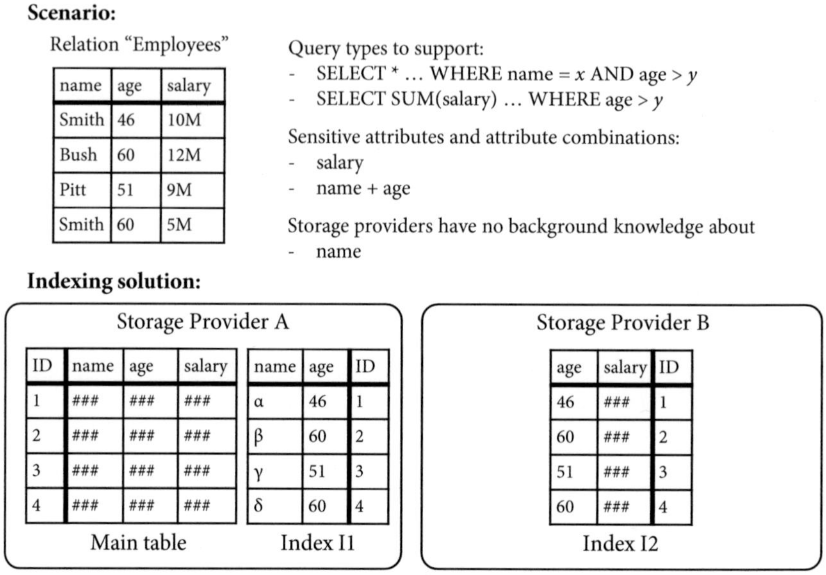

Figure 4.3: Data access in Securus for an exemplary scenario. Values printed as '###' are replaced by indistinguishable substitutes while Greek characters represent distinguishable substitutes. In this example, a hash index is used for attribute *name* in index I1 and homomorphic encryption is used for attribute *salary* in index I2.

4.3.2 Data Indexing

Securus outsources a data table by creating two kinds of data structures on one or multiple storage providers: the *main table* and one or multiple *index tables*. Figure 4.3 illustrates this concept. The main table is a direct duplicate of the data table and contains all of its columns and entries. However, all entries are encrypted probabilistically. Furthermore, an unencrypted *ID* column is added to the main table that assigns a unique identifier to each entry. As the whole main table is encrypted probabilistically, the contained data is sufficiently protected from the storage provider. However, this also means that the main table cannot be used by the storage provider in order to evaluate any queries.

For each kind of query that has to be evaluated, an index table is created. Each index table allows the respective storage provider to evaluate matching queries efficiently. The index table is thus stored on the storage provider that should process this kind of query. Usually, each index table is created on only one storage provider alone. However, it is possible to replicate an index table on multiple storage provider, for instance as a backup plan in case the "primary" storage provider is unavailable. As typically data has to be accessed by multiple kinds of queries, often multiple index tables have to be created. The index tables can (and will, most of the time) be created on different storage providers.

An index table contains a column for each attribute that the storage provider needs to access in order to evaluate a query. For instance in Figure 4.3, the storage provider has to select employes based on their name and their age. The corresponding index table thus contains the columns *name* and *age*. Furthermore, each index table contains an ID column that links the index table's entries to the main table's entries. The index tables' ID column thus serves as a secondary key. This allows the storage provider to answer the query `SELECT ... WHERE name = ''Smith'' AND age = 60` by first retrieving the IDs of the entries it needs to return from the index table *I1* and returning the (encrypted) entries from the main table.

As the storage provider has to operate on the index tables, they cannot be simply be encrypted probabilistically like the main table. The index tables thus pose a threat to data confidentiality. Securus has two means to prevent index tables from leaking sensitive information:

1. *Fragmentation*: If multiple non-colluding storage providers are available, index tables can be stored on different storage providers. This prevents each storage provider from linking the values stored in multiple index tables. Consider for example the scenario shown in Figure 4.3: if both index tables were stored on the same storage provider, the storage provider could link the name of an employee to her salary by joining both index table over the ID column. This is not possible if the index tables are stored on two different storage providers, as no storage provider has access to both index tables.

2. *Substitution*: As the index tables are merely used for identifying the entries that have to be returned, the columns' values can be replaced by *substitutes*, for example by hash values of the original data. In this case, Securus would for instance replace the query `SELECT ... WHERE name = ''Smith'' AND age = 50` by the query `SELECT ... WHERE name =` α `AND age = 50` where α represents the hash of the name "Smith". While the storage provider can still evaluate this query, the name "Smith" is not revealed. Many other similar confidentiality preserving indexing techniques (CPIs) exist that can be used by Securus. They differ in the kind of queries they support and the cryptographic properties of the created substitutes (compare Section 3.5).

Securus main problem is thus to decide (i) on which storage provider each index table should be created and (ii) which CPIs should be applied to which index table columns. The second question can be reduced to the question of which substitution category may be applied, as based on this information an appropriate CPI can be chosen directly from the catalog.

The stated problem can thus be rephrased: to outsource a table, Securus has to decide (i) on which storage provider each index table should be created and (ii) which substitution classes may be applied to each index table's columns. A solution to this problems allows Securus to distribute the index tables and select CPIs appropriately.

Securus solves this problem by converting it into an ILP problem that can then be solved by a generic ILP solver. In Section 4.5, this process is explained in detail.

Storage Provider A

name	age	salary	I_name	I_age
###	###	###	α	46
###	###	###	β	60
###	###	###	γ	51
###	###	###	δ	60

Main table + Index I1

Storage Provider B

name	age	salary	I_salary	I_age
###	###	###	###	46
###	###	###	###	60
###	###	###	###	51
###	###	###	###	60

Main table + Index I2

Figure 4.4: An optimized indexing variant of the index structures shown in Figure 4.3. The complete relation is encrypted probabilistically and stored on both storage providers. The index columns are appended to these tables. No ID columns are required.

4.3.3 Merged Index Tables

For the sake of clarity and simplicity, we explained Securus' indexing approach with the help of dedicated index tables. However, a more efficient approach is to fuse all main and index tables stored on the same storage provider into just one table. The reason for this is that this way just one table has to be accessed for any query that does not use joins. With dedicated index tables, two tables have to be accessed (the corresponding index table and the main table). While we will continue to speak from index *tables* for the rest of this thesis, Figure 4.4 illustrates the approach using fused index tables. As all tables can be joined anyway by the storage provider using the ID columns, both architecture are equivalent from a confidentiality point of view.

As depicted in Figure 4.4, only one table has to be created per storage provider. The table contains:

- A column for each of the outsourced attributes. The columns contain probabilistically encrypted values.
- All columns that would usually be created in the various index tables stored on this storage provider, with the exception of any ID columns.

The downside of this approach is that the data might be replicated on multiple storage providers, which results in increased storage consumption. However, in cases in which storage costs are relatively cheap and high access performance is required, this might constitute an acceptable tradeoff.

4.4 Policy Profiles

This section introduces policy profiles and explains their integral elements: *Access Policies*, *Confidentiality Constraints*, and *Inference Constraints*. Policy profiles allow the user to define her requirements with respect to the confidentiality and accessibility of the outsourced data. Securus than has to compute a *solution* that *satisfies* the specified policy profile. From the solution, a matching mediator can be generated. The concepts of a solution to a policy profile and of how a solution can satisfy a policy profile will be introduced in Subsection 4.4.5.

The foundation for a solution to be found is a formal definition of a policy profile. This definition plays a key role in the generation process and will be referred to continuously in this and the following sections. In the following, the definition will first be presented before its integral components will be described in the following subsections.

The term *policy profile* is defined as follows:

Definition 3 (Policy Profile) *A policy profile is a tuple* $L := (\mathcal{A}, \mathcal{S}, \mathcal{Q}, \mathcal{C}, \mathcal{F})$, *where*

- $\mathcal{A}$ *is a set of attributes for which the policy profile is defined*
- $\mathcal{S}$ *is a set of non-colluding storage providers*
- $\mathcal{Q}$ *is a set of* access policies
- $\mathcal{C}$ *is a set of* confidentiality constraints
- $\mathcal{F}$ *is a set of* inference constraints

Policy profiles are defined in the domain specific language *Securus-Latin* which we also present in this section. The language will be gradually introduced together with each presented policy profile element.

4.4.1 Attributes, Namespaces and Tables

A policy profile defines rules for data that is organized in tables. Securus organizes related tables in *Namespaces*. Each policy profile is defined for a specific namespace. All tables defined in this namespace are then accessible from this specific policy profile.

Namespaces can be declared in just one or multiple Securus-Latin files. These files have to be registered at Securus' registry for them to take effect. The registry manages all valid namespaces defined in a company and is the authoritative source for deciding which tables exist in a namespace. Tables can be added to a namespace by registering a new Securus-Latin file that specifies the same namespace.

Listing 4.1 shows an exemplary namespace definition in Securus-Latin. Two tables are added to namespace "medical" by this file. Tables are defined by the `DataStruct` directive followed by the table's name. Within brackets, a list of attributes follows. Each attribute represents a column in the corresponding table. An attribute definition consists of the attribute's name and its type. Currently, the types `String`, `Integer`, `Float`, and `Bytes` are supported. The example hence defines the table "Patient", which consists of the four columns "firstname", "lastname", "age", and "illnessId", and the table "Illness", which consists of the two columns "name" and "illnessId". Note that it is not necessary to define whether or not an attribute is used as a primary or secondary key.

```
Namespace medical {
  DataStruct Patient {
    firstname   : String,
    lastname    : String,
    age         : Integer,
    illnessId   : Integer
  }
  DataStruct Illness {
    name        : String,
    illnessId   : Integer
  }
}
```

Listing 4.1: Definition of namespaces and tables in Securus-Latin, file "namespace-medical.sl".

```
PolicyProfile medical-example {
  namespace medical
  APs {
    [Patient.firstname, Patient.lastname]
    [<Patient.age>]
    [<Patient.age> : COUNT()]
    [Patient.lastname, <Patient.age>]
    [Illness.name, Patient JOIN Illness ON Patient.illnessId ==
       Illness.illnessId]
  }
  CCs {
    [Patient.firstname, Patient.lastname]
    [Patient.lastname, Illness.name]
    [Patient.firstname, Illness.name]
    [Patient.illnessId]
    [Illness.illnessId]
  }
  ICs {
    [Illness.illnessId]
  }
}
```

Listing 4.2: An exemplary profile, written in Securus-Latin. File "medical-example.sl".

Each policy profile has to explicitly import the namespace it wants to use tables from with using the `namespace` directive. Listing 4.2 shows a policy profile that imports namespace "medical". It is not possible to import multiple namespaces.

Namespaces and tables are not represented in our formal definition. Instead, a policy profile's set $\mathcal{A}$ contains all attributes that are accessible from the policy profile, i.e., all attributes declared in the imported namespace. From a confidentiality perspective, Securus thus handles a policy profile that uses a single table the same way as if the table's attributes were defined in two tables. The reason for this is that it is very hard to judge whether or not any semantic relation between the entries contained in multiple tables can be inferred, especially if the tables' entries are queried together, for example by join-operations. It is thus always assumed that data distributed over multiple tables is as linkable as if it was stored in a single table only.

4.4.2 Access Policies

A policy profile can contain an arbitrary number of *Access Policies*. Each access policy defines a class of queries that the storage providers should be able to evaluate. Access policies are defined by (i) listing the attributes that the storage providers have to access in order to evaluate the query and (ii) stating for each attribute how the storage provider can access its values. The latter is done by choosing an appropriate *query category* (compare Section 3.5.3). Given these options, an access policy is thus a set of query category declarations for an arbitrary number of attributes. Multi declarations can be combined to create compound queries. These allow the storage provider to access multiple attributes for evaluating a single query.

Formally, access policies are defined as follows:

Definition 4 (Access Policy) *Given a policy profile* $L = (\mathcal{A}, \mathcal{S}, \mathcal{Q}, \mathcal{C}, \mathcal{F})$, *an access policy* $Q \in \mathcal{Q}$ *is a tuple* $Q := (E, R, G)$, $E \cap R = \{\}$ *where*

- E *is a set of attributes* $E \subseteq \mathcal{A}$ *that are used in* equality selections
- R *is a set of attributes* $R \subseteq \mathcal{A}$ *that are used in* range selections
- G *is a set of attributes* $G \subseteq \mathcal{A}$ *that are used in* aggregations

It should be noted that (with the exception of aggregations) the user does not have to specify which attributes should be returned by the access policy, as the storage provider does not have to decrypt any values it does not have to operate on. The storage provider can thus return any attribute the user requests.

In Securus-Latin, access profiles have to be defined within the *APs* section of the policy profile. All equality and range selections of the access policy are enclosed by brackets and separated by commas. Aggregations[2] are appended after a colon. Table 4.1 lists how each query category has to be defined in Securus-Latin and also provides a short SQL example for queries covered by the respective query category. The following constitutes an example for Securus-Latin's syntax:

[2]Out prototypical implementation currently supports the COUNT and SUM operations.

Query operation	SQL example	Securus-Latin
Equality selections	...WHERE name='Smith'	name
Range selections	...WHERE age<45	<age>
Aggregators	SELECT SUM(inc) ...	SUM(inc)

Table 4.1: Query categories in Securus-Latin. *Equality selections* correspond to SQL queries in which records are selected based on whether or not a specific attribute is equal to a term. For *range selections*, records are selected based on whether or not an attribute is within a specific range of values. *Aggregators* correspond to queries which require arithmetic operations to be performed on the stored data.

```
[P.lastname, <P.age>] :  SUM(P.timeInHospital)
```

This defines an access policy that specified that the storage provider should be able to perform equality selections on the attribute *P.lastname* and range selections on the attribute *P.age*. Furthermore, the storage provider should be able to calculate the sum over the records' values for the attribute *P.timeInHospital*.

Among others, the access policy matches the following SQL queries:

- SELECT SUM(timeInHospital) FROM P WHERE lastname = 'Smith' AND age >= 50
- SELECT * FROM P WHERE lastname = 'Smith' AND age < 20
- SELECT SUM(timeInHospital) FROM P WHERE age = 20

A special case of equality selections are *joins* [HM10]. In a join, two tables are combined to create their Cartesian product. Then, those entries are selected that fit a specific constraint. Currently, only *Natural-joins* are supported by Securus. In an Natural-join, entries of the Cartesian product are selected based on equality between two attributes (one of each table). Furthermore, duplicates are removed from the resulting list of entries. For all confidentiality concerns, each join over two attributes `A.a` and `B.b` can be considered equivalent to two equality selection being defined for the two attributes. In the following, all considerations mentioning equality selections thus also apply to joins, if not stated otherwise. In Securus-Latin, joins are defined by declaring the two involved tables and attributes as follows: *table1* `JOIN` *table2* `ON` *table1.attributeA == table2.attributeB*

4.4.3 Confidentiality Constraints

A *confidentiality constraint* (CC) is a set of attributes. It declares the relation between the specified attributes as *sensitive*: no storage provider may be able to reveal all of these attributes for any entry in the outsourced data. This concept is not new but has already been proposed by others, to our knowledge first by Aggarwal et al. [ABG+05]. Other studies that use this concept include [XGS11, CVF+10]. Following the definition used by Ciriani et al. [CVF+09], we define the term confidentiality constraint as follows:

Definition 5 (Confidentiality constraint) *Given a policy profile* $L = (\mathcal{A}, S, Q, C, \mathcal{F})$, *a* confidentiality constraint $C \in C$ *is:*

1. *a singleton set* $\{c \subset \mathcal{A}\}$, *stating that the values of the attribute are sensitive (*attribute visibility*); or*
2. *a subset of attributes in* $\mathcal{A}$, *stating that the association between values of the given attributes is sensitive (*association visibility*).*

In other words, at least one of these attributes has to remain concealed from the storage provider (*association visibility*). If a CC consists of only one attribute, then this attribute's values have to be encrypted (*attribute visibility*). It should also be noted that CCs can include attributes of different tables.

As a simple example, the user could define the combination of a patient's first and last name as sensitive, as together they identify a patient. They could thus not both be stored in the clear on any storage provider. However, this CC would allow to store either of both attributes alone at a storage provider in plaintext.

In Securus-Latin, a CC covering the attributes *a* and *b* is specified as `[a, b]`. CCs are declared within the policy profiles's section labeled "CCs" (compare Listing 4.2).

4.4.4 Inference Constraints

Securus might use deterministic encryption or hash functions to fill index columns with distinguishable ciphertexts. This often allows efficient evaluation of range or equality selections. However, the storage provider might be able to infer information from distinguishable ciphertexts if it possesses *background knowledge* about the outsourced data [CDV+05]. Background knowledge refers to any kind of information the storage provider might possess that allows it to deduce information from the outsourced data. Imagine for example that a storage provider knows that most patients in a hospital suffer from the flu. If the attribute *illness* of the table *Patient* is now outsourced using deterministic encryption, the same ciphertext will be stored in the column *illness* of all patients who suffer from the same illness. The storage provider would thus be able to infer which patients suffer from the flue, as the most common ciphertext would be stored as their illness.

An *Inference Constraint* (IC) constraints the inference capabilities of the assumed attacker on a single, specific attribute. The IC declares that the storage provider will not be capable to infer any knowledge from the corresponding attribute, even if it is stored using distinguishable ciphertexts. In particular, this assumption can be made under any of the following two conditions:

- The attribute's values are unique and uniformly distributed, as is commonly the case for primary keys and identifiers. Uniform distribution is only required if any range selections are defined for the respective attribute.
- It is impossible or very unlikely that the storage provider possesses any usable background knowledge about the contained data. However, it is far harder to judge whether or not this second statement applies to a user's scenario.

If a user does not specify any ICs, it is assumed that the storage providers are able to deduce information from any distinguishable ciphertexts found in the database. This technically prevents Securus from using a wide range of CPIs at all. It is thus important to assess carefully if ICs can be defined for any attributes. Often, previously unsatisfiable policy profiles can become satisfiable again if ICs are declared appropriately.

Inference constraints are formally defined as follows:

Definition 6 (Inference Constraint) *Given a policy profile* $L = (\mathcal{A}, \mathcal{S}, \mathcal{Q}, \mathcal{C}, \mathcal{F})$, *its set of* inference constraints $\mathcal{F}$ *is a subset of the policy profiles attributes* ($\mathcal{F} \subseteq \mathcal{A}$). *Each inference constraint states that no storage provider* $S \in \mathcal{S}$ *is able to infer any information from distinguishable ciphertexts of the corresponding attribute.*

ICs are defined within the *ICs* section of the policy profile. Each IC is declared by butting the respective attribute in brackets. For instance, the IC

```
[Illness.illnessId]
```

specifies that the storage provider is not able to infer any information from values of the attribute *illnessId* in the table *Illness*, even if they are stored using distinguishable ciphertexts. In this case, the reason is that the attribute is used as the primary key of the table.

4.4.5 Satisfying a policy profile

The mediator generated by Securus has to match the requirements defined in the corresponding policy profile. In order to do so, Securus has to decide (i) on which storage provider the index columns corresponding to each defined access policy should be stored, (ii) which attributes should be stored on which storage provider, and (iii) how the values of these attributes should be encrypted. This information constitutes a *solution* to the policy profile. Formally, we define a policy profile solution as follows:

Definition 7 (Policy Profile Solution) *Given a policy profile* $L = (\mathcal{A}, \mathcal{S}, \mathcal{Q}, \mathcal{C}, \mathcal{F})$, *a solution for this policy profile is defined as a tuple* $N := (\mathcal{M}, \mathcal{P}, \mathcal{D}, \mathcal{I})$, *where*

- $\mathcal{M}$ *is a set tuples* $M := (Q, S)$, *with* $Q \in \mathcal{Q}, S \in \mathcal{S}$. *Each tuple* M *states that access policy* Q *can be evaluated by storage provider* S.
- $\mathcal{P}$ *is a set of tuples* $P := (a, S)$, *with* $a \in \mathcal{A}, S \in \mathcal{S}$. *Each tuple* P *states that values of attribute* a *may be stored on storage provider* S *in* plaintext.
- $\mathcal{D}$ *is a set of tuples* $D := (a, S)$, *with* $a \in \mathcal{A}, S \in \mathcal{S}$. *Each tuple* D *states that values of attribute* a *may be stored on storage provider* S *as* distinguishable ciphertexts.
- $\mathcal{I}$ *is a set of tuples* $I := (a, S)$, *with* $a \in \mathcal{A}, S \in \mathcal{S}$. *Each tuple* I *states that values of attribute* a *may be stored on storage provider* S *as* indistinguishable ciphertexts.

The set $\mathcal{M}$ thus defines on which storage providers index tables have to be created, while the sets $\mathcal{P}$, $\mathcal{D}$, and $\mathcal{I}$ describe where and how the attribute's values may be stored without breaking data confidentiality. As with the exception of the index tables all outsourced data is encrypted probabilistically, the sets $\mathcal{P}$, $\mathcal{D}$, and $\mathcal{I}$ only have to map those attributes that are actually used in an access policy. Furthermore, the storage provider an attribute is mapped to has to match the storage provider that should support the corresponding access policy. More conditions exist that have to be fulfilled in order to not break any confidentiality constraint or access policy. If the solution fits all of these conditions, we say the solution *satisfies* the policy profile. Mediators can only be generated from solutions that satisfy the given policy profile. In the following, we define policy profile satisfaction.

Definition 8 (Policy Profile Satisfaction) *A solution $N = (\mathcal{M}, \mathcal{P}, \mathcal{D}, \mathcal{I})$* satisfies *policy profile $L = (\mathcal{A}, \mathcal{S}, \mathcal{Q}, \mathcal{C}, \mathcal{F})$, if and only if all of the following three conditions hold.*

Condition 1 *No storage provider may be able to reveal all attributes of any CC. An attribute is revealed by a storage provider S if its values are stored on S in plaintext. It is is also revealed by storage provider S if its values are stored on S as distinguishable ciphertext and no IC is defined for this attribute.*

$$\forall C \in \mathcal{C}, S \in \mathcal{S}, \exists a \in C, \begin{cases} \nexists\, (a', S') \in \mathcal{P} : a = a' \wedge S = S', & \text{if } a \in \mathcal{F} \\ \nexists\, (a', S') \in (\mathcal{P} \cup \mathcal{D}) : a = a' \wedge S = S', & \text{if } a \notin \mathcal{F} \end{cases}$$

Condition 2 *For every access policy there must be at least one storage provider who is responsible for evaluating matching queries.*

$$\forall Q \in \mathcal{Q}, \exists M = (Q', S) : Q = Q'$$

Condition 3 *Every storage provider responsible for evaluating queries matching an access policy must store all attributes used in the access policy's definition. Attributes used in equality and range selections must be stored in plaintext or as indistinguishable ciphertexts.*

$$\begin{aligned} \forall M = ((E, R, G), S) \in \mathcal{M}, ((\quad & \forall e \in E, \exists (a, S') \in (\mathcal{P} \cup \mathcal{D}) : a = e \wedge S' = S) \wedge \\ (\quad & \forall r \in R, \exists (a, S') \in (\mathcal{P} \cup \mathcal{D}) : a = r \wedge S' = S) \wedge \\ (& \forall g \in G, \exists (a, S') \in (\mathcal{P} \cup \mathcal{D} \cup \mathcal{I}) : a = g \wedge S' = S)) \end{aligned}$$

Condition 1 ensures that all confidentiality constraints are satisfied. It follows directly from the definitions of confidentiality and inference constraints (see Definitions 5 and 6 on page 53 ff.). Basically, it means that the values of at least one attribute per confidentiality constraint either have to be stored on a different storage provider than those of the other attributes, or they have to be replaced by sufficiently secure ciphertexts. Unless an inference constraint has been defined, only indistinguishable ciphertexts are considered "secure".

Conditions 2 and 3 together ensure that all access policies are satisfied as well. While Condition 2 simply allocates the responsibility for evaluating queries matching an access policy, Condition 3 ensures that the respective storage provider can access all the data that it requires in order to evaluate incoming queries. For being able to do so, an index table has to be created on the storage provider that contains a column for each attribute used in the corresponding access policy. The storage provider must hence be eligible for storing values of these attributes. Furthermore, a CPI has to exist in Securus CPI catalog that supports the type of query. Values have to be stored in plaintext or as distinguishable ciphertexts if the storage provider has to process equality or range selections, as no suitable CPIs exist that allow these operations to be processed on indistinguishable ciphertexts (see Section 3.5). With the help of (partial) homomorphic encryption, aggregations can be processed on all three kinds of substitutes.

4.5 Policy Transformation

4.5.1 Overview

This section describes the core of our approach: the generation of a mediator that meets the users requirements. As it was described in Section 4.4.5, a solution that satisfies a given policy profile has to specify (i) by which storage provider each access policy should be evaluated in the future and (ii) on which storage providers which kind of substitutes of each attribute's values may be stored.

The transformation process is based on the idea of formulating this problem as an ILP problem and adjusting it based on the specific policy profile. The problem can then be solved with the help of a generic ILP solver to create a solution to the ILP problem, which can then be converted into a blueprint of the mediator to create. This approach has multiple advantages:

- *Performance*: Many performance-optimized generic ILP solvers are available. As we will later see that the problem of satisfying a policy profile is NP-hard, we cannot expect to find an algorithm of a better complexity class for our problem without relying on heuristics or Monte Carlo algorithms.

- *Exact solutions*: The formulation as an ILP problem allows us to find exact solutions. In particular, it can be judged whether an solution is "optimal", i.e., no other solution exists that scores better on the optimality metric defined in our ILP formulation. Furthermore, ILP solvers also allow to determine whether or not an ILP problem is feasible, i.e., whether or not a solution exists at all. From this analysis, we can directly deduct whether or not the policy profile can be satisfied.

- *Formal meta model*: The formal specification of a policy profile makes it easier to study and discuss confidentiality and access requirements. It furthermore makes specification details more explicit which might otherwise remain hidden in Securus' source code.

For our implementation, we used Gurobi 5.0.0 [GO14], a fast commercial ILP solver. However, any generic ILP solver can be used.

Figure 4.5 presents an overview over the complete policy transformation process. The process starts with the definition of the policy profile by the user. As a first step, the policy profile is transformed into an ILP problem. The ILP constraint consists of a number of *ILP constraints* and an objective function. The ILP constraints are linear inequalities that have to hold while the objective function is minimized. To generate an ILP problem, Conditions 1 - 3 of the definition of a policy profile solution are formulated as ILP constraints. Choices that are part of the solution, such as *"Attribute i is stored on storage provider j"*, are modeled as variables the ILP constraints are comprised of, e.g., $x_{i,j} \in \{0,1\}$. In Subsection 4.5.2 it is explained in greater detail, how ILP constraints are deducted.

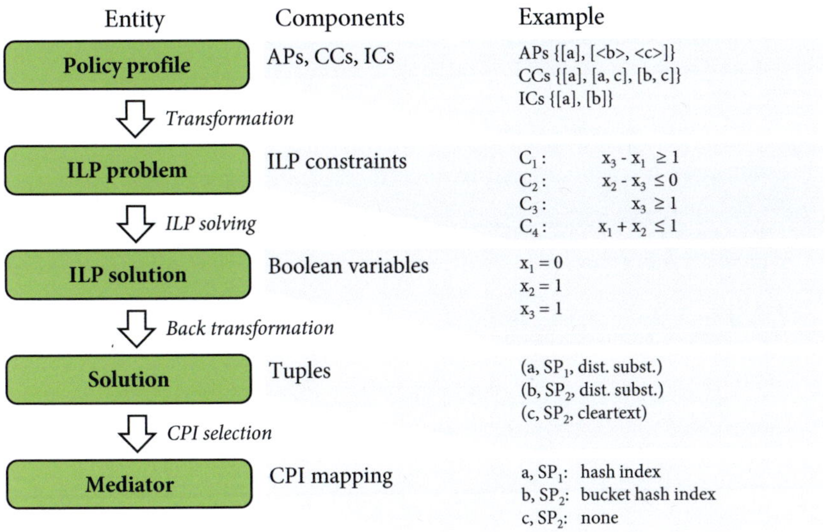

Figure 4.5: Overview over the policy profile transformation process.

When the formulation of the ILP problem complete, the problem is solved. The ILP problem's solution consists of individual values chosen for each of the defined variables. In a back transformation process, a solution for the policy profile is generated from the ILP solution. The solution of the policy profile defines for each storage provider which attributes have to be stored on it and which of them have to be replaced by substitutes of an particular class (plaintext, distinguishable or indistinguishable substitutes).

Furthermore, the solution describes by which storage provider each access policy will be supported. Section 4.5.3 illustrates this process.

In a last step, Securus picks an appropriate CPI for each attribute contained in the policy profile's solution from a table that maps substitution classes to CPIs. Using this information, the mediator can be generated directly.

4.5.2 ILP problem

As the first step towards the generation of a mediator, the policy profile has to be transformed into an ILP problem whose solutions satisfy the policy profile. ILP problems consist of an *objective function*, a number of *ILP constraints*, and the *variables* the function and constraints use. All of these elements are generated from the policy profile following a specific scheme. The scheme defines a fixed number of groups of variables and constraints. The number of elements each group contains depends on the policy profile. In the following, these groups will be described. The policy profile the ILP problem is build for is being referred to using its formal notation $L = (\mathcal{A}, \mathcal{S}, \mathcal{Q}, \mathcal{C}, \mathcal{F})$.

Variables

The ILP problem uses a large number of variables. These variables together constitute the ILP problem's solution. All variables may only be set to 0 or 1. We use the following index-based notation to refer to a number of related variables:

$v_{i \in \mathcal{X}}$: refers to $|\mathcal{X}|$ variables, one for each element in set $\mathcal{X}$.

The following variables are part of the ILP problem:

- $p_{a \in \mathcal{A}, S \in \mathcal{S}} \in \{0,1\}$: states whether or not values of attribute a are stored at storage provider S in plaintext.
- $d_{a \in \mathcal{A}, S \in \mathcal{S}} \in \{0,1\}$: states whether or not values of attribute a are stored at storage provider S as distinguishable ciphertext.
- $i_{a \in \mathcal{A}, S \in \mathcal{S}} \in \{0,1\}$: states whether or not values of attribute a are stored at storage provider S as indistinguishable ciphertext.
- $z_{a \in \mathcal{A}, S \in \mathcal{S}} \in \{0,1\}$: states whether or not values of attribute a are stored at storage provider S in plaintext or as distinguishable ciphertext. This is a set of helper variables that are required to express a certain ILP constraint. Another ILP constraint enforces the coherence of variables $z_{a,S}$, $p_{a,S}$, and $d_{a,S}$.
- $q_{Q \in \mathcal{Q}, S \in \mathcal{S}} \in \{0,1\}$: states whether or not storage provider S stores the index columns required by access policy Q.

Together, $(4|\mathcal{A}| + |\mathcal{Q}|)|\mathcal{S}|$ variables are used. The number of variables thus increases linearly with the number of storage providers, attributes, and access policies.

Objective Function

ILP problems use an *objective function* to define an optimization criterion. Depending on the function, the ILP solver tries to minimize or maximize the function. Whereas Securus makes extensive use of ILP constraints to model the policy profile's requirements, the objective function is of lesser importance for our approach. In future work, the objective function could allow to further optimize mediator performance by considering and comparing fine-grained performance differences between individual CPIs. The objective function could pose an appropriate place for implementing these changes.

In Securus' current state, we use the objective function to minimize the number of attributes whose values need to be encrypted:

$$min \sum_{S \in \mathcal{S}} \sum_{a \in \mathcal{A}} (d_{a,S} + i_{a,S}) \tag{4.1}$$

This criterion enforces that CPIs will not be applied unnecessarily: an optimal ILP solution will encrypt as few attributes as possible.

ILP Constraints

An ILP constraint is a linear inequality that has to hold while the solver tries to minimize the objective function. ILP constraints are the main instrument Securus uses to model the policy profile's requirements. As ILP constraints have to be defined for each variable, many ILP constraints are used in order to generate a solution that satisfies the policy profile. In the following, inequalities will be presented that represent groups of ILP constraints. Each single ILP constraint of a group uses a different set of variables.

Equation 4.2 represents a set of $|\mathcal{C}| * |\mathcal{S}|$ constraints. Each constraint enforces that a specific storage provider is not able to reveal all attributes of a specific confidentiality constraint. For doing so, each of these ILP constraints iterates over all attributes referred to by the specific confidentiality constraint C. For each attribute, the function $f(a, S)$ returns 1 if and only if storage provider S could reveal stored values. Else, 0 is returned. Depending on whether or not an inference constraint has been defined for the respective attribute either variable $p_{a,S}$ or $z_{a,S}$ are used for doing so. The ILP constraint then computes the number of attributes for which the $f(a, S)$ returned 1 by computing the sum of the function calls. As at least one attribute of the confidentiality constraint C must remain hidden from the storage provider, this sum must be smaller than the number of attributes defined in the confidentiality constraint. This group of constraints hence enforces Condition 1 of our policy profile satisfaction definition (see page 55).

$$\forall C \in \mathcal{C}, S \in \mathcal{S}: \qquad \sum_{a \in C} f(a, S) < |C|$$

with

$$f(a, S) = \qquad \begin{cases} p_{a,S} & \text{if } a \in \mathcal{F} \\ z_{a,S} & \text{else} \end{cases} \tag{4.2}$$

Equation 4.3 represents a set of $|\mathcal{A}| * |\mathcal{S}|$ constraints. The constraints enforce that each variable $z_{a,S}$ is set to 1 if and only if at least one of the variables $p_{a,S}$ and $d_{a,S}$ are 1. The variables $z_{a,S}$ are used as helper variables to implement Equation 4.2.

$$\forall a \in \mathcal{A}, S \in \mathcal{S}: \qquad p_{a,S} + d_{a,S} - z_{a,S} \leq 0 \tag{4.3}$$

Equation 4.4 represents a set of $x * |\mathcal{S}|$ constraints where x stands for the number of equality and range selections defined in the policy profile. Each constraint enforces that the values of a specific attribute that is used in the definition of a equality or range selection have to be stored either in plaintext or as distinguishable ciphertext on a specific storage provider, if the storage provider has to support the corresponding access policy. Together with the next one, this group of constraints thus enforces Condition 3 of our policy profile satisfaction definition.

$$\forall Q = (E, R, G) \in \mathcal{Q}, S \in \mathcal{S}, a \in (E \cup R): \qquad p_{a,S} + d_{a,S} - q_{Q,S} \geq 0 \tag{4.4}$$

Equation 4.5 represents a set of $y * |\mathcal{S}|$ constraints where y stands for the number of aggregations defined in the policy profile. Similar to Equation 4.4, this group of constraints enforces that values of all attributes used in aggregations are stored on the appropriate storage providers. As CPIs are available for each substitution category, it does not matter which one is used.

$$\forall Q = (E, R, G) \in \mathcal{Q}, S \in \mathcal{S}, a \in G: \quad p_{a,S} + d_{a,S} + i_{Q,S} - q_{Q,S} \geq 0 \tag{4.5}$$

Equation 4.6 represents a set of $|\mathcal{Q}|$ constraints. Each constraint enforces that at least one storage provider is responsible for evaluating queries matching a specific access policy. This group of constraints thus enforces Condition 2 of Definition 8.

$$\forall Q \in \mathcal{Q}: \qquad \sum_{S \in \mathcal{S}} q_{Q,S} \geq 1 \tag{4.6}$$

Equations 4.7 – 4.11 state that 0 and 1 are the only valid numbers for all defined variables. One constraint per defined variable $((4|\mathcal{A}|+|\mathcal{Q}|)\,|\mathcal{S}|)$ is required for doing so.

$$\forall Q \in \mathcal{Q}, S \in \mathcal{S}: \qquad q_{Q,S} \in \{0,1\} \tag{4.7}$$
$$\forall a \in \mathcal{A}, S \in \mathcal{S}: \qquad p_{Q,S} \in \{0,1\} \tag{4.8}$$
$$\forall a \in \mathcal{A}, S \in \mathcal{S}: \qquad d_{Q,S} \in \{0,1\} \tag{4.9}$$
$$\forall a \in \mathcal{A}, S \in \mathcal{S}: \qquad i_{Q,S} \in \{0,1\} \tag{4.10}$$
$$\forall a \in \mathcal{A}, S \in \mathcal{S}: \qquad z_{Q,S} \in \{0,1\} \tag{4.11}$$

In summary, $(5|\mathcal{A}| + |\mathcal{Q}| + |C| + x + y)\,|\mathcal{S}| + |\mathcal{Q}|$ ILP constraints have to be defined.

4.5.3 ILP solution and back transformation

The ILP solver generates a solution for the ILP problem by assigning a value (either 0 or 1) to each defined variable so that all ILP constraints hold and the objective function is minimized. From these variables, a solution $N = (\mathcal{M}, \mathcal{P}, \mathcal{D}, \mathcal{I})$ that satisfies the policy profile $L = (\mathcal{A}, \mathcal{S}, \mathcal{Q}, \mathcal{C}, \mathcal{F})$ can be deduced directly as follows:

$$\begin{aligned}
\mathcal{M} &:= \{(Q, S) &\mid& \quad q_{Q,S} = 1\} \\
\mathcal{P} &:= \{(a, S) &\mid& \quad p_{a,S} = 1\} \\
\mathcal{D} &:= \{(a, S) &\mid& \quad d_{a,S} = 1\} \\
\mathcal{I} &:= \{(a, S) &\mid& \quad i_{a,S} = 1\}
\end{aligned}$$

The helper variable $z_{a,S}$ is not used in this process.

Note that solutions might be generated that let multiple storage providers support the same access policy. This can only happen if the respective access policy can be satisfied by assigning the *plaintext* category to all attributes referred to by the access policy, as else the ILP problem's objective function would not be minimal. In our implementation, we chose to simply ignore duplicates when generating the mediator in order to avoid adding more constraints to the ILP problem.

Policy profiles can be unsatisfiable. Consider for instance a policy profile that contains the access policy `[a, b]`, the confidentiality constraint `[a, b]`, and no inference constraints. To satisfy the access policy, the values of both attributes have to be stored on at least one storage provider in plaintext or as distinguishable ciphertexts. However, the confidentiality constraint forbids exactly this. The policy profile can thus not be satisfied. Securus is unable to generate a solution if and only if the policy profile is unsatisfiable.

To resolve a conflict within a policy profile and make it satisfiable again, the user has to either change the access policy, confidentiality constraint, or add a new inference constraint. In [KJH14], Köhler et al. extend Securus by a mechanism that is able to detect conflicts and present them to the user. This allows the user to more easily identify conflicts and adjust the policy profile appropriately.

4.5.4 CPI selection

Based on the solution, appropriate CPIs can be chosen from the CPI catalog. For doing so, Securus iterates through all access policies. For each attribute used in the access policy, the corresponding substitution category, the storage provider the attribute should be stored on, and the query type is retrieved. An appropriate CPI is then selected from the cell in the CPI catalog that matches the individual attribute's substitution category and query type (compare Table 3.1 on page 31). The corresponding index column will be created on the storage provider defined by the solution.

5 Evaluation and Discussion

In the previous chapters, Securus, its vision, and its technical foundation have been introduced. In the following and last chapter of the first part of this thesis, the suitability of the Securus approach during daily operation is evaluated and discussed. In order to do so, we highlight the following deployability aspects:

- *Security*: Against which classes of adversaries can Securus protect the outsourced data when compared to other solutions?
- *Operation*: How easy is it to deploy and maintain Securus in a business environment?
- *Performance*: What query evaluation performance can a user expect to achieve with a generated mediator? How long does it take to generate a mediator?

Subsequently, Section 5.6 provides an outlook about promising future research opportunities and remaining challenges. Section 5.7 concludes the Securus approach.

5.1 Security

When modeling the attacker's capabilities, one can differentiate between the attacker's *monitoring capabilities*, i.e., whether she has not only access to the data but is also able to monitor queries, and her *background knowledge* on the outsourced data. In the following we will discuss our assumptions in this regard and compare them to those made by other approaches.

Regarding the attacker's *monitoring capabilities*, Securus assumes an adversary that has access to the outsourced data only but does *not* monitor updates or queries. To our knowledge, this assumption is shared between all other published DaaS frameworks. However, Securus is more robust than other approaches against adversaries that are able to monitor a limited number of queries.

One cause for this is that Securus does not consider multiple fragments that are stored on a single SP to be unlinkable but instead assumes that all columns that are stored together on a storage provider can be linked. Approaches such as [DCdVFJ+13, For10] depend the unlinkability of multiple fragments that are stored on one storage provider. However, if the attacker is able to monitor a single updating or insert operation targeting the fragmented table, she might be able to link fragments. Securus is not vulnerable to this kind of attack.

Another cause is that Securus does not employ CPIs that allow to evaluate equality or range selections on indistinguishable ciphertexts, as these CPIs have the potential to already weaken the achieved protection level when a single query is monitored. Consider for example a query that selects all employees from a table whose name is "Smith". Assume that names are stored as indistinguishable ciphertexts. If two employees with the name "Smith" exist in the database, the attacker can immediately infer that the two returned employees share the same name, if she monitored the query. Effectively, the indistinguishable ciphertexts thus provided not more protection than distinguishable ciphertexts. Securus is robust against this issue. It is thus ensured that indistinguishable ciphertexts can not be linked by monitoring single queries.

Regarding the attacker's *background knowledge*, Securus differentiates only between two cases: the probability that the attacker may have (any) background knowledge about a specific attribute and the absence of this probability (compare Section 4.4.4). We feel that this is a reasonable model mainly because in practice, it is often hard to judge in detail which kind of knowledge an attacker might possess. It is thus easier for the user to accept the default level (an attacker might have complete background knowledge) for most attributes and defining exceptions rather than having to analyze each attribute in detail.

5.2 Operational Aspects

Contrary to other approaches such as CryptDB [PRZB11] that do not provide hard security guarantees, Securus requires the user to specify her access and confidentiality requirements beforehand and expects them to remain unchanged. However, in practice this obviously is not always the case. In the following, we will discuss under which occasions a policy profile would have to be redefined and how Securus would cope with such an event.

Attributes and tables can be added and removed freely from the database, as long as the sets of confidentiality constraints, inference constraints, and access policies remain unchanged. Attributes can easily be added by adding a new, probabilistically encrypted column to the main table, while "removed" attributes could even simply be ignored from now on without touching any data.

Confidentiality constraints describe the inherent dependencies and semantics of the data. In general, it is thus not very likely that they have to be modified very often, if they were chosen correctly in the beginning. Possible scenarios which could force the user to alter her specifications include changes in the companies legal environment – e.g., new laws could require certain information to always remain encrypted.

Inference constraints might have to be removed from a policy profile in case that attacker's are assumed to suddenly have gained more background knowledge. An example for a possible reason for this to happen is that a third party's data center has been compromised.

Access policies are the most likely candidates to change. For instance, the user might have to access old data differently or she might have to add and access a new table that represents a new product.

If an access policy or confidentiality constraint is added to an existing policy profile or an inference constraint has been removed, three outcomes are possible:

1. It is possible to generate a backward compatible mediator. The mediator does not require any previously outsourced data to be restructured or re-encrypted.
2. It is not possible to generate a backward compatible mediator, but a normal mediator can be generated that reflects the changes made by the user. Previously outsourced data has to be restructured and re-encrypted.
3. The new policy profile is not solvable. It has to be relaxed in order for a mediator to be generated.

In order to check which is the case, the ILP problem is modified as follows. First, the currently used ILP solution has to be "frozen" by converting all defined variables to constants. Then, new ILP constraints can be added that enforce the new access policies or confidentiality constraints. If any inference constraint has been removed, those existing ILP constraints have to be modified that were defined in Equation 4.2 and refer to the respective inference constraints. If the resulting ILP problem can be solved, it is possible to generate a backwards compatible mediator that does not require to restructure any previously outsourced data. If no solution exists, the new (modified) policy profile has to be solved without freezing the old solution. Any generated mediator will have to restructure and probably re-encrypt the previously outsourced data. While this procedure can be costly, it can be performed automatically and only has to be performed once.

5.3 Expressiveness

An often stated requirement on confidential DaaS frameworks is that they are able to support most or all queries involved in everyday use. With equality and range selections, joins, and aggregations, Securus already supports a wide range of relational-algebra constructs. However, Securus concept is universal enough to be extended to support further operators.

Consider for example the "LIKE" operator. LIKE selections can be evaluated an plaintext values or even on distinguishable attributes, if searchable encryption schemes are also considered. In order to support LIKE selections it would thus be enough to define a new group of ILP constraints that states that values of the corresponding index table's column have to be stored in plaintext only (plaintext or as indistinguishable ciphertext in case SSE searchable encryption schemes are considered). In a similar fashion, Securus can be extended to support other operators such as "GROUP BY" [KJ14].

5.4 Transformation Performance

In Securus, a mediator typically has to be generated only once. As this process is furthermore performed outside normal operation routines, its performance is of lesser importance. However, as the underlying optimization problem that has to be solved is proven to be NP-hard [KJH14], one could wonder whether policy profiles of typical complexity levels are solvable in reasonable time.

For this reason we evaluated the performance of the policy transformation process by generating policy profiles of different complexities and measuring the time needed to transform them into mediators [KJ14]. The experiment was designed as follows: "For each complexity level we randomly generated policy profiles consisting of the stated numbers of attributes, policies and SPRs. The number of attributes referenced by the APs and CCs was chosen from an exponential distribution with $\beta_{CC} = 3$, $\beta_{AP_{Sel}} = 3$ and $\beta_{AP_{Aggr}} = 0.3$. The proportion of range selections and equality selections was uniformly chosen as $2:8$. We continued to generate policy profiles and measure the transformation time until 5000 satisfiable policy profiles of each category had been generated." [JKH12] The experiment was run on a commodity computer with 4GB RAM and a 2.93GHz Dual Core CPU. The experiment's results are shown in Table 5.1. It can be seen that with mean transformation durations of less than 5.5 sec, Securus' ILP problems can typically be solved quickly for reasonably sized scenarios and "hard" problem instances occur rarely. For large policy profiles that contained 80 attributes, 80 access policies, and 100 confidentiality constraints, transformation could take up to 690 seconds. As mediators have to be generated only once, these duration lengths are acceptable.

5.5 Query Evaluation Performance

In general, Securus' query evaluation performance is determined by the CPIs that are used to evaluate the respective query. The expected performance is furthermore strongly influenced by the concrete database management system used, the technical infrastructure of the storage provider, and the client's network connection. It is hence not possible to make generalized statements about the performance of a generated mediator. For a specific evaluations, we refer the reader to performance measurements conducted by the original authors of the respective CPIs (compare Section 3.5). However, Securus uses CPIs only then for a specific query category, if the CPI is able to evaluate matching queries *efficiently*. In the following, we will analyze Securus' query evaluation performance on a higher level. This analysis as-

Number of policies/elements					Duration (s)	
Attr.	APs	ICs	CCs	SPs	mean	max
10	5	1	10	3	0.004	0.056
20	10	2	40	4	0.015	0.217
20	15	2	10	4	0.016	0.330
40	40	3	50	4	0.555	8.169
40	40	3	60	4	0.658	6.714
80	40	3	40	4	0.036	0.812
80	60	3	80	4	0.887	16.602
80	80	3	100	4	5.474	692.235

Table 5.1: Time required to generate a mediator from policy profiles of various sizes [KJ14].

sumes that the more optimized mediator variant, which uses merged index tables, is used(compare Section 4.3.3).

When using the optimized mediator variant, every query that matches one of the defined access policies can be evaluated (i) in a single communication round and (ii) by accessing a single data table only[1]. It should be noted that this includes compound queries which combine multiple selections or aggregations. As every query has to match at least one access policy to be evaluated, all this is true for all valid queries.

Most CPIs furthermore have to encrypt or hash data that has to be transmitted and decrypt returned values. With the exception of homomorphic encryption schemes, most calculations are performed on a limited number of values on the client machine and are comparatively cheap [PRZB11]. Depending on the concrete scheme used, homomorphic encryption can take considerably more time.

Some CPIs induce additional overhead by requiring the mediator to transfer longer queries (for example by chaining multiple *AND* clauses) or by having the storage provider return false positives. This can lead to a higher amount of data having to be transferred. From the currently supported CPIs, only bucket hash indexes suffer from this phenomenon. For bucket hash indexes, the number of false positives in general decreases for higher numbers of buckets while the number of additional *AND* clauses increases. Section 3.5.4 on page 32 illustrates the CPI's behavior in greater detail.

The combination of multiple CPIs in compound queries allows to optimize evaluation performance by reordering query trees analogously to optimization conducted in relational database systems [Cha98], especially if CPIs are used that might produce false positives. While such fine-grained performance optimization models could prove to be valuable, we consider them out of the scope of this thesis.

[1]The only exception are Joins, which require the storage provider to access every joined table.

5.6 Outlook

While Securus already provides a rich set of features to preserve data confidentiality, we see various options for future additions to and enhancements of Securus. In the following, the most promising ideas will be discussed.

In order to balance access and confidentiality requirements, both dimensions are currently divided into three levels (three substitution categories and three *query categories*). Furthermore, Securus differentiates between two levels of background knowledge: the storage provider is assumed to either possess complete background knowledge or non at all. The ILP problem is build by analyzing interdependencies between these levels. While we limited the numbers of levels deliberately in order to ease policy profile definition, additional levels could be added to each of these dimensions to allow for a more fine-grained policy profile definition. This would allow to include new CPIs that are currently not be supported by Securus because their confidentiality assumptions are to weak or their performance is inferior. In order to not overburden the user, the use of these new features could remain optional.

For example, order-preserving encryption schemes (see Section 3.5.5) produce distinguishable ciphertexts that also leak their order. This makes them very susceptible to attackers with limited background knowledge. If, for instance an attacker knows that a column contains order-preserving ciphertexts of the salaries of an company's employees, she can assume that the company's CEO is among the records with the highest value in the salary column. Due to this susceptibility, we did not include these schemes in Securus. However, when compared to bucket hash indexes, order-preserving encryption schemes have the advantage of permitting more efficient query evaluation as no false-positives are returned. By adding a new substitution class between the categories *plaintext* and *distinguishable ciphertexts*, and starting to differentiate between different levels of background knowledge, order-preserving encryption schemes could fill a niche in Securus in which the user defines explicitly that no background knowledge is available to any attacker. Per default, a higher level of background knowledge could be assumed. In a similar fashion a new query category could be introduced that represent queries that select records based on string-similarity to a given argument. In SQL, the *LIKE* operator would fall into this category. The addition of this category would allow to include searchable encryption schemes (see Section 3.5.5) in Securus.

Furthermore, Securus could be extended to (optionally) also provide support against attackers that are able to monitor queries and data modifications. Securus does currently not protect against attackers of this kind as the matching CPIs typically require a logarithmic number of sequential communication rounds to evaluate a query. Query evaluation is thus considerably slower than a conventional database. However, including these kinds of CPIs could allow Securus to better meet the user's demands in cases in which a high level of confidentiality is required and query evaluation performance is secondary.

Another direction for further improvement is to make Securus more easily integrable into existing IT infrastructures. Desirable features would for example be to provide full SQL support, or an integrated access control.

Lastly, Securus could target other protection goals besides data confidentiality. In particular, data integrity and anonymity constitute often desired features. To ensure data anonymity, several approaches have been proposed [MKGV07, Swe02] that resemble CPIs and could probably be combined in a similar manner.

5.7 Conclusion

In previous three chapters of this thesis, we presented Securus, a confidential DaaS approach that allows to satisfy hard confidentiality requirements when outsourcing sensitive data. As a new step in the user's workflow, Securus lets the user define her access and confidentiality requirements as a *policy profile* prior to outsourcing her data in the domain specific language Securus-Latin. A custom-tailored software adapter that enforces these requirements by fragmenting the outsourced data and applying an appropriate set of CPIs is then generated. Securus computes which security mechanisms it has to apply by transforming the policy profile into an Integer Linear Programming (ILP) problem, which is designed so that its solution directly determines the architecture of the adapter to generate.

Securus is the first confidential DaaS solution that at the same time provides strong confidentiality guarantees, combines data fragmentation and encryption, and is able to utilize multiple non-colluding storage providers. Securus furthermore isolates the required security knowledge and makes it easily reusable. The user thus does not have to be both security and domain expert any longer.

In particular, the Securus approach includes the following scientific contributions:

- *Meta model* for access and confidentiality requirements: Through the use of policy profiles, a meta model is provided that allows to express access and confidentiality requirements. It is specific enough to define confidentiality demands in sufficient detail to compute an appropriate mix of security techniques, but abstract enough to not require the user to possess any cryptographic expert knowledge. By making worst-case assumptions by default that can be relaxed by the user, it is furthermore tailored towards providing hard security guarantees.

- *Combination of fragmentation and CPIs*: Securus advances the field of confidential DaaS research by being the first framework that allows to combine CPIs with data fragmentation on multiple, non-colluding storage providers. This approach is more generic and can cope with stronger attacker models than solutions that rely on CPIs only or rely on data fragmentation on a single storage provider. At the same time, Securus does not depend on the existence of multiple storage providers.

- *Universal problem formulation*: Securus underlying optimization problem is based on the concept that a scenario's requirements can be categorized in multiple dimensions: the supported kind of queries, the protection level of the stored data, and the capabilities of the attacker. Interdependencies between the dimensions are modeled as constraints of an ILP problem. This concept allows Securus to be easily extended, for example by introducing more levels of a dimension in order to permit an even more nuanced distinction of CPIs. This makes Securus a very sustainable approach.

Part II

Performance Management in DHTs

6 Towards a Basic DHT Service

6.1 Motivation

Distributed Hash Tables (DHTs) are Peer-to-Peer networks that allow users to store and retrieve key/value pairs without relying on central services. DHTs reached widespread use due to their inclusion in popular file-sharing applications such as BitTorrent[1] and eMule[2]. High resilience against external shut-down attempts combined with the networks' good scalability are some reasons for the success of the DHT technology in this field of interest. As of today, millions of users contribute simultaneously at any time at the three largest public DHTs – the BitTorrent Mainline DHT (MDHT), the Azureus DHT, and KAD [ZDWR11, JAH11, SENB09]. Studies like [CKC⁺13] analyze the motivation behind file-sharing uses further.

Despite their reputation, DHTs were designed as a fundamental building block for general, decentralized applications rather than to advance (illegal) file-sharing. To achieve this goal, they provide a directed routing functionality that is required by most decentralized applications: identifying those peers that are responsible for storing a specific key/value-pair[3] in logarithmic time. This process is called a *Lookup*. The ability to perform lookups constitutes a DHT's main functionality. Besides storing arbitrary values, lookups can be used to build more advanced services such as locating other peers, forming groups of peers, and many others. Other desirable properties include a DHT's ability to self-organize its peers, its lack of central components and hence lower maintenance costs, and its ability to scale well with an increasing number of peers.

Due to these properties, many DHT-based systems have been proposed by academic research. Examples include content dissemination protocols like Swift [OGJK12],

---

[1] http://www.bittorrent.com, [last visited in October 2014]

[2] http://www.emule.com, [last visited in October 2014]

[3] Values are typically stored redundantly on a small number of peers to cope with peer dynamics.

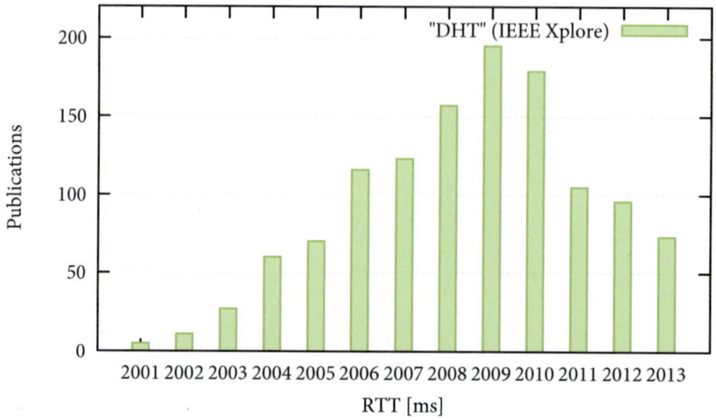

Figure 6.1: Number of publications per year that include the keyword "DHT".

distributed file systems like CFS [DKK+01] or PAST [RD01b], web caches [FFM04], distributed DNS [Bau08], and traffic information services [RSKM09].

Furthermore, much research has been done to further improve DHTs and the quality of the services they provide. Figure 6.1 visualizes the tremendous impact that the advent of DHTs have had on the academic world. It lists the number of publications in this field of research during the last twelve years. For each year, the figure shows the number of IEEE publications that contained the search term "DHT" in their metadata – for instance in the publication's title or its assigned keywords. The searches were conducted with the *IEEE Xplore* search engine[4] on April 26th 2014. The graph shows a rapid growth of publication numbers in the field of DHTs since 2001, with almost 200 publications a year at its peak.

The decline in publication numbers since 2009 shows a strong resemblance to *Gartner's Hype Cycle* [LF03], a model developed by the American IT research firm *Gartner, Inc.* to describe the maturity, adoption, and application of technologies. According to this model, emerging technologies have to progress through two subsequent "hype phases": the first positive hype phase is characterized by overenthusiasm and inflated expectations. The second, negative hype phase is characterized by disillusionment and exaggerated depreciation. During the subsequent third phase, real-world benefits and weaknesses are beginning to get accepted, triggering mainstream adoption of the respective technology. In this phase, a level of maturity is eventually reached that allows wide-spread adoption of the technology. Figure 6.1 suggests that the DHT technology might currently be at the verge of the third phase: core issues – such as elemental routing mechanisms – have indeed been getting increasingly well understood and DHTs are starting to mature. Furthermore, the community has recently started focusing mostly on bringing DHT-based applications to live. As one promising idea, the concept of sharing a single DHT as a kind of *basic service* between a multitude

[4] http://ieeexplore.ieee.org/, [last visited in October 2014]

of decentralized applications has been proposed by many researchers. Among the first, Rhea et al. started the project *OpenDHT* [RGK+05]. OpenDHT was a centrally administered platform that allowed researchers to explore application-side problems of decentralized applications. Along OpenDHT were many other projects that shared a similar idea such as *JXTA* [Gon01], *OpenChord* [www14c], Hazelcast [www14a], and lately *Maidsafe* [www14b]. As one of the most advanced DHT-based application platforms, Maidsafe provides decentralized storage, authentication, and single sign on. In [ZWXY13], Zhang et al. provide a more detailed picture of the field of DHT platforms.

Although many of the proposed systems had tremendous academic success, for years few had a large impact in the non-academic world. This changed when the first companies started to leverage *private DHTs* to build privately managed, decentralized systems that require low maintenance when compared to centralized approaches. A private DHT is a DHT that is under the central control of a single party, i.e., the DHT consists exclusively of peers that are managed by the same party. Private DHTs are thus examples for Single-Party Systems. *Public DHTs* on the other hand are formed by peers that are controlled by individual users and thus constitute prime examples for Multi-Party Systems.

A popular example for a system that is based on a private DHT is Amazon Dynamo [DHJ+07]. Amazon's infrastructure consists of "tens of thousands of servers and network components located in many datacenters around the world" [DHJ+07]. To provide a reliable key-value storage system, Amazon Dynamo lets the devices form a DHT. The DHT allows to manage the continuous failing of components. The system thus harnesses the DHT's self organization capabilities to more easily cope with failures that are very hard to predict in advance.

One reason for the earlier success of private DHTs when compared to public DHTs is that they do not face many challenges that Multi-Party Systems have to cope with, in particular peer dynamics and peer heterogeneity. While these problems remain far from being solved, major improvements have recently been made: studies such as [JOK11, FPJ+07] have helped to increase lookup performance and stability considerably, and security features have been standardized recently [Nor14a].

With these improvements, more and more commercial applications that use a public DHT as their foundation started to arise in the recent years. The application *Tribler* [ZCBP11], for instance, provides P2P-based video streaming on demand. Tribler uses the MDHT to locate data items among its users. Another application that leverages the MDHT is *BitTorrent Sync*[5] [FSK14]. BitTorrent Sync allows to synchronize files between personal computers and other devices. Different from other popular synchronization services like Dropbox, BitTorrent Sync does not transfer files to any central servers, in order to comply with privacy concerns. In December 2013, BitTorrent Sync had over 2 millions of registered users[6]. With *Bleep*[7] a

[5] http://www.bittorrent.com/sync, [last visited in October 2014]

[6] http://blog.bittorrent.com/2013/12/05/bittorrent-sync-hits-2-million-user-mark/, [last visited in October 2014]

[7] http://blog.bittorrent.com/2014/07/30/bittorrents-chat-client-unveiled-bittorrent-bleep-now-in-invite-only-pre-alpha/, [last visited in October 2014]

DHT-based and decentralized chat and voice over IP client was released in July 2014. Through the use of encryption and the abstinence of the use of any servers, Bleep targets a privacy-aware audience.

The success of these systems does not only show that it is possible to build competitive solutions on the foundation of public DHTs, but also that users are willing to participate in these kind of systems, even if they have to contribute some of their computer's resources in order to do so. However, this new class of DHT-based applications demands a far higher quality of service than file-sharing applications: while generally only one lookup has to be performed to download a file, lookups can be much more frequent for other applications. At the same time, many applications are much more sensitive to lookup delays than file-sharing applications [JOK11]. These requirements have to be met reliably for such a *Public DHT Service* to be viable. The goal of the second part of this thesis thus is to ensure that public DHTs can provide a high quality of service as reliably as possible. For doing so, the performance characteristics of public DHTs have to be understood: how peer autonomy affects a DHT's performance, and how one can cope with the identified challenges. With this background in mind, we state our motivational question as follows:

How can public DHTs provide the ongoing and reliable quality of service modern DHT-based applications demand?

6.2 Challenges and Research Questions

As Multi-Party Systems, public DHTs face unique challenges that often prevent them from achieving the performance and predictability of private DHTs. These challenges are caused by the lack of control over the DHT's environment, namely (i) the *behavior* of the peers' users, (ii) the client *implementations* they use, and (iii) the *technical infrastructure* the peers use to connect to each other. Each of these three aspects leads to issues that private DHTs lack and that have the potential to severely affect a DHT's reliability and performance:

Firstly, as peers are controlled by natural persons instead of a single organization with a clearly defined agenda, peers will join and leave the network unpredictably. This phenomenon is called *churn* and strongly affects lookup performance. Furthermore, users might lose interest in using the DHT altogether. Secondly, public DHTs are formed from compatible but not identical client implementations that have the potential to influence each others performance and might receive updates at any time. Thirdly, public DHTs are typically realized as an overlay network on top of the Internet, a much more diverse technical infrastructure than private DHTs rely on. As peers are coming from all over the world, inter-peer latencies are way less predictable than within private DHTs. Furthermore, peers use widely different kinds of network links, might be hosted on constrained hardware, or might be located behind NAT gateways or firewalls. We will later show that especially the latter poses a great challenge for public DHTs, as those peers typically experience one-way connectivity only.

Public DHTs are thus composed of a heterogeneous mass of ultimately unpredictable peers. Key properties of the DHT thus fluctuate and might even suddenly shift on occasion. However, because of the high numbers of participating peers, these peer dynamic also lead to more predictable long-term trends. Examples for such short- and long-term changes that we observed are the sudden duplication of peer numbers due to a bug in a popular BitTorrent client in May 2014, and a the gradual increase of the number of peers that come from Russia. We will describe both events in greater detail in Chapter 8.

Today, neither peer composition in public DHTs nor its evolution is understood well. While several measurement studies exist that target public DHTs [WK13, SENB09, MRGS09, JOK09, SR05b], and other properties have been analyzed analytically [RSS13, WTN06], none provides both a comprehensive picture coupled with ongoing measurements that allow to identify and judge trends early. A second problem is that the community still lacks the tools to evaluate the impact that changes within a public DHT's composition have on the DHT's performance, at least not on a satisfying level of detail. Most probably, it would still be impossible to predict every fluctuation in a global DHT, even if these problems were solved. It is thus necessary that peers adapt optimally to unpredicted changes in the DHT. We will see that in this area today's DHT clients fall short of our expectations.

In summary, the following challenges inhibit the viability of today's public DHT's as a platform for decentralized applications:

1. The composition of public DHTs is heterogeneous, not well understood, and changes over time.
2. It is unclear how specific changes of the DHT affect lookup performance.
3. Despite their reputation, DHT clients are bad at adapting to changing DHT properties.

In this part of the thesis, we tackle these challenges by covering the following research questions. The research question were directly derived from the stated three challenges.

1. How do public DHTs perform and evolve over time?
2. How can we better understand performance inhibitors and assess how they affect lookup performance?
3. How can clients more reliably provide high lookup performance despite the inherent dynamics of public DHTs?

6.3 Structure

The second part of this thesis is structured as follows:

We begin in Chapter 7 by assessing the behavior of lookup algorithms in public DHTs. In order to do so, we first present the technical background by explaining the used protocols and introducing the BitTorrent Mainline DHT (MDHT) as the main object of our studies. We explain why we chose the MDHT instead of other public DHTs and outline DHT characteristics. We then analyze lookup algorithms in greater detail. The analysis allows us to identify by which factors lookup performance is affected the most.

In Chapter 8 we analyze the peer composition of the MDHT and quantify peer dynamics. Our analysis is based on a long-term and ongoing measurement study that we conducted on the MDHT. The measurements were first started in August 2010.

Based on these measurements and other studies, we built a simulation model of the MDHT that allows for a simulation-based prediction of real-world lookup performance. In Chapter 9 we describe our model in detail and elaborate on the trade-offs we had to make to balance prediction accuracy, ease of use, and simulation performance. The model is validated by comparing the simulated performance of typical lookup algorithm variants to their real-world performance.

Chapter 10 present an approach that aims at letting clients more reliably provide high lookup performance, even if the DHT evolved in an unforeseen manner. The approach is based on the idea of dynamically optimizing the client though tuning its parameters at run-time. For doing so, different configurations are automatically tested and compared.

This part of the thesis in concluded together with its first part in Chapter 11.

7 Lookup Algorithm Analysis

Lookup algorithms are the heart of any DHT client, as they empower the client to retrieve values by *get(key)* calls or storing them by *put(key, value)* calls. These procedures are performed in two steps, with the *lookup* being the first. As illustrated in Figure 7.1, the lookup returns a number of peers that are responsible for managing the specified key and the corresponding values. In the following, we will call these peers *target peers*. Target peers have to store any value that is assigned to the corresponding key and return it if requested. During the second step of any *get* or *put* operation, one or multiple of these peers are contacted in order to either store or return a value.

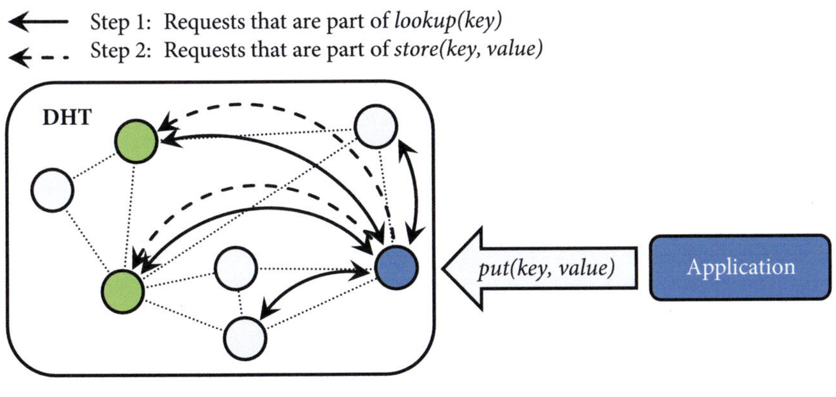

Figure 7.1: Storing of a *value* under a specific *key* in a DHT. In step one, two green target peers are identified by a performing a*lookup* for *key*. In step two, the value is pushed to all target peers.

To define which peers have to be returned for a given key, DHT protocols specify a proximity metric that calculates the distance between peers and keys. The target peers for a given key can then be defined as the k peers closest to the key. In public DHTs, k is usually greater than one to reduce the chance that all target peers leave the DHT at the same time and previously stored values are lost. In order to share the load of being a target peer between all participating peers, DHT protocols try to distribute both peers and keys uniformly over the ID space created by the used metric (compare Figure 7.2). This is typically achieved by assigning random, uniformly distributed IDs to peers at start-up and hashing keys.

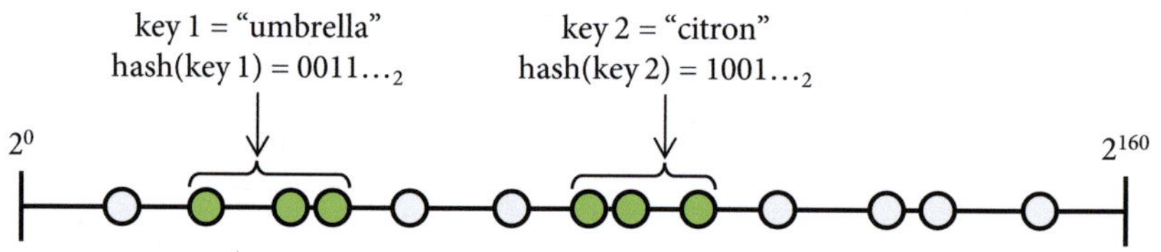

Figure 7.2: 160-bit ID space. Peers are assigned a random ID whereas keys are hashed. In this example, the three peers closest to a key are responsible for storing the corresponding values ($k = 3$).

Lookup algorithms identify those peers among the currently participating ones that are closest to the key with respect to said metric. A plethora of different algorithms have been proposed and / or implemented for various DHTs (among others: [JOK11, SCB10, FPJ+07, SR06a]). Typically, lookup algorithms even differ significantly within the same DHT, as multiple compatible clients are available to the user. In [JOK11], Jiminez et al. studied the market share of different competing DHT clients within the BitTorrent Mainline DHT, one of the most widely used public DHTs. While 60.0% of all checked peers used µtorrent, at least four other implementations could be identified. Furthermore, 32.5% of all peers did not identify their implementation.

Lookup algorithms can be assessed in multiple ways. Among the most important qualities a good algorithm should provide are the following:

- **Speed:** Lookup algorithms should ideally identify and return the target peers quickly, i.e., the duration of a lookup should be low.
- **Low overhead:** Lookup algorithms should induce low computational load and require to send as few network messages as possible. It can further be differentiated between the overhead induced during the execution of a lookup and the overhead induced during idle periods of time.
- **Accuracy:** In public DHTs, lookup algorithms will occasionally be unable to reliably identify all target peers, especially ones with few connections to other peers. For instance, recently joined peers might remain invisible to most peers for some time until more and more peers are getting aware of their presence [SENB07]. We call the capability of a lookup algorithm to miss as few peers as possible as the algorithms *accuracy*.

This chapter aims at providing a deeper understanding about lookup algorithms, their performance, and proposed optimizations. This analysis also serves as a foundation for the following chapters. First of all, Section 7.1 introduces the Kademlia protocol, which is used by the currently most widely used public DHT, the BitTorrent Mainline DHT. As the remainder of this part of the thesis will focus on the MDHT, its prominent role is being justified before the DHT's most characteristic properties are introduced. In Section 7.3, different lookup algorithm variants are presented and discussed. The analysis starts with a description of a set of implementation recommendations that are widely considered as a reference implementation for any lookup algorithm that aims at being compatible to the MDHT. As, however, these recommendations are not very strict, often proposed optimizations are presented and discussed. With *JKad*, we designed a configurable lookup algorithm that is able to "mimic" many commonly proposed optimization. As most measurements and experiments we report on in the rest of this thesis were performed with the help of JKad, we introduce the lookup algorithm used by JKad in greater detail. In Section 7.4, we propose a definition of "lookup algorithms". The definition is deliberately broad to match most if not all previously proposed optimizations, but still allows to place later statements on a more stable foundation. Section 7.5 presents *KademliaPlot*, a tool and graphical notation that allows to depict the workflow of single lookups. When integrated into simulation frameworks or DHT clients, *traces* of lookups can be stored and easily visualized. In Section 7.6, we analyze JKad's performance within the MDHT.

7.1 Kademlia

This section introduces *Kademlia* [MM02], the protocol used by the largest public DHTs. Kademlia was originally published in 2011 by Petar Maymounkov and David Mazières [MM02] as a DHT protocol that "has a number of desirable features not simultaneously offered by any previous DHT." [MM02]. Among these features are the fact that routing information spreads automatically as a side-effect of lookups, the flexibility to send multiple requests in parallel to speed up lookups by avoiding timeout delays, as well as formal provability of key Kademlia properties, such as its scalability. Although it was published one year later than its four competitors CAN [RFH+01], Pastry [RD01a], Tapestry [ZHS+04], and Chord [SMK+01], these characteristics enabled the protocol to reach a much bigger impact on public DHTs, as Kademlia is today used by all major public DHTs that experience widespread adoption. Among others, these DHTs include the *Kad network*, the *Vuze* network, and the *BitTorrent Mainline DHT* (MDHT). In the following, we provide a brief description of Kademlia's main elements – the *XOR metric*, the the defined *remote procedure calls* (RPCs), and the *routing table* design. Note that while most Kademlia-based DHTs adopt these original recommendations, implementations differ in detail as we already mentioned. At places where the paper by Maymounkov et al. is especially ambiguous, we resort to the *BEP5 specifications* [Loe08], a document that specifies how the Kademlia protocol has to be implemented by clients that aim for MDHT compatibility.

7.1.1 XOR Metric

Most of Kademlia's defining features stem from the use of the *XOR metric* that is used to define distances between entities of an 160-bit ID space. At start-up, each peer is assigned a 160-bit integer as an ID, chosen at random. Keys are placed by computing their SHA-1 hash. Distances are then calculated by computing their bitwise exclusive or (XOR) and interpreting the result as an integer ($d(x, y) := x \otimes y$).

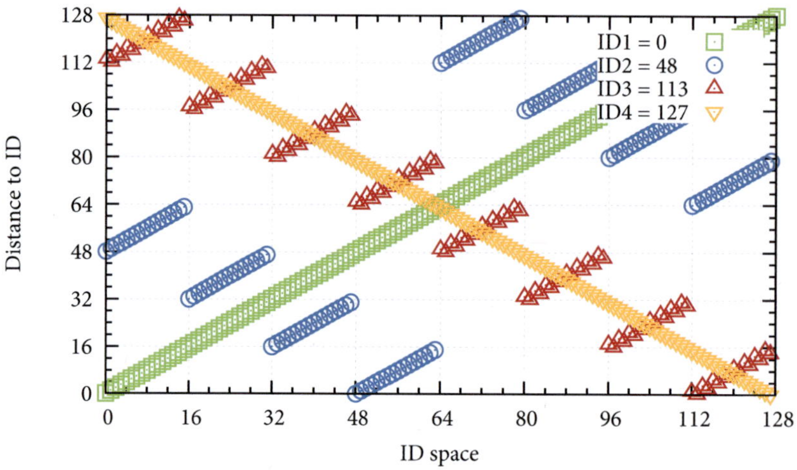

Figure 7.3: XOR Metric: distance graphs for four exemplary IDs.

Figure 7.3 illustrates the XOR metric by depicting the distances to other peers for four starting peer IDs ID_1 to ID_4. For clarity, we chose an ID space of only 2^7 IDs in this example. It can be seen that any peer found in the same half of the ID space as the starting peer is closer than any peer from the other half. In fact, the distance graph looks the same in both halves with the exception that it is shifted along the y-axis. The same is true when further separating each half into smaller fractions. The routing table's structure utilizes this property for its peer management.

7.1.2 Remote Procedure Calls

Kademlia defines for Remote Procedure Calls (RPCs): Ping, Store, Find_Node, and Find_Value. Each RPC is performed by sending a single UDP packet, the *request*. The recipient responds with another single UDP packet, the *response*. The RPC's behavior is defined as follows:

- Ping: This RPC checks whether or not the recipient is online. A peer that receives a Ping request has to respond immediately with a Ping response.
- Store: This RPC transfers a key-value pair to the recipient and asks the peer to store it for later retrieval.

- Find_Node: This RPC asks the recipient to return the k peers it knows that are closest to a *target ID*, according to the XOR metric. The target ID is an ID taken from the 160-bit ID space and typically constitutes the hash of a key that is searched for in a lookup. The response contains not only the peers' IPs and port numbers, but also their IDs.
- Find_Value: This RPC behaves exactly like Find_Node, unless the recipient currently stores a key-value pair that matches the target ID. In that case, the key-value pair is returned instead of the list of peers.

Due to their importance for the execution of lookup algorithms, we will call both Find_Node and Find_Value RPCs simply as *requests* in this thesis.

7.1.3 Routing Table Management

Every peer maintains a routing table to store the IDs and IP-addresses of a number of peers. The routing table consists of a number of *buckets*. Each bucket contains up to k (typically k is set to eight) peers of a similar distance to the peer the routing table's owner: the distance of any peer x in bucket n to the routing table's owner z is $2^{(159-n)} < d(x,z) \leq 2^{(160-n)}$. Due to the use of the XOR metric all peers found in on bucket originate from a precisely defined part of the ID space. For instance, all peers found in bucket 0 are coming from the half of the ID space that does not contain z, while all peers found in bucket 1 are coming from those of the remaining two quarters that does not contain z. Hence, bucket n covers $1/2^{(n+1)}$ of the ID space. Figure 7.4 illustrates this concept. As each bucket can only hold a fixed number of peers but buckets cover a smaller part of the ID space the closer they come to the ID of the routing table's owner, peers store in general many peers more in their direct vicinity than in a greater distance.

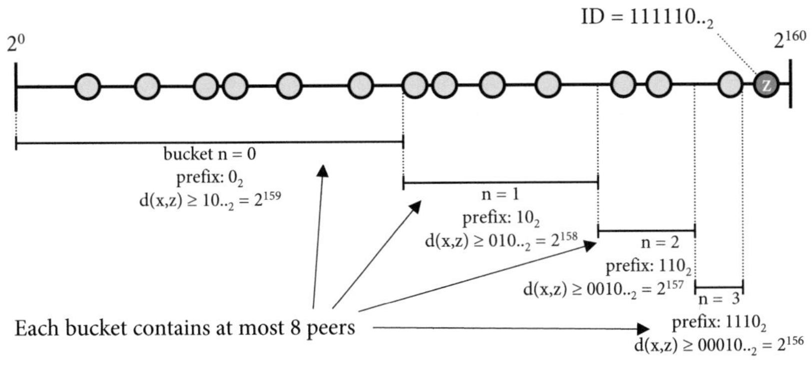

Figure 7.4: Buckets and Distances. This figure depicts which parts of the ID space are covered by the first four buckets of a peer with an ID starting with the bits 111110. Furthermore, a lower bound for the distance of any of the buckets' peers is given.

Whenever a packet is received, the sending peer is added to the routing table. For doing so, the appropriate bucket index is determined by computing the distance between to the sender of the packet and counting the number of leading zeros in its binary representation. If, e.g., the first three bits of the two IDs are the same then the bucket index would be 3.

In case that the identified bucket and all buckets with a higher index are empty, the peer is inserted into the highest bucket that is not empty instead. If this bucket gets filled completely at a later point in time, it is *split* by moving all its peers that do not belong here to the next higher bucket index. This way, more and more buckets are filled over time.

If at least one other bucket with a higher index exists that is not empty, i.e., the peer does not have to inserted into the last bucket, it is attempted to add it to the bucket with the correct bucket index. Three things can happen now:

1. If the bucket is not full or it contains at least one *bad* entry, the new peer is inserted, potentially replacing the bad peer.

2. If the bucket contains any *questionable* peers, these peers are pinged. If any of them does not respond, it is replaced. If all respond, the new peer is discarded.

3. Else, i.e., if the bucket contains only *good* peers, the new peer is discarded.

A peer is considered *good* if it ever responded to a request and sent us any packet (request or response) in the last 15 min. If the peer either did not have a chance to respond as it was not yet queried or if it did not sent a packet in the last 15 min, then it is considered being *questionable*. If the peer was queried but did not respond it is considered being *bad*.

7.1.4 Bootstrapping

Bootstrapping is the process in which a new peer joins a DHT, makes itself known to other peers, and fills its routing table. The process can be separated into two parts: first, the discovering of an initial peer and second, the advertising of the joining peers presence.

An initial peer can be discovered in multiple ways. A fully decentralized approach called *Random Address Probing* was published by Dinger et al. in 2009 [DW09]. In order to identify the initial peer, peers search for peers by "probing" (i.e., port-scanning) random IP addresses. This approach has the advantage of not-relying on any central servers but can be more time-consuming and harder to implement than other concepts.

For this reason, DHT implementations typically employ dedicated central servers that are used for bootstrapping only. The IP addresses and port numbers of these servers are hard-coded into the client or can be configured by the user. Some of the bootstrapping servers that are used by MDHT clients can be reached under *router.bittorrent.com* and *dht.transmissionbt.com*, both on UDP port 6881. While a centralized bootstrapping is surely easier to implement, we will later see that the reliance on central servers can provide a serious risk for an otherwise fully decentralized DHT. In Chapter 8, we will report on measurement reports that show that the MDHT's size dropped by approximately 25% in periods in which one of the more commonly used bootstrapping servers was unreachable. To our knowledge, all commercial MDHT clients make use of central bootstrapping servers.

After an initial peer has been found, the client has to fill its routing table and propagate its presence to other peers. It does that by starting a lookup for its own ID. The routing table is filled automatically in the process with the peers contacted during the lookup. When the lookup is finished, is bucket that is not empty at this point in time is additionally refreshed by starting a lookup for a random ID from the corresponding bucket.

7.2 The BitTorrent Mainline DHT

As mentioned earlier, the Kademlia protocol is used by multiple public DHTs. The three largest of them are the *BitTorrent Mainline DHT* (MDHT), the *Azureus DHT* (also known as *Vuze DHT*), and KAD. The MDHT is formed by clients that are compatible to the Mainline implementation of the BitTorrent client [1], a popular file-sharing application. The Azureus DHT is used by a competing – but incompatible – BitTorrent client called Vuze [2]. The KAD network is built by *eMule* clients, another popular file-sharing application [3].

In this section, we provide a glimpse on the MDHT before we will analyze it thoroughly in the following chapters. We also elaborate on the MDHT's significance as an important study object, as due to its enormous size and complexity it not only allows us to analyze and quantify real-world challenges for decentralized applications but also to gain valuable insight about user behavior.

7.2.1 The BitTorrent Ecosystem

With millions of users, BitTorrent has been one of the most popular file sharing applications for years. The first BitTorrent client was published in July 2001 by Bram Cohen [4]. Today, a wide spectrum of compatible clients is available, typically free of charge.

The BitTorrent client is just one component of the ecosystem that is required for BitTorrent to work. Beside the *peers*, it furthermore consists of *peer discovery mechanisms*, and *torrent-discovery sites*. Each file that is shared between BitTorrent peer is identified by a *infohash*, which is derived by a hashing mechanism. The set of peers that participate in sharing a specific file at a specific time are called a *swarm*.

To join a swarm, a user first needs the file's infohash. Infohashes are distributed by torrent-discovery sites in the form of *.torrent files*. Popular torrent-discovery sites in-

[1] http://www.bittorrent.com, [last visited in October 2014]

[2] http://www.vuze.com, [last visited in October 2014]

[3] http://www.emule.com, [last visited in October 2014]

[4] https://groups.yahoo.com/neo/groups/decentralization/conversations/topics/3160, [last visited in October 2014]

clude The Pirate Bay (http://thepiratebay.se/) and Mininova (http://www.mininova.or g/). These sites can be browsed to find and download .torrent files. Among other data, a .torrent file contains the file's infohash and the IP addresses of one or more *Trackers*.

A tracker is a server that manages a file's swarm. Any peer that wants to join a swarm must retrieve the .torrent file and register at at least one of the listed trackers. The peer can then obtain a list of other swarm members from the tracker and start to download the file from them. At the same time, other swarm members will ask the peer to upload already exchanged pieces to them. Zhang et at. provide a good overview over the BitTorrent ecosystem in its state of 2011 [ZDWR11].

Originally, trackers were the only peer discovery mechanism supported by BitTorrent. BitTorrent clients did not yet include a DHT implementation at this time. In 2005, BitTorrent clients began to offer a second "trackerless" peer discovery mechanism to their users. For trackerless peer discovery, a DHT plays the role of the tracker. A file's swarm is thus managed by the DHT instead of a tracker. In order to do so, a *get(key)* call has to be performed with the key being the file's infohash. The DHT then returns a list of all members of the swarm as a response. To register itself as a new member of the swarm, the peer has to issue a *put(infohash, <IP address, port>)* call. The main advantage of DHT-based peer discovery is that it eliminates the single point of failure that a central tracker constitutes.

7.2.2 Comparable public DHTs

When BitTorrent clients started to include DHT implementations, the Kademlia protocol [MM02] was chosen. However, some clients used incompatible DHT variants. The BitTorrent Mainline client used a variant that the authors specified in the *BitTorrent Enhancement Proposal 5* (BEP5) [Loe08] while the Azureus client used a different variant. The peers using the Mainline and compatible clients formed the MDHT, whereas the Azureus peers formed the Azureus DHT. Today, most clients share compatibility with the MDHT, while some peers, such as the Azureus client itself (now re-branded as *Vuze*), are compatible with both DHTs.

The third major public, Kademlia-based DHT is the KAD network. The KAD network is formed by *eMule* clients, another popular file-sharing application.

7.2.3 Significance as an Object of Study

All three major DHTs have been studied extensively during the last couple of years. Like this thesis, most studies focus on improving lookup performance [JOK11, SCB10, OHKY10, FPJ+07, BS07, SR06a, RGRK04] or quantifying the DHTs' robustness and stability [CSM11, SENB09, CW07, BL07] in order to establish DHTs as a viable option for building public and fully decentralized systems.

Whereas the three DHTs have many challenges in common, the MDHT is of particular significance as an object of study mainly because of its size and ongoing popularity. For instance, Salah et al. [SS13] reported on decreasing numbers of participating peers in KAD, going down from 1.2 - 1.8 million in 2009 as measured by [YLX+11] to 0.5 millions in 2013. In 2008, Steiner et al. estimated the Azureus DHT to contain around

1.1 million peers [SB08]. In comparison, we found the size of the MDHT to fluctuate between six and eleven million peers, depending on the current season, weekday, and time [JAH11]. This makes the MDHT the by far most widely used public DHT. Our measurements further show that the MDHT is growing continuously at least since 2010, which is when we started our measurements. We will report on these results more thoroughly in Chapter 8.

While the MDHT is on the one hand very popular among users, it on the other hand also has unique properties that make it harder to study. First and foremost, differently from smaller DHTs like KAD, the MDHT is comprised of a multitude of different client implementations. Jiminez et al. studied the market share of competing DHT clients and estimated that 60.0% of all checked peers use the µtorrent client, 7.3% use the libtorrent client [5], and the client used by 32.5% of all peers could not be identified [JOK11]. Furthermore, the source code of the most common client, µtorrent, is not publicly available, which makes it harder to understand and predict the behavior of remote peers. These facts might explain why, despite its popularity, the MDHT is less intensely studied than the KAD network.

In the remaining chapters of this thesis, we focus on the MDHT due to its huge and still increasing popularity. We argue that its size and heterogeneity make it a more realistic and interesting object to study real-world challenges of large-scale decentralized applications, the type of systems whose viability we ultimately strive to support. In particular, we see the MDHT as a good candidate for studying the following aspects:

- **Real-world issues**: In studies that rely on analytical models or simulation alone, real-world issues of deployed DHTs have often been either neglected or oversimplified, assuming a more idealized model of the Internet that does not suffer from issues like NAT gateways or client heterogeneity. However, real-world lookup performance still often falls short of expectations. To pave the road for decentralized systems, a better understanding of the underlying causes is necessary. The analysis of a large, real-world DHT is a requirement for this.

- **User behavior**: The performance and stability of public DHTs is greatly affected by their users' behavior, e.g., their session lengths. As the MDHT is comprised of millions of peers coming from almost all parts of the world, it is an ideal candidate to study user behavior in public DHTs.

- **Long-term evolution**: DHTs are highly dynamic systems that change and evolve over time. Properties such as the DHT's size, topology, the users' behavior, or the proliferation of NAT gateways are bound to change over time. Long-term monitoring of the MDHT allows us to gain insight about the DHT's stability and to estimate the likelihood of these kinds of events.

[5] http://www.rasterbar.com/products/libtorrent/, [last visited in October 2014]

7.3 Lookup Algorithms and Optimizations

The official standardization document for the MDHT, the BitTorrent Enhancement Proposal 5 (BEP5) [Loe08], does not define a lookup algorithm in detail but rather sketches its behavior roughly. Clients thus have to choose their own algorithm, which is why lookup performance varies significantly between implementations. In this section, we introduce the standard lookup algorithm specification and commonly proposed optimization. We furthermore analyze the algorithms used by some popular MDHT clients. We then present *JKad*, the lookup algorithm we used for most of our measurements. JKad is highly configurable and can be used to "mimic" commonly proposed lookup optimizations.

7.3.1 Standard Lookup Algorithm (BEP5)

Lookup algorithms can be implemented either iteratively (the source peer sends all requests) or recursively (the peer receiving a request executes the next request). As in reality most DHTs, including the MDHT, support only iterative lookups we focus on this variant only.

The BEP5 specifications go only so far as to state that lookup algorithms should use multiple FIND_NODE requests to iteratively approach the target ID. Figure 7.5 illustrates this process. The peer that initiates a lookup for a target ID (in the following, we will call this peer *source peer*) sends FIND_NODE requests to those peers from its routing table that are closest to the target ID. These peers then return the closest peers they know, i.e., that are contained in their routing tables. This process is repeated until no even closer peers can be found. The eight peers closest to the target ID that were queried and did respond are then returned as the lookup's result (the *target peers*). Due to the routing table's structure, lookup duration will be in $O(\log n)$, with n being the size of the DHT [MM02].

Note, that if one can be sure that all values stored for a specific key are the same, a lookup does not necessarily need to identify all eight target peers if it only wants

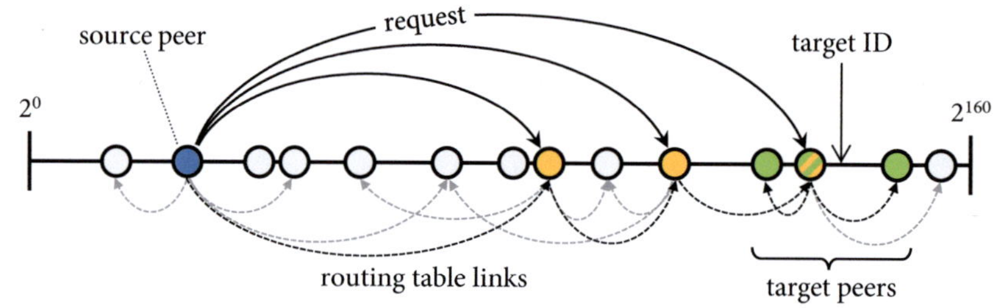

Figure 7.5: Overview over an iterative lookup algorithm's behavior. The source peer queries the peer from its routing table that is closest to the target ID. The queried peer then returns the closest peers it knows and the source peer sends another request. This way, the target ID is approached iteratively.

to retrieve a key's value. Instead, the lookup can be stopped immediately when one peer is found that holds the desired key. Hence, this lookup variant is much quicker but it can only be used to retrieve values, not to store them. In this thesis we will focus on the stricter, more general variant.

7.3.2 Popular Optimizations

Many studies have been published that focus on improving lookup performance. Many of them rely on altering the lookup algorithm alone, while some also try to improve the routing table's structure or maintenance routines. In the following, we present the most common optimization proposals.

Parallel Requests

Parallelism has often been proposed as a means to speed up lookups: by sending more than one *Find_Node* requests in parallel, the impact of unresponsive peers or late responses can be diminished [SCB10, FPJ+07, SR06a, SR05b]. In [FPJ+07], Falkner et al. use this technique to speed up lookups in the Azureus DHT. In [SR06a], Stutzbach et al. employ the same strategy in KAD. An analytical examination of the optimal degree of parallelism is presented by Wu et al. in [WTN06]. Based on measurement results on the KAD network given in [SR05b], the authors find a parallelism degree of 2 or 3 to be optimal. The study furthermore compares iterative and recursive routing strategies analytically.

Decreased Timeout Thresholds

Another often proposed idea is to decrease the *timeout threshold* as much as possible. The timeout threshold specifies how long the lookup algorithm waits for a response to a previously sent request. After this time, the algorithm typically considers the queried peer as being unresponsive and sends a new request to a different peer. Hence, choosing an adequate timeout threshold is a trade off between aborting too many queries prematurely and waiting unreasonably long for pending, but eventually failing requests. In [FPJ+07], the authors propose to use measured response probabilities to introduce "soft" timeout thresholds: instead of abandoning pending queries, the rate at which additional requests are being sent is derived from the measured probability. Steiner et al. advise in [SCB10] to derive the timeout threshold from measured inter-peer round trip delays.

Some studies have proposed to systematically favor peers with low expected round trip delays [KLKP08, JOK11]. In the KAD network, Kaune et al. introduced two new techniques (*proximity neighbour selection* and *proximity route selection*) that aim at filling the routing table preferably with peers that are geographically close. In a simulation of 10,000 peers, the authors their method to reduce lookup duration to a third of its previous value [KLKP08]. Similar to this approach, Jiminez et al. let the client replace existing routing table entries with a certain probability, if a new peer possesses a shorter round trip delay [JOK11].

Increased Bucket Size

Lookup performance can be improved by increasing the capacity of the routing table's buckets, i.e., the *bucket size*. A similar idea, which is already mentioned in the original Kademlia publication [MM02], is to add more buckets to the routing table. Both ideas have been studied analytically for the KAD network in [SR06a] with the conclusion that their performance gain is virtually identical, but an increased bucket size comes at lower costs in terms of implementation complexity and bandwidth consumed for routing table maintenance. In [JOK11], the authors propose to increase bucket sizes proportionally to the ID space the buckets cover. This technique allows to limit the maintenance traffic increase. In a measurement study, in which one modified peer is brought into the MDHT, the authors find only a small performance gain.

Adaptive Parametrization

Typically, lookup algorithms use static parameters that are set by the developer based on one-time measurements. Often, a better lookup performance can be achieved by *adaptive parametrization*, i.e., choosing the values just-in-time. For instance, Steiner et al. proposed in [SCB10] to dynamically adapt the number of parallel requests, the timeout threshold, and other parameters. In Chapter 10, we will present how parameters can reliably and efficiently be optimized at run-time.

Other Proposals

In their study from 2011, Jiminez et al. presented a client for the MDHT that not only combines parallel requests, favoring of low-RTT peers, and increased bucket sizes, but also includes a *quarantine* and an *improved routing table maintenance* feature [JOK11]. The quarantine feature was originally proposed in [JOK09]. It adds new peers to routing table only if they respond to at least one request during a quarantine period of three min. This mechanic prevents peers that suffer from limited connectivity from being added to the routing table. The improved routing table maintenance feature send a Ping request to the most stale routing table entry every six seconds. This helps ensuring each bucket contains fresh entries.

7.3.3 JKad

Our studies required an open source client that is compatible to the MDHT, is able to handle a high number of simultaneous lookups, and is reliable enough to run unsupervised for months. Popular MDHT libraries such as libtorrent were not able to satisfy these needs. We thus implemented our own client, called *JKad*. JKad is written in Java and available under GNU General Public License, version 3 (GPL)[6]. JKad has already been presented in [JH14]. In terms of routing table structure and management, JKad follows the BEP5 recommendations as closely as possible. However, JKad uses a lookup algorithm that combines several optimizations that we previously presented, namely *Parallel Requests*, *Decreased Timeout Thresholds*, and *Adaptive Parametrization*. The algorithm also implements the new idea of using different

[6]http://dsn.tm.kit.edu/jkad.php

parallelism degrees in different phases of a lookup. By changing the parameters' values, the algorithm is furthermore able to "mimic" other algorithm. For instance, it is possible to configure the algorithm to behave like a pure BEP5 client or to just use the Parallel Requests optimization.

The algorithm makes extensive use of request parallelization. This allows the algorithm to continue making progress even if some queried peers fail to respond or respond late. As furthermore more peers will be returned, convergence towards the target ID is accelerated. However, this performance increase comes at the cost of additionally sent queries. If the probability of timeouts to occur is small, a sequential algorithm might be able to provide similar performance at lower costs. A lower parallelism degree should thus be chosen for low timeout probabilities. JKad's lookup algorithm hence adapts to different timeout probabilities by changing the number of requests that are allowed to be pending at the same time. We call this variable the *parallelism degree* l.

The algorithm is divided into two phases: *approximation* and *covering*.

- **Approximation Phase:** During approximation, the algorithm's goal is to approach the target ID quickly until it is "close" to the target ID, but without sending to many requests to limit the induced overhead. It does so by sending a request to each of those l peers it knows that are closest to the target ID. Whenever a response is received or a timeout occurs, the algorithm sends a new request to the closest known peer not yet contacted. Hence, l requests will be pending at any time. Most peers that are returned during approximation will be still distant to the target ID. As they will thus most likely not be part of the lookup's final result, the algorithm should not send more requests than necessary to avoid being forced to wait for timeouts to expire. The parallelism degree l thus has to be minimized in order to maximize efficiency.

  When peers cease to return peers that are closer to the target than they are, the algorithm assumes that it has reached the target ID's direct vicinity. It thus ends the approximation phase when the b closest peers it knows have all been queried without responding with any closer peers. The parameter b is called the *covering threshold*. If a smaller value is used for b, the algorithm will detect the target ID's vicinity earlier. However, approximation phase is also more likely to end prematurely in case some peers are accidentally unable to return any closer peers, for instance because their routing tables are not filled yet.

- **Covering Phase:** Covering phase begins after approximation is complete. The algorithm assumes at this point in time that it has reached the direct vicinity of the target ID. It thus does not expect to receive many more even closer peers. However, it still has to make sure that the closest eight peers did not return any closer peers. As those peers have to be queried anyway, the algorithm cannot save bandwidth by using a low parallelism degree. It thus queries the eight closest peers in parallel. It should be noted that more than eight peers can be sent during covering phase in case that some peers do not reply or they return closer peers.

7.3.4 utorrent

As mentioned before, μtorrent is by far the most commonly used BitTorrent client today. Both Zhang et al. and Jiminez et al. estimate that around 60% of all users use this client [ZDWR11, JOK11]. This client implementation is particularly important for the MDHT not only because it affects the most users directly, but also because issues can severely affect the MDHT itself because of the implementation's dominating market share.

μtorrent is developed by *BitTorrent, Inc.*, an American, privately held company. The company was founded in 2004 by Ashwin Navin and Bram Cohen, the inventor of the BitTorrent protocol. Among others, the company actively drives the development of the BitTorrent protocol. In this process, MDHT changes are also introduced and specified in BitTorrent Enhancement Proposals (BEPs)[7]. The last MDHT-related change was the addition of a security feature in January 2014 [Nor14a].

Unfortunately, μtorrent's source code is not publicly available. In [JOK11] Jiminez et al. reverse engineered some aspects of the client to compare it to their own implementation. Their implementation showed higher performance and fewer maintenance traffic than μtorrent. According to Arvid Norberg, a developer working for *BitTorrent, Inc.*, the μtorrent client was later improved and now includes not only the changes suggested by the authors but also employs further optimizations [Nor14c, Nor14b]. In the following, we describe all mentioned optimizations.

The μtorrent client uses an increased number of buckets as was already suggested in the original Kademlia publication [MM02]. Each bucket contains 8 peers. Initially, a μtorrent client separates the ID space in 32 buckets with each bucket covering a 5 bit range. As usual, only the bucket in which the client's own ID lies will be split. The client also spreads out maintenance traffic more evenly over time, as was suggested in [JOK11].

Furthermore, μtorrent favors peers based on their RTT and their position inside their bucket. Peers have a higher chance of being added to a bucket if they have a low RTT and if their addition leads to a more even peer distribution within the bucket. Norberg described the position-based favoring as being stronger than the RTT-based favoring [Nor14c].

As another optimization, μtorrent does not use a fixes parallelism degree but tries to always query the closest αpeers immediately. This is the same behavior as JKad uses during its *covering* phase (compare Section 7.3.3. The parameter $\alpha$is set to 3 or 4.

7.4 Defining Lookup Algorithms

In the previous sections, we have explained that no strict standard for lookup algorithms in the MDHT exist. Both the original Kademlia publication [MM02] as well as the BEP5 specification [Loe08] only provide recommendations that are furthermore fuzzy in key areas. Most algorithms that make use of the four Kademlia RPCs can be deemed compatible to the MDHT. In practice, the lookup algorithms used by

[7] http://www.bittorrent.org/beps/bep_0000.html, [last visited in October 2014]

virtually any pair of two MDHT clients differ or use at least different parameters. This makes it hard to make general statements about how "lookup algorithms" behave in general, e.g., in order to improve or predict their performance.

In the following, we thus propose a definition that defines a set of minimal requirements for lookup algorithms. The definition is deliberately broad to fit most previously proposed lookup optimizations. Its main idea is to forbid communication by other means than sending requests, but leave most other points unspecified.

Definition 9 (Lookup Algorithm) *A* lookup algorithm *is an algorithm that matches the following requirements:*

- ***Fixed Target ID**: Each lookup is initialized with a 160 bit* target ID. *The target ID is fixed and does not change until the lookup is complete.*

- ***Requests only**: The algorithm communicates with other peers* only *by sending* FIND_NODE *or* FIND_VALUE *requests and receiving the corresponding results as specified by the BEP5 standard. The requests' target ID parameter is always set to the lookup's fixed target ID. The lookup algorithm is free to decide when and how many request to send, but requests are only sent to* known *peers. In the beginning of a lookup's execution only the peers currently contained in the source peer's routing table are considered known. When a peer is returned by a request it becomes known as well.*

- ***Termination**: The lookup algorithm terminates every lookup at some point in time. Upon termination, the lookup chooses 8* known *peers (or all available ones, if less than 8 peers are known) to return.*

As mentioned before, the definition fits virtually all previously proposed lookup optimizations. For example, it fits all 8 variants proposed by Jiminez et al. in [JOK11] (including the 2 variants of their BEP5 implementation), as well as the lookup algorithm proposed by Falkner et al. in [FPJ+07]. Note, however, that not every lookup algorithm that matches this definition would be considered a "good" lookup algorithm: for instance, an algorithm could just terminate instantaneously and return 8 randomly chosen peers from its routing table. While this algorithm would be very fast, it would be very unlikely that any of the target peers would be returned.

Most importantly, the definition implies that lookup algorithms use FIND_NODE or FIND_VALUE requests as the only means of communication. This allows us to model the algorithms communication with the DHT completely by three types of events, which we call *Lookup Events*: *Request Transmission*, *Request Timeout*, and *Response Reception*. As any request can be modeled by just these three types of events, and any lookup can be interpreted as a concatenation of multiple requests, any lookup can be described by these three types of events as well. In the next section, we will illustrate these event types in greater detail with the help of a graphical notation.

7.5 A Graphical Lookup Notation

In order to be able to visualize the behavior of specific lookup algorithms better, we developed a graphical notation that allows to plot individual lookups. The notation is based on Definition 9 introduced in the previous section and its use of *Lookup Events*. A lookup event is a specific point in time at which a query was either started (*Request Transmission*), aborted (*Request Timeout*), or successfully completed (*Response Reception*). Figure 7.6 illustrates the graphical representation of lookup events.

A lookup can be visualized by plotting all of its lookup events as seen in Figure 7.7. The figure shows the behavior of a single, exemplary JKad lookup. For this lookup, the parallelism degree l was set to 2 and the covering threshold b was set to 8. The timeout threshold t was set to 1 second. With these parameters, the lookup algorithm will never enter its covering phase and thus behave similar to a strict BEP5 implementation.

The x-axis of the diagram shows the elapsed time in milliseconds whereas the y-axis shows the encountered peers' distances to the target ID on a logarithmic scale. The dashed vertical line on the right denotes the completion of the lookup. Each empty (white) circle represents the discovery of a formerly unknown peer. Peers are normally detected when they are returned by successful FIND_NODE-requests, but the very first peers are taken from the source peer's routing table. A white circle at (x, y) hence represents a peer that was discovered x ms after the lookup was started and whose distance to the target is y. A horizontal arrow means that a request was sent to the peer (white circle) left of the arrow. The beginning of the arrow represents the *Request Transmission* event. Often, peers are not immediately queried when discovered.

The arrowhead specifies that the query terminated at a certain time: if the arrowhead ends in an 'X', a *Request Timeout* occurred, i.e., no response was received and the request was aborted after a set duration. Else, the arrow ends in a filled (black) circle, which represents the *Response Reception* event. The peers that were returned by the response are also drawn as white circles and connected to the Response Reception event through a vertical, dotted line. Note that because only formerly unknown peers are depicted, often less than the expected 8 peers are shown. Those successfully queried peers (black circles) that form the lookup's end result are surrounded by another circle.

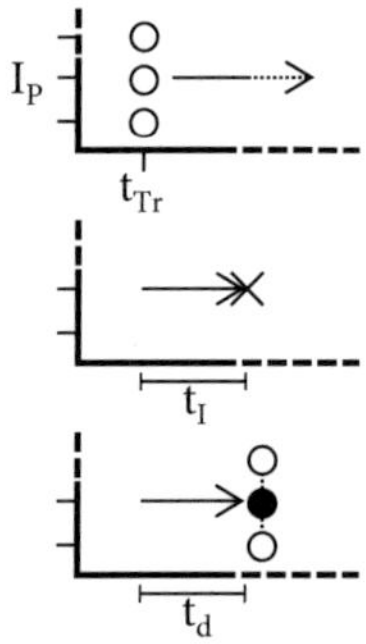

(a) Request Transmission. At t_{Tr} ms a request is sent to the peer using the ID I_P.

(b) Request Timeout. At t_l ms after the request was sent, the lookup algorithm triggers a timeout.

(c) Response Reception. At t_d ms after the request was sent, a response is received containing a number of previously unknown peers.

Figure 7.6: Illustration of Lookup Events.

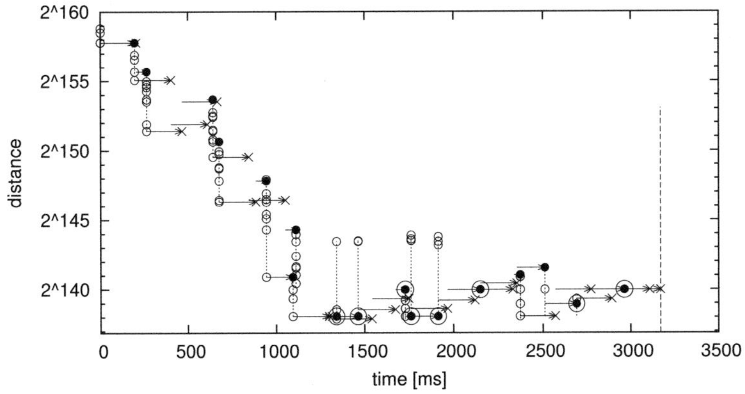

Figure 7.7: Lookup Events forming an exemplary lookup. At each point in time, the algorithm runs 2 requests in parallel. Requests time out after 200 ms without a response.

Diagrams like this are useful to get a quick, intuitive impression of a lookup's performance and the algorithm's behavior. For instance, it can be seen in Figure 7.7 that at every time exactly two requests are pending, with the exception of the very end of the lookup. One can thus assume that the lookup algorithm uses a parallelism degree of two. The diagram furthermore shows that the speed at which the algorithm approaches the target ID decreases logarithmically during the first 1.0 - 1.5 seconds, as the depicted lookup events form a approximately linear line on the logarithmic scale. This behavior is caused by Kademlia's routing table structure. It can also be seen, that starting around the 1.4 seconds mark request stop returning any closer peers, as most black circles are only connected to peers above them, and thus further away from the target ID. This point in time marks the beginning of the covering phase that JKad would normally try to detect, if the covering threshold b was set to a lower value. All of the lookup's result peers were identified in this phase.

When analyzing the lookup's performance, it is easy to see that the covering phase was responsible for more than half of the lookup's duration. The use of a higher parallelism degree during this phase could have prevented that. The plot also makes it obvious that at several points in time the algorithm did nothing but wait for requests that eventually timed out. In fact, the lookup algorithm did nothing else for **XXX**% of the lookup duration. A shorter timeout threshold or higher parallelism degree might help decrease this fraction. The plot also shows that the majority of the peers returned by the lookup were around 2^{139} units away from the target ID, which is an important factor to judge the lookup algorithms accuracy.

In summary, we see that the used graphical notation allows to quickly get a first impression about a lookup algorithm's behavior. While it is no substitute for a numerical, statistically significant analysis, it has the potential to be of great use for researchers and developers alike.

7.6 Lookup Performance

7.6.1 Performance Metrics

Besides the duration, the performance of a lookup can be measured by various metrics, for instance the induced network traffic. In the following, some of the most important metrics will be introduced and discussed.

Lookup Duration

The *lookup duration* or *lookup latency* is typically considered as one of the most important performance metrics. It can be defined in multiple ways: one way is to measures the time until the lookup algorithm has found 8 peers that did reply to a request but did not return any peers that were even closer to the target ID.

Another common definition is to measure the time until at least one peer has been found that stored the value belonging to a specific key. This definition is, for instance, used by Jiminez et al. [JOK11]. This definition has the advantage that it more closely represents the time the user in practice actually has to wait for a lookup, as in most cases lookups are used to retrieve rather than store values. However, a disadvantage of this definition is that the measured lookup performance depends on the popularity of the used key-value pair: the more popular it is, the higher the chances rise that a peer that stores the correct value can be found quickly.

In this thesis, we will use the first definition. As this definition leads to higher lookup durations, care should thus be taken when comparing results with studies that use the second definition.

Requests sent

Measures the number of requests sent on average during a lookup. Unanswered requests are counted. This metric is an important indicator for a lookup's efficiency as it directly describes the algorithm's bandwidth consumption. Also, sending many requests can introduce considerable strain on a possible NAT gateway that protects the sending peer, as for each sent request a new entry has to be created within the NAT gateway's connection table.

Responses Received

Measures the number of responses received on average during a lookup. As every request results in a timeout or a response, this metric also shows how well the variant "avoids" causing timeouts.

Timeout Block Time

We define *Timeout Block Time* (TBT) as the cumulative duration per lookup in which only requests were pending that later resulted in timeouts. The TBT is a good indicator about how strongly an algorithm variant is affected by timeouts, as it describes the time that is lost due to timeouts.

Target Distance

The target distance of a lookup is computed as the average distance that the 8 returned target peers had from the target ID. Target distances are usually very large as only a couple of millions of peers are spread over the entire ID range which has a length of 2^{160}. Because routing tables are structured logarithmically, outliers in both measurement as well as simulation can lead resulting distances being magnitudes larger than normally. As these outliers would dominate the calculation of a variant's average target distance, we typically use median target distances for this metric.

7.6.2 Performance Inhibitors

Although *private* DHTs exhibit great lookup performance with delays of below 100 ms [DHJ+07, LM10], lookup performance in *public* DHTs still has a long way to go with latencies often being a magnitude higher [JOK11][8]. The main differences between lookups run in private and public DHTs are higher network latencies and especially the high likelihood for *timeouts* to occur.

Timeouts are probably the biggest threat to lookup performance in public DHTs. They occur if no reply is received to a Find_Node request in time. Timeouts impair lookup performance as they delay the lookup's progress without helping to discover any new peers. Depending on the specific lookup algorithm used and the current state of the routing table, a large percentage of initiated requests typically remain unanswered. For different configurations of JKad, we observed timeout ratios of 35 to 70%.

Timeouts are caused by different effects:

- *Churn*: The queried peer has already left the DHT, i.e., the user has stopped the client.
- *Guarded Hosts*: Despite being online, the queried peer did either not receive the request or the response did not reach the querying peer. The most prominent reason for this is that the queried peer was located behind a NAT gateway or firewall.
- *Network Latency*: The response reaches the querying peer too late, i.e., after a specific timeout threshold set by the lookup algorithm expired. Either the request, the response, or both packets could be delayed. For instance, delays can be caused by congested passages in the Internet or the user's IT infrastructure. Besides increasing the probability of a request to time out, high network latencies impair lookup performance in another way, as they also delay the reception of responses that did not time out.

In the following, each of this causes will be discussed in greater detail.

Churn

Churn is a term often used in the marketing world and is derived from the words *change* and *turn*. In this context, the churn rate is for instance used as a measure to

[8] In this paper, the second definition (compare Section 7.6) for lookup latency was used.

describe at which pace customers join or leave a specific market. Within the P2P community, it describes the rate at which peers join and leave a P2P-network.

A high churn rate constitutes an important problem for lookup performance in public DHTs, as it causes an routing table's entries to become *stale* more quickly. A stale routing table entry is an entry that refers to a peer that is no longer reachable, for example because it has gone offline. If this entry is queried, a timeout occurs. Clients hence employ different maintenance techniques to hold their entries up-to-date, from which some have already been introduced in Section 7.1.3. Typically, it is ensured that peers are regularly queried. If they do not respond to a specific number of requests, they are removed from the routing table.

Due to its great importance, churn in public DHTs has been the subject of numerous studies [MCPCLG13, LWZ+12, OHKY10, BL07, WTN06, SENB07, SR06b, SR05b, LSM+05, SW04, RGRK04]. An analysis of most of these studies will be given in Section 8.6 of the following chapter, as our own measurements will then have been introduced. We will, however, provide in the following a brief view on the introduced models.

Churn has mostly been modeled as a combination of two factors [SR06b]: the *inter-arrival time*, which is the time interval between two subsequent peer arrivals in the DHT, and the *session length*, which specifies the duration for which a specific peer participates continuously at the DHT until it leaves the network. Stutzbach et al. found in their empirical study in different public DHTs that session lengths follow a Weibull or log-normal distribution, but are ill-explained by the exponential distribution.

Guarded Hosts

Guarded hosts are peers that are located behind a NAT gateway or firewall and thus suffer from connectivity problems. Depending on the type of firewall or NAT gateway, guarded hosts will not be able to send or receive packets, resulting in queries to time out.

Peers hidden behind a firewall will typically not be able to receive *any* incoming Kademlia packets at all, but might still be able to send requests. These peers will thus never answer requests. For this reason, most maintenance mechanisms are very good at filtering them from the routing table. Our measurements that we report on in Section 8.4.4 show that only a small percentage (11.8%) of around 290.000 tested peers showed behavior that could have been caused by a firewall.

NAT gateways will block incoming packets depending on whether or not the sender of the incoming packet has been contacted in the recent past. If it has been, packets originating from the respective peer will be accepted for a certain time, typically 2 min [JOK09, RWHM03]. This leads to the problem, that during these period of time the guarded host appears completely reachable to the peer it contacted although it cannot be reached by other peers. To our knowledge, this effect was first defined a *non-transitive connectivity* by Freedman et al. [FLRS05]. In their study, Freedman et al. provide a thorough analysis of connectivity problems of guarded hosts. A similar assessment is presented in [JOK09]. In both studies, non-transitive connectivity is identified as a major issue for DHT networks.

RFC3489 [RWHM03] defines four types of NAT gateways: *full cone*, *restricted cone*, *port restricted cone* and *symmetric*. The type determines whether the sender is identified by its IP address (*restricted cone NAT*), its IP address and port number (*symmetric* or *port restricted cone NAT*), or not at all (*full cone NAT*). Full cone NAT gateways thus "accept" packets from completely different IP addresses.

Any kind of NAT gateway thus allows a peer located behind it to receive *responses* from any contacted peer, as the response should come from the same IP address and port number the request was sent to. The peer will, however, in general not be able to receive *requests*, as those are typically not preceded by an outgoing packet. The fact that affected peers will still be able to send requests makes them harder to filter from routing tables. In our measurements, we estimated ratio 33.8% of all tested peers to be located behind any kind of NAT gateway.

Network Latency

The network latency denotes the time required for a UDP packet to reach its destination. For lookup algorithms, the *Round Trip Time* (RTT) typically is the more important metric. The RTT is defined as the time interval between the transmission of a request and the reception of the corresponding response. It is thus influenced twice by the network latency, as both the request and the response are affected.

Packets can be delayed at any section on their way to the recipient: at the sender's local IT infrastructure (say, for instance, its NAT gateway), at the Internet, and / or at the recipient's local IT infrastructure. While geographically distant peers certainly show higher network latencies introduced by the routing through the Internet, these delays account typically for far below 200ms. The local IT infrastructure of a user, on the other hand, may introduce far higher latencies, if overloaded: NAT gateways, which are often used to connect to the ISP, may introduce delays of over a second when they cannot handle a high number of incoming and outgoing packets any more [DW09]. Such delays are likely to exceed even the most conservative timeout thresholds and cause timeouts. Unfortunately, this phenomenon can be caused directly by extensive file-sharing use, which is why it is not uncommon in the MDHT.

In order to reduce the issues caused by peers that suffer from high network latencies, the idea has been proposed to favor peers with low RTTs, i.e., let low-latency peers replace routing tables entries that refer to high-latency peers. This approach has already been explained in Section 7.3.

7.6.3 Lookup Performance in the MDHT

Figure 7.8 illustrates the lookup performance of different JKad variants. For each tested configuration, 10,000 lookups were started with JKad (V. 0.7.159). All experiments were run on a Linux machine (Intel T7200 Dual Core @ 2 GHz, 2GB RAM) that was directly connected to the Internet using a 2 GBit/s connection. It was not protected by any NAT- or Firewall-capable devices. For each set of 10,000 lookups, a new JKad instance was started. To build its routing table, the client was started and left idle for 120 s. Then, a new lookup was started every second. For each lookup, a new target ID was chosen at random. After the last lookup had been started, the client was given 30 more seconds to wait for incoming responses before it was stopped. The measurements were conducted between 10 am and 2 pm CET during November 2013.

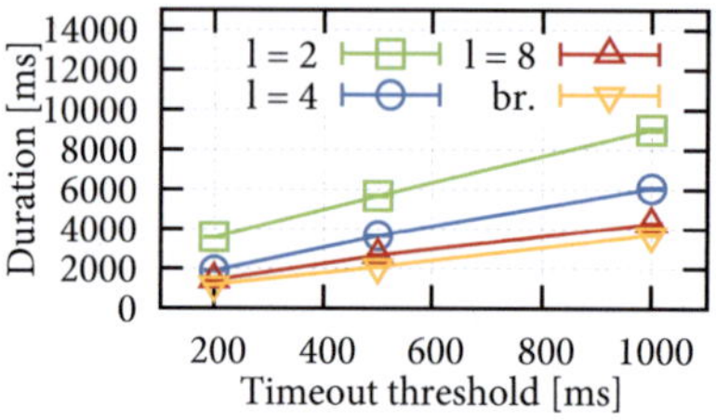

(a) Average lookup durations for the tested variants.

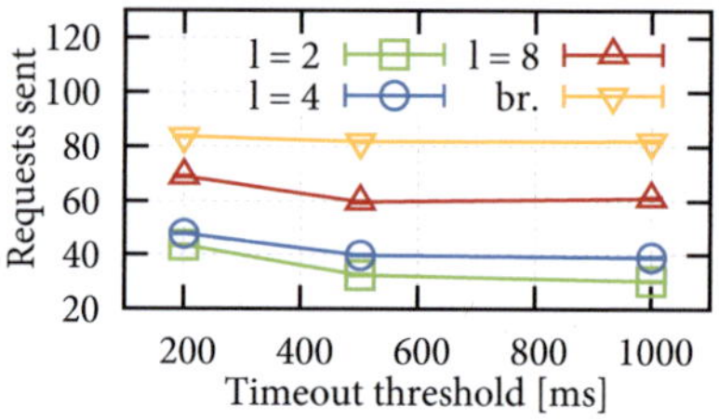

(b) Average requests sent per lookup for the tested variants.

Figure 7.8: Two of the most important lookup performance metrics for differently parametrized jKad variants, including 95% confidence intervals. All measurements were conducted in the MDHT. The parameter l denotes the parallelism degree of the variant, while *broadcast mode* means that parallelism degree was set to 0 and the broadcast threshold b was set to 8, i.e., the 8 closest nodes were always instantly pinged (compare Section 7.3.3).

Figure 7.8a depicts the average lookup duration as a function of the chosen timeout threshold, while Figure 7.8b depicts the number of requests sent on average per lookup.

The chosen algorithm variants displayed vastly different lookup durations ranging from around one to ten seconds. Lookup duration increases linearly with higher timeout thresholds and lower parallelism degrees. In broadcasting mode, lookups were especially fast.

Furthermore, the number of sent requests differs greatly between variants. Higher parallelism degrees lead to more requests being sent. Low timeout thresholds increase the number of sent requests as well, as more requests are prematurely aborted and need to be repeated.

8
DHT Measurement

In the two previous chapters, we motivated the significance of the MDHT as an object of study and provided an glimpse on how DHT properties such as the peers' session lengths or the prevalence of NAT gateways affect lookup performance. In this chapter, we present a thorough assessment of the MDHT and quantify these and other properties. Our analysis is based on results we obtained by long-term measurements that are running continuously since August 2010 and still ongoing. To our knowledge, this makes this study the most long-term and comprehensive measurement study of any widely deployed public DHT.

The work presented in this chapter has partly been published in [JAH11] and [JADH10]. Parts of this chapter are based upon these publications.

The chapter is structured as follows:

Section 8.1 introduces the objective of our measurement study. In Section 8.2, *BitMON* - the framework, with which our measurements are conducted - is presented. In the following section, it is explained how BitMON is able to collect peer samples that are representative for the whole DHT. These samples are the basis for different analyses. In Section 8.4, measurement results are presented, analyzed and discussed. In the end of the section, the results are briefly summarized. Section 8.5 lists three selected incidents that occurred since 2010 and analyzes their effect of the MDHT. Among these incidents are the Arabic spring, the Japanese Tōhoku earthquake of 2011, and the sudden growth of the MDHT to twice its previous size in May 2014. Section 8.6 presents related measurement methodology and related measurement studies. Section 8.7 concludes this chapter.

8.1 Objective

Our need to monitor the behavior and evolution of the MDHT originally arose due to requirements of the project *KAI* which has already been introduced in Section 2.5 on page 18.

An integral part of the envisioned system was the *user discovery service* that returned the IP addresses of all currently active users. When a user connected to the system, she used the discovery service to connect to the other users and establish encrypted connections. As the system was required not to rely on any central services, the discovery service was implemented with the help of the MDHT: immediately after a user got connected to the Internet, the discovery component connected to the MDHT and stored the peer's current IP address and port number in the MDHT, using a pre-configured key that was shared between all users. The discovery component thus just had to perform a *get(key)* call on the shared key to receive a list of all active peers.

Typical MDHT clients however still use central services to bootstrap, i.e., to connect to the MDHT (compare Section 7.1.4). The discovery service hence had to rely on decentralized bootstrapping. For doing so, the client sends Ping requests to random IP addresses (*"Random Address Probing"*). In [DW09], Dinger and Waldhorst describe the approach in detail. Obviously, the effectiveness of Random Address Probing depends severely on the number of available MDHT peers and the port numbers they listen on. The more peers are listening on a specific port, the higher the probability to quickly guess a matching IP address by chance. The effectiveness of the KAI system thus depended on the popularity of the MDHT and their users' port number preferences. It was thus required to monitor the MDHT to ensure the system's reliability.

Besides our use-case, many other systems exist whose performance relies on comparable properties of public DHTs. The application *Tribler* [ZCBP11], for instance, provides P2P-based video streaming on demand. Recently, Tribler was extended to support the *Swift* protocol [OGJK12], which allows to search for items in a information-centric rather than location-specific fashion. Tribler uses the MDHT to locate data items among its users. Because of Tribler's on-demand nature, lookup performance and reliability is of utmost importance [JOK11]. As lookup performance depends on the number of participating peers, the prevalence of NAT gateways, and other factors that are bound to change over time, changes in the MDHT could influence user experience severely. The MDHT is used in a similar way by *BitTorrent Sync* [1], an application that allows to synchronize files between personal computers and other devices. Different from other popular synchronization services like *Dropbox* [2], BitTorrent Sync does not transfer files to any central servers, to comply with privacy concerns. In December 2013, BitTorrent Sync had over 2 millions of registered users [3]. In [FSK14], Farina et al. provide a deeper analysis of the service. Another example are DHT-based Content Delivery Networks (CDN) like Coral [Fre10, FFM04] that aim at delivering data items – such as websites – quickly.

[1] http://www.bittorrent.com/sync, [last visited in October 2014]

[2] https://www.dropbox.com/, [last visited in October 2014]

[3] http://blog.bittorrent.com/2013/12/05/bittorrent-sync-hits-2-million-user-mark/, [last visited in October 2014]

In order to assure a satisfying performance for systems that are based on public DHTs, it is thus necessary to monitor the respective DHT for unexpected changes and trends. Our goal was to provide such a long-term monitoring for the MDHT. Whereas our initial incentive was to support the KAI project, we quickly recognized the demand of similar projects and extended our monitoring engine. The objective of our measurements is twofold:

- Firstly, we aim at monitoring and publishing key properties of the MDHT automatically for projects and applications that directly depend on the MDHT. Among these key properties are the MDHT's size, the geographic origin of peers, and many others. Our goal is to provide a valuable tool to ease the management of DHT-based systems.
- Secondly, we aim at gaining a better understanding of the real-world behavior of public DHTs in general. Therefore, we analyze the MDHT's long-term evolution and analyze the DHT for stability and its reaction to global events. We hope that our results help other researchers to better understand public DHTs and to develop new large-scale DHT-based applications.

8.2 BitMON

For our measurements, we created a measurement platform called *BitMON* [JADH10]. BitMON was originally created in 2009 and received smaller updates over the years. The tool was written in Java. BitMON does not only conduct the various supported measurements but can also create diagrams from the collected data. It thus combines measurement and data analysis. BitMON comes with a graphical user interface (GUI) that allows to start and stop measurements and to display diagrams. A screen shot of the GUI is shown in Figure 8.1.

In 2014, the tool received a makeover to make it easier to handle the vast amount of data it collected during the last years. *BitMON 2* still uses the same measurement and analysis routines as BitMON, but stores all collected data in an Apache CouchDB [4] database. Previously, measurement results were stored in individual files. BitMON 2 furthermore discards the old user interface in favor of an interactive, web-based replacement. As the measurement engine remained unchanged, we will in the following use the name "BitMON" for both versions of the tool, when discussing the measurements or their results.

BitMON was build as a framework to make it easier to support new monitoring demands. BitMON can be extended by three kinds of *modules* to provide new functionality:

- **MeasurementProviders** implement the measurement routines used by BitMON. They perform the actual measurements, for instance by crawling the MDHT, and produce *Measurement Results*.

[4] http://couchdb.apache.org/, [last visited in October 2014]

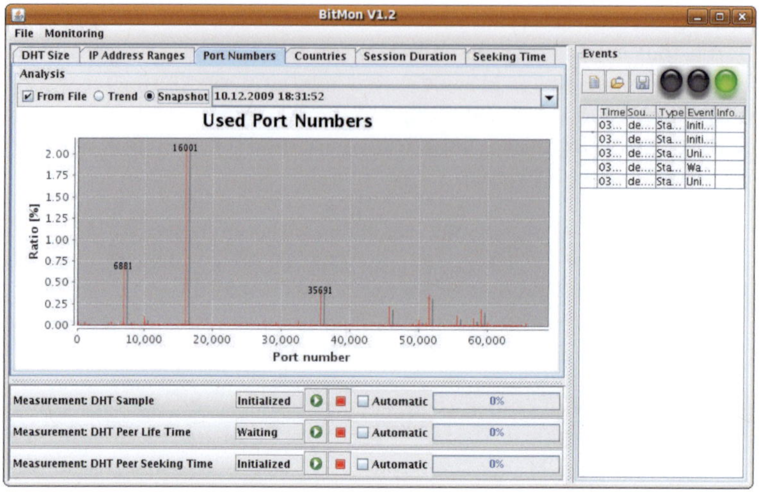

Figure 8.1: Graphical user interface of BitMON.

- **Analyzers** consume measurement results and analyze the raw data. As output, the create two kinds of plots, *Snapshots* and *Trends*. Snapshots are created from a single measurement result and visualize a certain aspect of the MDHT at the time of the measurement, for instance the current distribution of port numbers used by the peers. Trends are created from multiple measurement results and visualize the evolution of a specific aspect over time. A trend could for instance plot the weekly fluctuation of the MDHT's size.

- **Thresholds** monitor the analyzers' results for sudden changes. If a certain threshold is exceeded, a warning message is generated. In BitMON 2, thresholds are not used any more.

In Figure 8.1 three measurement providers are used. Each one can be controlled by its own control panel. Multiple measurements can be running concurrently. On the right, a log of recent warnings and other events is shown. Above the providers' control panels, the analyzers display their plots in multiple tabs.

8.3 DHT Sampling

In order to draw universally valid conclusions about a DHT's peers, two options exist: observing every participating peer extrapolating from a smaller but representative subset (or "sample") of peers. A full crawl of a public DHT consisting of more than ten million peers takes much longer than a partial crawl and has a much higher memory footprint. As a result, full crawls are not only inconvenient to process and store for later analysis, but also less accurate on the timescale. We thus decided to rely on representative samples.

Our sampling process is based on the idea of finding all peers within a small interval of Kademlia's ID space [JAH11]. The interval represents the 256th part of the ID space and hence spans 2^{152} IDs. Peers are retrieved by running lookups for a large number of IDs taken from the interval. As peers are uniformly distributed over the ID space, it is possible to generalize conclusions drawn from the peers found within a specific partition of the ID space.

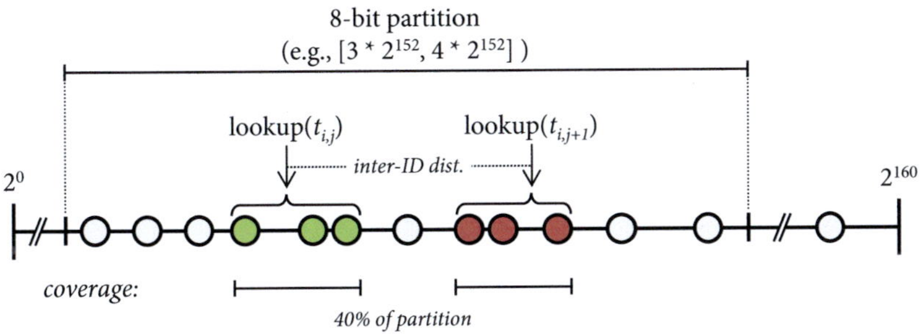

(a) Sampling process using a high inter-ID distance. In this example, the fourth 8-bit partition of the ID space is scanned using a high inter-ID distance. As the scanned areas do not overlap, many peers are missed and only a small part of the whole partition can be considered *scanned*.

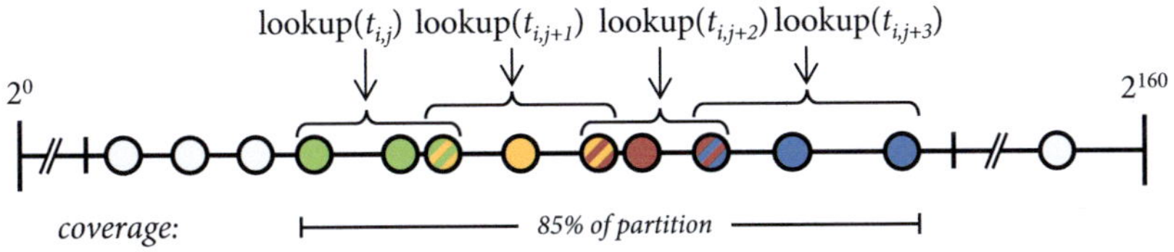

(b) Sampling process using a low inter-ID distance. This time, the same partition as shown in Figure 8.2a is scanned again, but with a lower inter-ID distance. Some peers are returned by multiple lookups and a much larger ratio of the partition can be considered *scanned*. However, a higher number of lookups need to be run.

Figure 8.2: Lookup-based DHT sampling.

To completely scan a partition of the ID-space, we leverage the fact that lookups return the eight closest peers to the target ID. The probability that a peer that lies "between" the returned peers is missed should thus be very low. As a result, the area between the peers with the lowest and highest IDs can be considered *scanned*. If IDs that are close to each other are targeted by consecutive lookups, the scanned areas will likely overlap, creating a consolidated scanned interval in which all peers have been detected. With decreasing distances between targeted IDs, a larger and larger part of the partition will be covered, eventually approaching a *coverage* of 100%, as illustrated by Figure 8.2. With low inter-ID distances, scans are thus more accurate as they are able to detect a higher ratio of peers. On the down side, more lookups need to be run for doing so, potentially slowing down the crawling process. Thus, an appropriate tradeoff has to be chosen.

Our crawler supports two modes: one in which the partition is scanned once per crawl (*fixed accuracy mode*) and one, in which the partition is repeatedly scanned in multiple cycles, while the number of executed lookups is doubled from cycle to cycle (*progressive accuracy mode*). In progressive accuracy mode, the crawler is able to automatically determine an appropriate number of lookups to conduct, but might overestimate peer numbers slightly, as the same ID interval is scanned multiple times. In the following, we will describe both modes.

8.3.1 Progressive Accuracy Mode

In progressive accuracy mode, the ID partition is scanned in multiple cycles, as depicted by Figure 8.3. In the ith cycle, 2^i IDs are looked up. The IDs targeted during the same cycle are evenly distributed over the whole partition. This is done by separating the partition into 2^i parts and using the IDs in the center of each of these parts. More formally, the jth target ID $t_{i,j}$ of cycle i can be computed as follows:

$$t_{i,j=0,\dots,2^i} := l + \left\lfloor \frac{2j+1}{2^{i+1}} w \right\rfloor \tag{8.1}$$

where l is the lower boundary of the crawled partition, and w is the width of the crawled partition. Note that no ID will be targeted twice:

$$\forall i, i', j \in \{0, \dots, 2^i\}, j' \in \{0, \dots, 2^{i'}\} : t_{i,j} = t_{i',j'} \Leftrightarrow i = i' \wedge j = j' \tag{8.2}$$

Because of this, the lookup results of different cycles can be combined: Any peer that is returned at least once by a lookup during any cycle is included into the the collected sample.

The *scan rate*, which is defined as the number of lookups sent per second, stays fixed during the whole crawl. Hence, each cycle takes twice the time of the previous one. With higher cycle numbers, coverage converges against 100% of the partition, as illustrated by Figure 8.2. When a satisfying threshold is exceeded (we use 95%), the crawl is stopped after completing the current cycle. At which cycle this happens depends on the current size of the DHT, as the area covered by a single lookup depends on the number of participating peers: with higher peer numbers, the returned peers will likely be closer to the target ID and thus cover a smaller area of the ID space. This way, the crawler is able to adapt to different DHT sizes.

An issue of the progressive accuracy mode is that it is susceptible to overestimating the DHT size in the presence of higher churn rates, e.g., when the peers' session lengths are short. The reason for this is that over multiple cycles the crawler will look up IDs that are very close to each other with considerable delay (up to multiple minutes). As a result, peers that were already counted by the first lookups might leave the DHT while new peers that join the DHT might be counted by subsequent lookups. On average, our estimations made in progressive accuracy mode deviation are 10% higher than those made in fixed accuracy mode.

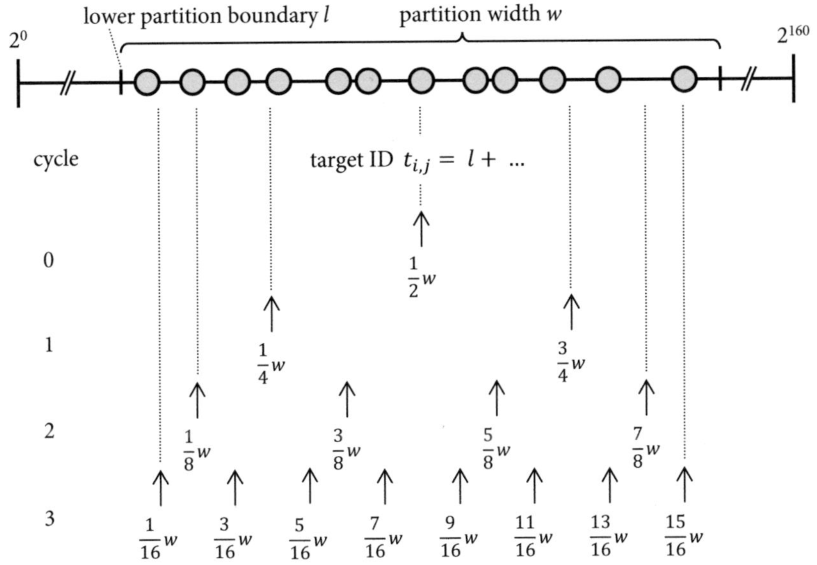

Figure 8.3: Progressive accuracy mode. In this mode, the partition is scanned in multiple cycles. In each cycle, the number of initiated lookups doubles. The rate at which lookups are started stays constant.

8.3.2 Fixed Accuracy Mode

In fixed accuracy mode, the crawler scans the partition in a single cycle of a pre-configured depth i. The coverage of the scanned area does not serve any purpose in fixed accuracy mode. In all other respects, the crawler behaves exactly as it would in progressive accuracy mode. In depth $i = 14$, $2^{14} = 16,384$ lookups would thus be run in a single cycle before the crawl ends.

Compared to the progressive accuracy mode, a fixed accuracy crawl suffers to a far lesser extent from the overestimation problem as far less time elapses between lookups targeting close IDs because IDs are looked up strictly in ascending order. However, the user is required to "guess" an appropriate cycle depth to configure the crawler properly. This number could, for instance, be derived by running the crawler first in progressive accuracy mode.

8.3.3 Configuration and Statistics

For our long-term measurement, we ran BitMON in progressive accuracy mode until we switched to fixed accuracy mode in August 2014. In progressive mode, the crawler always stopped after processing the 13th cycle, hence $\sum_{i=0}^{13} 2^i = 2^{14} - 1 = 16,383$ lookups were run per scan. We used a scan rate of 10 lookups per second. One crawl thus took 27 minutes and 20 seconds. In fixed accuracy mode, we used a cycle depth of 14, so a crawl took approximately the same time as before. Our database currently (as of October 10th 2014) contains 70.752 DHT samples, each containing between 15.000 to 105.000 peers.

8.3.4 Measurement Accuracy

Like any other DHT crawler, out approach might miss peers when trying to scan an ID interval completely. We argue that the impact of this probability is negligible and does not spoil the representativeness of collected samples. Our rationale is based on two arguments: (i) peers that are missed have not been bootstrapped properly and (ii) peers that have not been bootstrapped properly are not contributing to the DHT and thus (per definition) not part of the DHT.

Our crawler is configured so that every peer has multiple chances to be detected: with 2^{14} lookups being run per scan and 8 peers returned per lookup, up to 2^{17} peers can be detected per scan, which would suffice for DHT sizes of up to $2^{17} * 256 = 2^{25} \approx 32$ million peers. In every lookup for target ID t, at least the eight eventually returned peers have been queried for any even closer peers (compare Section 7.3). A missed peer thus must not have been known by any of these peers, i.e., it must not have been contained in their routing tables. As these eight peers are closest to t, the missed peer would belong in the deepest bucket of each of these peers. The deepest bucket cannot be full, as if it was, it would be split and a new, not completely filled bucket would be created (compare Section 7.1). The missed peer can thus not have been dropped from the other peers' routing tables for the reason of them being full: if it is not contained, the peer thus must have never contacted these peers. However, any peer has to repeatedly lookup its own ID as part of its bootstrapping process. In this process, it would have sent requests to at least some of the eight and thus be added to their routing tables. A peer that has been missed by multiple lookups can thus not have been bootstrapped properly. It should be noted that any peer that replies to requests will over time be propagated to other peers and as a result be part of more and more routing tables, until it is eventually known to the peers in its direct vicinity. At that point, lookups will be able to find the peer.

If a peer is missed, it can not be found by lookups and is thus not propagated to enough peers, most probably because it either just joined the DHT or does not reply to requests. Such a peer does not (yet) contribute to the DHT as it will not be able to store key/value pairs. We do not consider such peers as being part of the DHT. Missing those peers does thus not spoil our samples. In Section 8.6.2, it will furthermore be shown that our results are in-line with other measurement studies.

8.3.5 Comparison to other Crawlers

The idea of relying on lookups only is different from many other crawlers [WK13, SENB07] that use Find_Node requests to query any available peers in a breadth-first search. Whenever these crawlers receive a response, more peers become available. This way, every peer within a DHT can eventually be queried. Compared to these crawlers, our approach has multiple advantages:

1. A lookup-based crawler accesses the MDHT the same way DHT-based applications will: by running lookups. Thus, peers will only be included into a sample if they will also be used by DHT-based applications. Created samples thus represent a user's view on the MDHT by definition. Depending on the specific method used, alternative crawlers are subject to a higher risk of over- or under-representing certain groups of peers, for instance in case not the entire DHT can be scanned.

2. The approach allows to scan a partition of the MDHT selectively and thus enables the user to choose the size of collected samples, simplifying the handling of the results while maintaining representativeness. To create representative samples using an algorithm that is based on a simple breadth-first search, the whole DHT needs to be scanned.

3. Moreover, the approach is relatively easy to implement, deploy, and manage. Our approach only requires a DHT client that is capable of handling ten lookups per second. The crawler can be deployed on a single machine and has low CPU and memory requirements: our crawler runs seldom produces a higher CPU load than 20% on a T7200 dual core CPU @ 2 GHz and consumes less than 500 MB RAM, with multiple measurement providers running at the same time.

However, a disadvantage of our approach is that a single crawl takes longer when compared to other crawlers.

8.4 Analysis

8.4.1 DHT size

We define the *size* of a DHT as the number of concurrently participating peers. This number should not be confused with the number of deployed DHT clients, which is much higher [SR06b]. We argue that the number of participating peers reflects the popularity of the MDHT better than the number of client deployments and is more useful to characterize peer behavior. While our initial interest in the number of participating peers arose because of its significance for the KAI project, the metric is an important indicator for several other properties:

- *Popularity:* The DHT size is a direct indicator for the current popularity of MDHT-based applications. It can also be used to estimate long-term trends.

- *User Behavior:* The DHT size also constitutes a foundation to analyze short-term user behavior, such as the likelihood of users to use a MDHT-based application at a certain time.

- *Impact on Lookup Performance:* Because of the logarithmic organization of Kademlia's routing table, $O(\log n)$ hops are needed to reach a randomly chosen ID, with n denoting the DHT size [MM02]. The DHT size thus directly influences the lookup performance and is an important parameter for every lookup performance model.

- *DHT stability:* A long-term analysis of the DHT size allows to judge the MDHT's stability and resilience to global events such as natural disasters or changes to the Internet's topology to a certain extent.

In the following we report on our estimations of the DHT size. All presented results are estimations gained from extrapolating from collected representative samples as we explained in Section 8.3. The numbers were computed by multiplying the number of peers found within the 256th part of the ID space by 256.

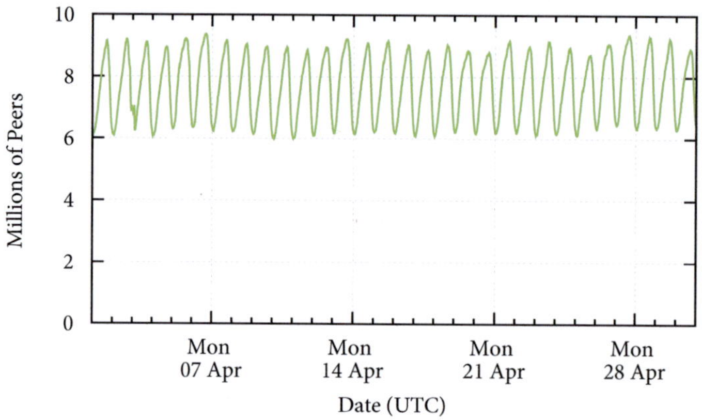

Figure 8.4: Monthly fluctuation of DHT size.

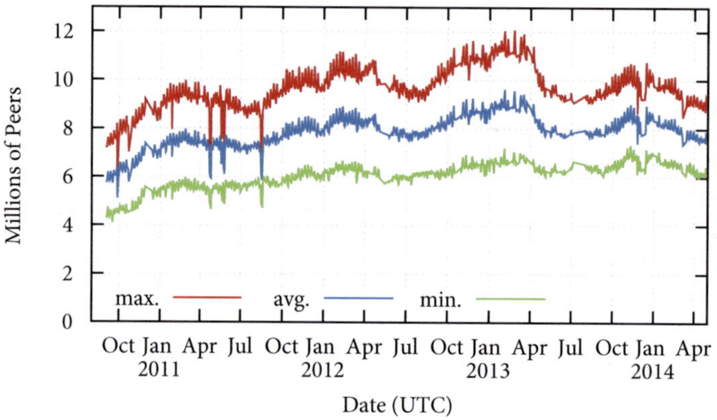

Figure 8.5: Daily minimum, maximum, and average DHT size.

Figure 8.4 plots the fluctuations of the DHT size in a typical month. A strong diurnal cycle is apparent with its daily peek lying in the central European evening and the daily low lying in the middle of the central European night. Similar patterns have been found within the KAD network by Steiner et al. [SENB07]. For example, on May 1st only 6.3 million peers were online at 01:30 am UTC (03:30 CEST), but 8.9 million peers participated at 17 pm UTC (7 pm CEST). This means that the DHT grew by by 41% from its daily low to its high. The DHT also shows a weekly pattern which becomes even more noticeable when looking at a whole month as depicted in Figure 8.4. During the weekend, more peers seem to participate so that on Sundays the DHT size rises to a peak that is 3 to 5% higher than that of common weekdays.

In Figure 8.5 we illustrate long-term trends in the MDHT. The figure plots the daily minimum, average, and maximum DHT size since 2010. The average value is calculated as $avg = (min + max)/2$. The figure shows that the DHT grew from an average number of 6 million peers (September 2010) to over 8 million peers (Jan 2014). Peer numbers increased comparatively quickly until the growth slowed down in the beginning of 2011. Moreover, a strong seasonal pattern is apparent. During northern hemisphere winter, more users seem to use the DHT. The daily peak furthermore seems to be more affected by this phenomenon than the daily low. We assume that this is due to the fact that users are more likely to stay indoors during winter rather than going out. We can thus conclude that the popularity of the MDHT remains undiminished and in fact still increasing.

8.4.2 Peer Origin

In the following, we analyze the distribution of the peers' countries of origin. To determine a peer's country of origin we used the *Maxmind GeoIP* database [5] to map the peer's IP address to a country. Details about each country, such as the number of inhabitants and the continent it belongs to, were taken from the *GeoNames* geographical database [6]. An estimation of the number of Internet Users per country was retrieved from the *Internet World Stats* database [7]. As our analysis is based on our representatively collected samples, all presented results can be seen as representative as well.

Peer Numbers per Continent

Figure 8.6 illustrates how the composition of the MDHT changes during a typical day. Each point on a specific line represents the sum of all peers coming from the corresponding continent that were found in a DHT sample collected at a specific time (X-value). Each continent has a different point in time during the day at which its share on the MDHT's population is the highest. These points match the evening hours of the continent's most prominent time zones nicely. For Europe, the daily peak lies at 17:30 UTC while the daily low lies at 1:30 UTC. The diurnal fluctuation is also most prominent for the European continent, which is explained by the low number of time zones it spans. At its daily low, little more than 2 million European

[5] http://dev.maxmind.com/geoip/legacy/geolite/, [last visited in October 2014]

[6] http://www.geonames.org/countries/, [last visited in October 2014]

[7] http://www.internetworldstats.com/list2.htm, [last visited in October 2014]

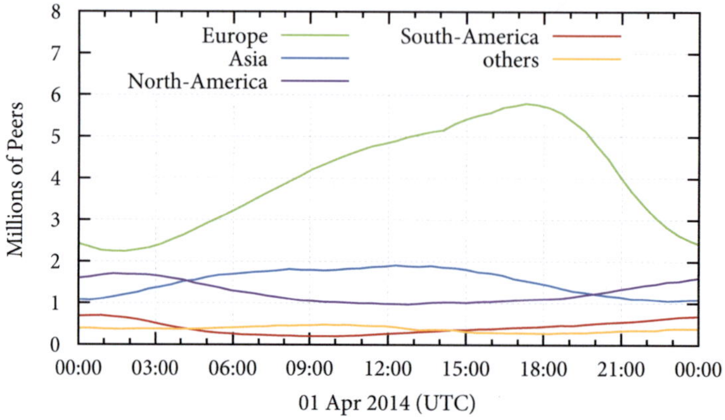

Figure 8.6: DHT participation by continent (day).

peers participate at the DHT. Until its daily high is reached, European participation increases by over 150% to almost 6 million peers. Asian and North-American peers are much less common during any time of the day. Their daily peaks and lows are furthermore much less distinct. At their daily lows, both continents contribute around 1 million peers to the DHT, while around 1.9 million Asian peers can be found at Asian peak time (12:30 UTC) and 1.7 million North-American peers at North-American peak time (1:30 UTC, which is 17:30 PST and 20:30 EST). South-America shows similar daily fluctuations as North-America, but significantly lower number of peers, reaching only 0.7 million concurrently active peers during its peak time. All remaining countries together reach similarly low numbers. As can be seen in Figure 8.7, the shown fluctuations are regular and periodic.

Peer Numbers per Country

The previously presented results show that the MDHT is dominated by European peers. Figure 8.8 displays the 15 countries of origin that were most commonly encountered during our measurements in June 2014. For each country, the fraction of all peer *sightings* collected in this time interval is depicted that could be attributed to the country. A peer *sighting* is defined as a peer entry that is contained in a DHT sample. If the same peer is contained in multiple samples, multiple sightings are counted for this peer. More formally, if $s_{c,i}$ denotes the number of peers in sample i that came from country $c \in C$ and $s_i := \sum^{c \in C} s_{c,i}$ denotes the number of all peers contained in sample i, the ratio depicted in Figure 8.8 is calculated as:

$$r_c := \frac{\sum_{i=0}^{n} s_{c,i}}{\sum_{i=0}^{n} s_i}$$

The figure thus illustrates the cumulative amount of time that peers coming from each country spent in the MDHT. It can be seen that Russian peers alone account for 18.8% of all peer sightings, followed by peers coming from the United States

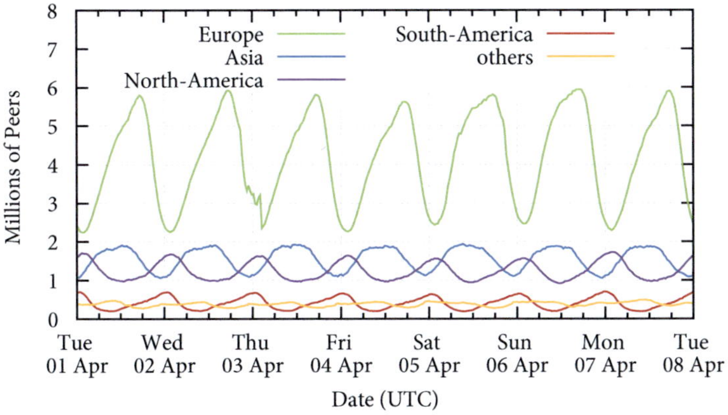

Figure 8.7: DHT participation by continent (week).

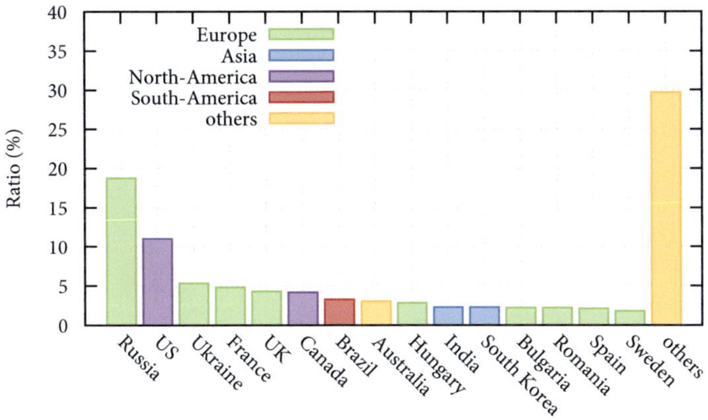

Figure 8.8: Countries with the highest absolute MDHT participation during June 2014.

(11.0%). Ukraine and France together account for another 10.1% of all peer sightings. Interestingly, some large and industrialized countries are not to be found in the top 15. Germany, for instance, is found on rank 46 and accounts for only 0.43% of all peer sightings, beyond countries like the Netherlands (rank 17, 1.27%) Israel (rank 21, 1.11%), and Serbia (rank 31, 0.64%). As another example, China, is placed only on rank 16 with 1.44% of all peer sightings, despite its 1.3 billion inhabitants.

Popularity per Country

In order to put these numbers into a better perspective, Figure 8.9 shows by which factor a country's number of sightings is overrepresented in the MDHT when compared to the country's number of inhabitants. With 9.5 million inhabitants Sweden, for instance, only accounts for 0.14% of the world population but for 1.78% of all peer sightings in the MDHT. It is thus overrepresented by a factor of $1.78/0.14 \approx 12.8$. The overrepresentation factor is thus a good indicator for how popular the use of the MDHT is in a country. Only the countries with the 16 highest factors are depicted. To avoid outliers, we furthermore filtered countries with less than 10,000 sightings (around 0.01% of all sightings).

The figure shows that the MDHT is most popular in Northern and Eastern Europe. For example, Bulgarian, Slovenian, and Hungarian peers are all around 20 times more common than the size of their countries would make you suggest. Furthermore, users from Canada, Australia, and Israel seem to also to use the MDHT quite commonly, as they are overrepresented by factors of 8.5 to 10.4. The high factors found for Iceland and New Caledonia might partly be caused by measurement inaccuracies as these countries have extremely few inhabitants.

In Figure 8.10 the countries' number of peer sightings is compared to the (estimated) number of Internet users in that country, rather than its number of inhabitants. While the factors are lower than in the previous analysis, the plot shows the high MDHT popularity in Eastern Europe even more pointedly.

As of now, the most prominent reason to use the MDHT still is the file-sharing use case. However, the popularity of file-sharing is hugely different between countries, even between those of comparable wealth and level of industrialization, as Figure 8.11 shows. The figure plots the overrepresentation factor per Internet user for the 20 major economies of the world (*Group of Twenty*, G-20) . The European Union was omitted in this plot as it is composed of multiple countries. Strikingly, Germany is underrepresented by a factor of 0.15 while France and the UK, countries with a similar culture and standard of living, are overrepresented by a factor of 2.3 and 1.9, respectively. Similarly, we see quite different factors for Canada (3.5) and the US (1.0). Among the selected countries, popularity is highest in Russia (7.5). We suspect anti-piracy campaigns and the likelihood of legal prosecution to be the cause for the popularity differences between individual countries.

Popularity Evolution

Figure 8.12 illustrates at the example of selected countries how differently a country's participation rate can evolve over time. The figure shows how many peers were coming from certain countries at each point in time since 2010.

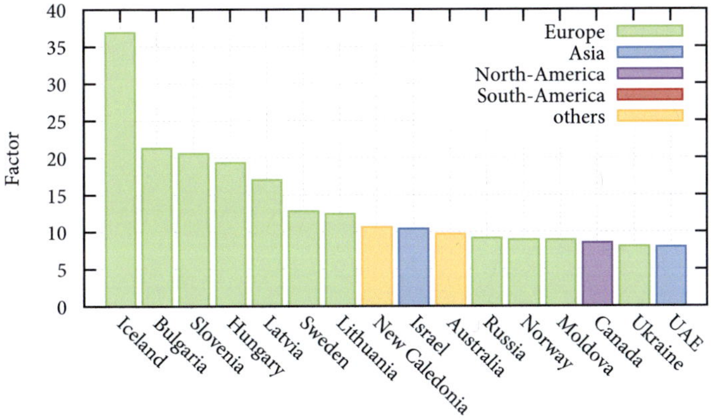

Figure 8.9: MDHT popularity relative to inhabitant numbers. The graph depicts the factor by which a country's share of all peer peer sightings was higher than its share of the world population would suggest.

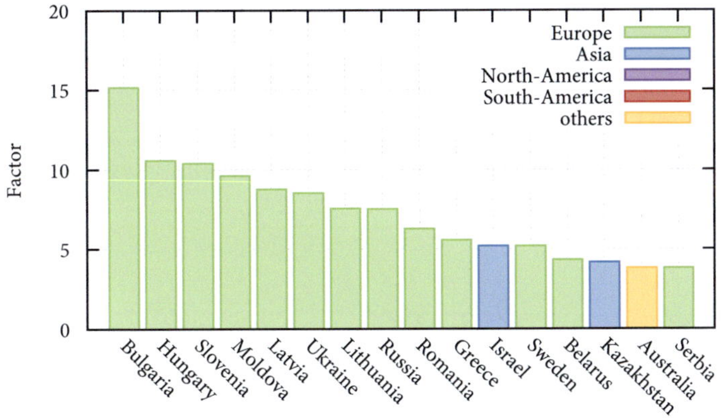

Figure 8.10: MDHT popularity relative to a country's number of Internet users. The graph depicts the factor by which a country's share of all peer peer sightings was higher than its share of the global number of Internet users would suggest.

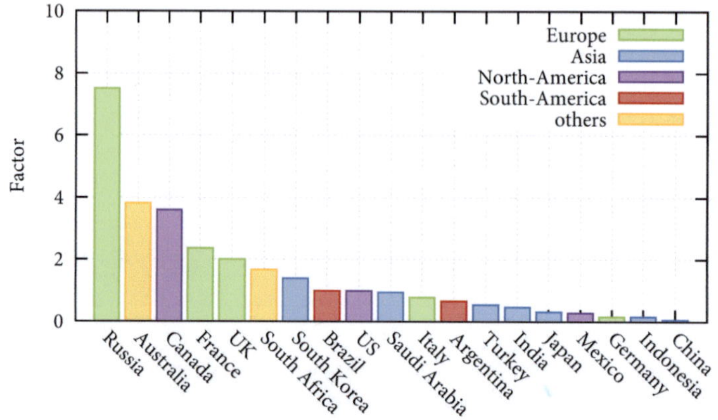

Figure 8.11: MDHT popularity among G20 countries, per Internet users.

First it can be seen that the number of peers coming from the United States remained almost constant since 2011. The number of Russian peers though increased at a rapid rate, from around 700k peers in 2010 and to more than 1.5 million peers in spring 2014. We hence assume that file-sharing popularity has drastically increased in Russia but remained largely unchanged in the US. For China, we detected a slow but steady increase in peer numbers until growth started to increase rapidly in summer 2013, reaching peak numbers of over 2 million concurrently active Chinese peers in November 2013. Beginning in December and January 2014, the number of Chinese peers suddenly started to drop to around 0.2 million peers in April 2014. We expect the cause for this unexpected behavior to be changes in a client that is only used by Chinese peers. In comparison, German peers became rarer over time peer numbers started to increase again in January 2014. However, German peers remain drastically underrepresented as was already discussed before.

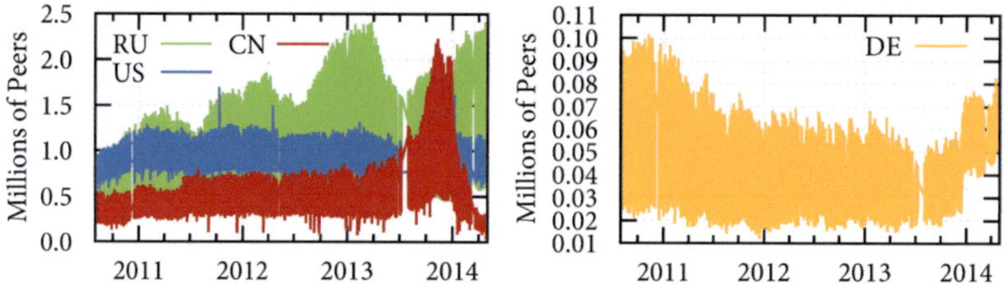

(a) Russia, United States, China.

(b) Germany.

Figure 8.12: Development of DHT participation for selected countries.

8.4.3 Session Length

Measurement Methodology

The *session length* is defined as the duration between the point in time T_j at which a peer joins the DHT and the moment T_l at which it leaves. The session length thus compute as $T_s = T_l - T_j$. We will see that session length in public DHTs are typically short (50% of all MDHT sessions are shorter than 115 min). Short session length are an important metric that describes *churn* rates, as we already introduced in Section 7.6.2.

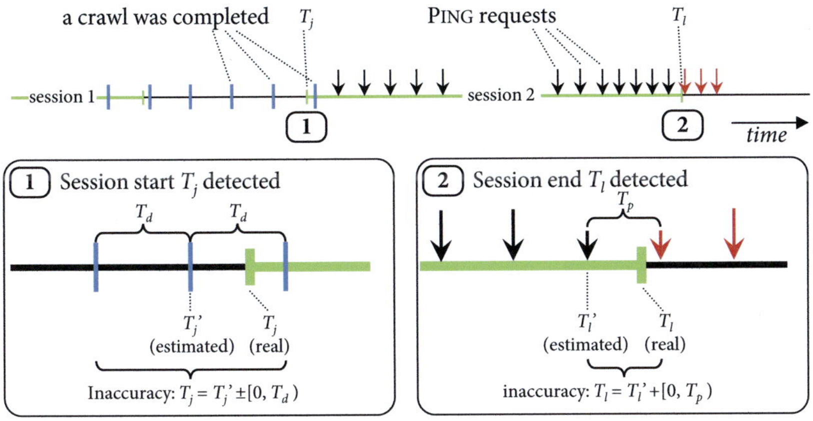

Figure 8.13: Measuring a peer's session length. At point (1), the monitored peer has not been seen for at least 60 minutes. When the peer is detected again, it is unclear whether the peer joined during the last crawl or during the crawl before. The estimated start of the session might thus differ from the real one at most by the duration of a single crawl. At point (2), three consecutive PING requests have failed. The session is thus estimated to have ended at T_l', the time the last packet was received successfully.

To determine the length of a peer's current session, one has to measure both T_j and T_l. In particular, it is hard not trivial to detect T_j, as it is not easy to decide whether or not a peer has already been online before it was seen. We solve this problem by comparing the samples collected continuously by our crawler. Figure 8.13 illustrates the approach. If a peer was not contained in any sample during the last 60 minutes but it is present in the newest one, it is assumed that the peer joined during one of the last two crawls. T_j is thus set to the starting time of the most recent crawl which is equal to the ending time of the second-most recent crawl. The inaccuracy of this estimation is thus within the interval $\pm [0, T_d)$, where T_d denotes the duration of a single crawl. During our long-term measurements T_d was 27 minutes.

Following this procedure, the measurement provider continuously checks completed crawls for started sessions. If a session start is detected, the corresponding peer is inserted into a set of currently tracked peers. The measurement provider continues to check for each tracked peer if the peer is part of any following collected sample. If it is not, the peer is removed from the set. As soon as enough peers are being tracked, the set of peers is sealed and the measurement provider starts trying to detect the end of the peers' sessions. BitMON is currently configured to start this procedure when 2000 peers are being tracked. Meanwhile, the provider continues to track new session starts as a foundation for following measurements.

To track the end of a peer's session, the provider sends Ping requests to the peer continuously. Each second, 10 peers are contacted. If a peer does not answer to 3 consecutive requests, T_l is set to the time at which the last response was received (cmp. Figure 8.13. With 2000 peers being tracked on average, the maximum delay between two Ping requests sent to the same peer was $2000/10\ \text{s} \approx 3\frac{1}{3}$ min. In reality, the session ends thus up to 200 seconds later than our measurements suggest. This number is even smaller for long-living peers, as fewer peers need to be queried at later stages of the measurement.

Results

Figure 8.14 shows the session length as a complementary cumulative distribution function (CCDF). The shown plot was created by averaging 46 session length measurement runs that lasted 25 hours each and were taken between September and November 2013. Together, 92,000 peers were tested.

As the tracked peers have to be present in at least two DHT samples before the set of tracked peers is sealed and the measurement engine starts to sent Ping requests, peers are not pinged for 27 minutes, which is the time required to collect one DHT sample. It is thus first detected that a peer timed out after less than 27 minutes when it is first pinged. As no pings were send previously, the measurement engine is unable to estimate the session end more precisely. As a result, sessions that timed out in less than 27 minutes are depicted as having lasted 0 minutes in the figure.

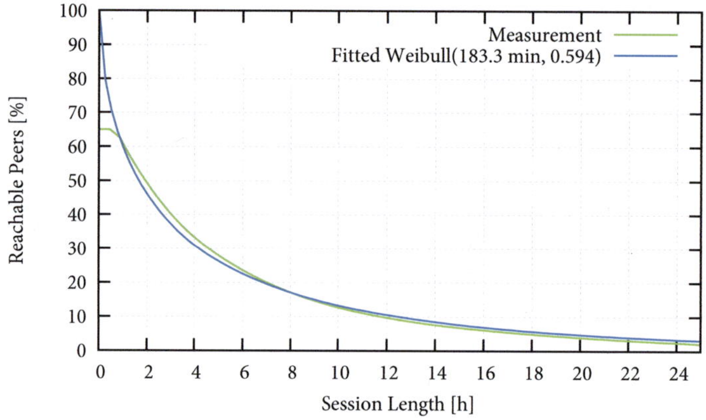

Figure 8.14: Comparison of the session length model to the measured distribution as complementary cumulative distribution functions (CCDF). As peers were not pinged before 27 minutes had passed, shorter session lengths were incorrectly detected as having lasted 0 minutes only.

The results show that only 30% of sessions last 4 hours or longer. The shortest 50% of sessions last below 115 minutes while the longest 5% last at least 17 hours and 48 minutes. Session lengths thus show a heavy tailed distribution. While many authors found session lengths to follow heavy tailed distributions [SENB09, SW04, BQ04], Stutzbach et al. showed that the Weibull distribution is a good fit [SR06b]. Our results confirm this finding. We found that our results are well-described by a Weibull distribution with scale $\lambda = 183.4\,\text{min}$ and shape $k = 0.594$. This function is also plotted in Figure 8.14. In Chapter 9, the function will be used in a simulation model of the MDHT.

The figure shows that most sessions are rather short

8.4.4 Guarded Hosts

Measurement Methodology

Guarded hosts are peers that are located behind a firewall or NAT gateway [WCZJ04]. Depending of the configuration of the used device, guarded hosts are often unable to receive packets from peers they did not contact before. We differentiate between four types of NAT gateways: *full cone*, *restricted cone*, *port restricted cone* and *symmetric*. These types are defined in [RWHM03]. In Section 7.6.2, we already outlined their individual behavior.

In [JAH11], we describe our measurement approach as follows: "For measuring the number of guarded hosts we used a similar experiment design as described in [JOK09]: our measurement engine had access to 3 different UDP sockets A_1, A_2 and B, where A_1 and A_2 were bound to the same IP address, but different ports. Socket B was bound to a second IP address. For becoming popular among other peers, we were continuously sending FIND_NODE queries to peers that were returned by previous requests. We limited our sending rate to a maximum of 1000 queries per second. Whenever a packet coming from a peer that had not been queried yet was received on socket A_1, 3 PING queries were sent from each of our 3 sockets (9 queries in total). Each packet was sent after a delay of 30 sec. We then categorized the peer depending on which of our sockets we received replies."

Due to its high overhead, we ran this measurement provider for a limited time only, beginning in September 2010 and ending in March 2011. We continued these measurements in August 2014.

Results

Table 8.1 lists the shares of the peers for each kind of behavior as measured in September 2014. During these measurements, which lasted from September 1st to September 19th, 209.994 peers were assessed in 99 individual measurement runs. Each measurement took approximately 4 hours.

- The category **FULLY_ACCESSIBLE** refers to peers that responded to packets sent from each of our three sockets. Most likely, the tested peer was connected to the Internet directly or behind a correctly configured *full cone* NAT or activated port-forwarding [RWHM03].

Category	Replied to	Ratio [%]
FULLY_ACCESSIBLE	A_1, A_2, and B	51.7
IP	A_1, and A_2	2.8
IP_AND_PORT	A_1	31.0
FIREWALL	None.	11.8
OTHER	Any other combination.	2.5

Table 8.1: Guarded Host distribution.

- Peers of the **IP** category answered only to sockets that used the same IP, but different ports. This behavior is expected of peers that are located behind a *restricted cone* NAT gateway. This type of NAT gateway seems to be rather uncommon.
- The **IP_AND_PORT** category refers to peers that did only respond to packets sent from the same socket. This behavior is typical for peers that are located behind a *symmetric* or *port restricted cone* NAT gateway. These types were most common in our measurements.
- Peers that did never respond were grouped in the **FIREWALL** category. Using a firewall is a common reason for missing responses.
- Any other combination of unanswered requests is reflected by the **OTHER** category. We cannot match this behavior to any type of firewalls or NAT gateways and expect random packet losses to be the reason. Only 2.8% of all assessed peers fell into this category.

It can be seen that every second assessed peer suffered from limited connectivity. It should be noted that this does *not* necessarily mean that 50% of all peers in the DHT suffer from limited connectivity, as we can only check peers that contact us first and impaired peers might have a higher or lower probability than normal peers for doing so. All other studies we are aware of suffer from the same problem (e.g., [JOK09]). However, the ratio is a good estimator for predicting the likelihood that a previously unknown peer that just sent us a query is a guarded host. This information is useful for configuring routing table maintenance algorithms correctly.

In general, our results match the observations made in [JOK09] very well. However, we found more fully accessible peers (51.7% over 38.2%) and less peers that did not respond (11.8% over 18.2%).

To reduce the number of guarded hosts, countermeasures should be taken. A popular tool are hole punching techniques as described in [DW09, FSK05]. Other solutions can directly be included into the DHT client, such as the exclusion of guarded hosts, favoring fully accessible peers [BMR+06] or higher choosing a higher parallelism degree to speed up lookups [FPJ+07]. Some of these have in fact already been implemented in clients such as µtorrent (compare Section 7.3.4). Further recommendations are given in [JOK09].

8.4.5 Summary

In this section, we analyzed the MDHT with respect to the number of concurrently participating peers, the peers' origin, the peers' session lengths, and the prevalence of guarded hosts. The focus of our analysis laid on studying whether or not the MDHT is dominated by any particular countries, on determining the relative popularity of MDHT clients in specific countries, and on evaluating whether or not these properties evolve over time. In particular, the collected data allows to draw the following conclusions:

- *European dominance:* The MDHT is currently dominated by European peers. With around 2-6 Mio. concurrently participating European peers, at most times more peers can be found that come from Europe than from Asia and North-America combined, the two next-most prevalent continents, which contribute just 1 to 2 Mio. peers. The European peak contribution is thus three times as high as Asian or North-American.
- *Strong diurnal, weekly, and seasonal fluctuation:* The number of concurrently participating peers that originate from a specific country shows multiple regular wave-like patters. Peer numbers peak once a day in the home-country's evening hours, at which time typically multiple times more peers are online than during the night or early morning. Furthermore, peer numbers are higher during the weekends.
- *Russia and US currently most prevalent:* During summer 2014, 18.8% of all peers are coming from Russia, followed by the US, which contributes another 11.0%. Other European countries, such as the Ukraine, the United Kingdom, and France are responsible for less than 6% each. For Asia, India and South-Korea are top contributors. Interestingly, peers from some other countries are way less common than one might have expected. For example, only 1.4% of all peers are Chinese and only 0.4% are German.
- *MDHT most popular in Eastern and Northern Europe:* In relation to the number of a country's inhabitants or its number of Internet users, the MDHT is most popular in Eastern and Northern Europe. For example, Bulgarian peers are 15 times as common as the country's number of Internet users would suggest. According to this metric, the MDHT is also very popular in Russia, Australia, Canada, and France, while it is very unpopular in China, Germany, Mexico, Japan, and India. The United States take a middle ground. We assume a different level of law-enforcement pressure on file-sharing users to be one reason for this discrepancies.
- *Drastic shifts in popularity are common:* Historically, we see that many of these findings are prone to change over time. For example in 2010, Russian peers were much less common than peers coming from the US and only marginally more common than Chinese peers, which were more prevalent than those

coming from most Eastern European countries. While most of these properties changed gradually, we also saw an example of a sudden, drastic shift, as the average number of Chinese peers dropped from over 1 million peers to less than 500000 in just 2 months.

8.5 Selected Incidents

Till now, we presented mostly regular or slowly evolving metrics of the MDHT that were influenced by changing user behavior and other effects. Now, we will report on a selected number of fairly irregular and sudden incidents we observed during our long-lasting measurements. These phenomenons illustrate how easily a public DHT like the MDHT can be affected if no preventive measures have been taken.

8.5.1 The MDHT doubles in Size (May 2014)

Beginning on May 9th 2014, we observed a drastic increase of the MDHT's size. As depicted in Figure 8.15, the growth started suddenly and continued for ten days. For a limited time span our measurement engine was unable to cope with the increased number of peers, until we fixed the problem. The short gaps seen in the figure are caused by this problem. The growth of the DHT suddenly stopped on 19th and the DHT's size remained stable for three weeks until it started to decrease again on June 10th. Both in- and decrease happened at approximately the same pace. Since June 19th, the size of the MDHT remains stable again at 9 to 14 million peers. The DHT size thus did not normalize completely but remained at an around 50% higher level.

We inquired other BitTorrent developers to find the cause of the phenomenon, among others by sending an email to the official discussion group for BitTorrent developers [8] on May 16th. Unfortunately, this group is not publicly accessible. We received a response [Norl4d] from the developers of the µtorrent client that stated that they believed a recently introduced security feature to be the cause. They confirmed this suspicion on May 24th and promised to release a hotfix soon [Norl4e].

According to the µtorrent developers, the phenomenon was caused by two bugs that were related to the implementation of the BEP42 proposal [Norl4a]. The document proposes to choose a peer's ID based on its external IP address to defend against the Sybil attack [DH06]. The bug was apparently related to receiving messages that did not state their own external IP explicitly. In this case, the DHT client would occasionally restart and in process choose a new ID. As one and the same client could now be found under two different IDs in the DHT, the number of peers in the DHT increased artificially. As the bug was distributed to millions of µtorrent peers in parallel, the MDHT could double in size in only a couple of days.

The DHT size hence increased because peers joined the MDHT multiple times. This behavior can cause problems as an affected peer might "poison" other peers' routing tables by changing its own ID. Any older routing table entries of other peers will still link to the previous ID. The affected peer will thus fill a position in the wrong

[8] https://groups.google.com/a/bittorrent.com/d/forum/bt-developers, [last visited in October 2014]

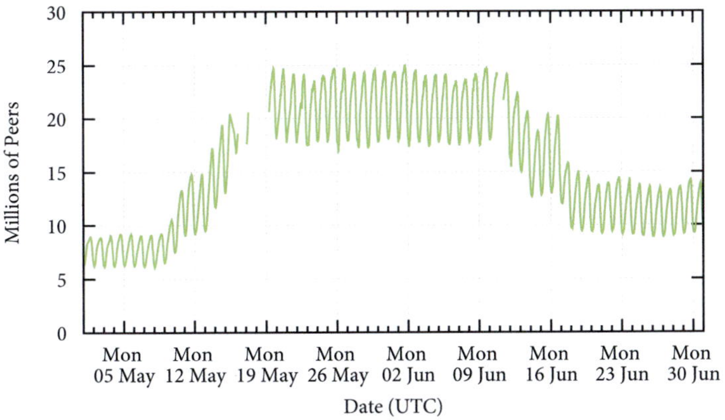

Figure 8.15: Size of the MDHT since May 2014.

bucket, leading to suboptimal results when queried. The quality of its own routing table might also suffer as whenever the ID is changed the routing table has to be rebuild. Although we saw a significant improvement after the hotfix was deployed beginning on June 10th, the problem apparently has not been fixed completely. In fact, we still find entries in our client's routing table that refer to peers with the same ports and IP addresses, but different IDs. We notified the µtorrent team about our findings.

This incident demonstrates how severely and quickly a public DHT can be affected if issues arise in a client implementation that dominates the DHT. It also shows how important it is to stakeholders to monitor the DHT continuously in order for detecting problems as early as possible.

8.5.2 Dependency on Bootstrapping Routers

As we already explained in Section 7.1.4, most clients use central *bootstrapping servers* in order to connect to the MDHT. The addresses of these servers are hard-coded into the clients and return a list of currently available clients when queried. Popular bootstrapping servers are *router.bittorrent.com* and *dht.transmissionbt.com*, both on UDP port 6881. Despite their simple nature, bootstrapping servers are very important for the MDHT as most clients rely on their availability.

On multiple occasions during our measurements, the bootstrapping server with the hostname *router.bittorrent.com:6881* went unavailable for an extended period of time. All incidents occurred in 2011: from April 22nd through April 26th (5 days), from May 18th through May 21th (4 days), from May 23rd through May 26th (4 days), and from August 14th through August 18th (5 days). As an example for the ramifications these events had on the MDHT, Figure 8.16 depicts the DHT's size in May 2011. It can be seen that peer numbers dropped by around 25% during this periods of time but recovered quickly when the server came online again. This illustrates how strongly public DHTs depend on central components, despite their otherwise decentralized architecture.

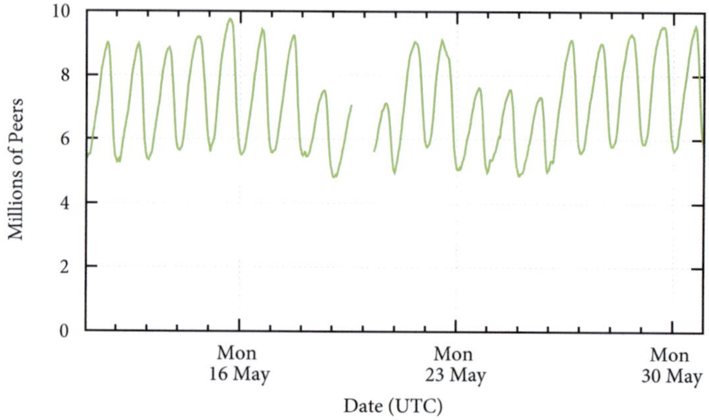

Figure 8.16: Impact of the unavailability of *router.bittorrent.com:6881* on the MDHT in May 2011.

Since 2011, we did not notice any more comparable incidents. This hints that the reliability of the bootstrap servers has improved significantly, possibly because the operators recognized their great importance. However, the idea that an otherwise completely decentralized systems depends on a small number of centralized servers should pose threatening to potential developers of DHT-based applications. To remedy this issue, fully decentralized bootstrapping mechanisms should be implemented, for instance as described in [DW09]. To our knowledge, no publicly available client supports a comparable approach yet.

8.5.3 Natural Disasters and Other Regional Events

Continuous monitoring also allows to assess how well the MDHT is able to cope with natural disasters and other events that impair peers coming from a specific region of the world. As an example, we analyzed two major events of this kind: Egypt's cut-off from the Internet during the Arabic Spring and the Japanese Tōhoku earthquake in 2011. Figures 8.17 and 8.18 depict the number of peers coming from the respective countries during these events. In the case of Egypt, the duration of the measures taken by the Egyptian government can be clearly seen as peer numbers dropped to zero instantly. In the case of Japan, a sudden decrease of peer numbers right when the earthquake hit is visible as a spike would have been expected at that time of day. However, the impact of this major earthquake was rather small, even when looking at Japanese peers only as participation completely normalized in under a week.

When comparing these results to Figure 8.5 in Section 8.4.1, one can see that the two events did not have a major effect on global peer numbers, especially when compared to the failure of a single bootstrap server. This highlight both strengths and weaknesses of the current state of the MDHT: a high potential resilience against even massive global disturbances but also a high susceptibility against issues of key components.

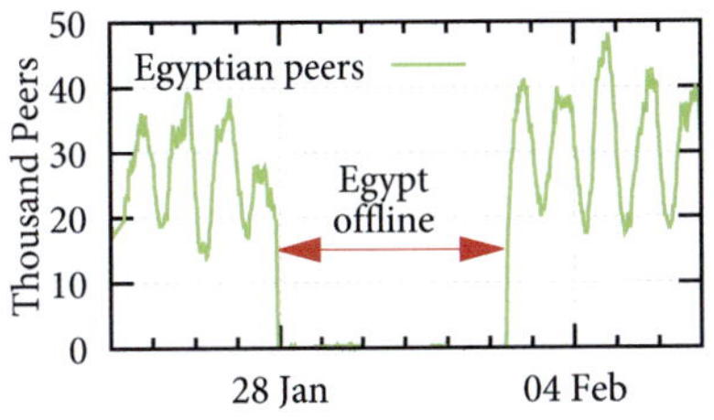

Figure 8.17: Impact of the Arabic Spring 2011 on peer numbers.

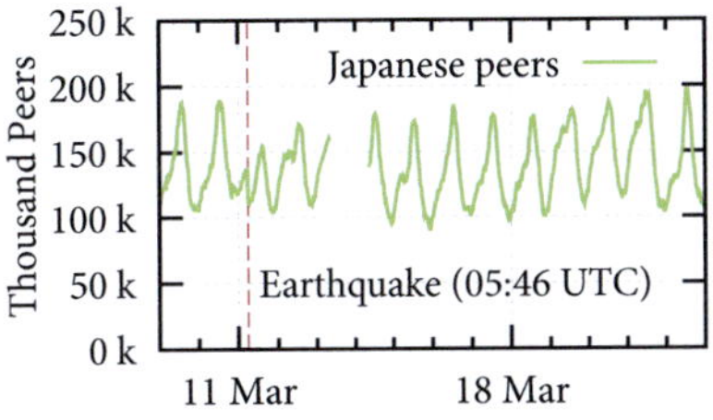

Figure 8.18: Impact of the major earthquake of 2011 on Japanese peer numbers.

8.6 Related Work

During the past years, many studies have been published that aim at attaining a better understanding about the MDHT, its quirks, and its users' behavior and incentives. We divide this huge field of research into three groups: (i) studies that present measurement methodology, (ii) studies that focus describing certain MDHT characteristics that are important for lookup performance and reliability, and (iii) studies that focus on gaining insight about the behavior of BitTorrent users over the world. These groups are not disjunct, i.e., papers may appear in multiple categories. In the following, we will discuss the relation of our work to research done in each of these fields.

8.6.1 DHT Measurement Methodology

Multiple different measurement engines have been proposed that target public DHTs. However, most of them focus on the KAD or Azureus, rather than the MDHT. Furthermore, most other crawlers use *graph exploration* for peer sampling, i.e., they try to retrieve and follow the peers' routing table entries. Compared to our crawler, this approach has the advantage that it is generally faster and produces less overhead, but it is also harder to judge whether the collected samples represent the whole DHT well. In the following, we will provide an overview of commonly used crawlers.

Steiner et al. use the crawler *Blizzard* for their various measurement studies [SCB10, SENB09, SB08, SENB07, SBEN07]. The crawler was developed by the authors themselves and first introduced in [SENB07]. Blizzard targets the KAD network, but was later extended to also cover Azureus [SB08]. The crawler uses a graph exploration approach. The crawler is very fast as the authors state that they crawled the full KAD network (1.5 to 2 million peers were contacted) in 8 min [SENB07]. In order to achieve this, the crawler exploits the fact that KAD and Azureus peers use persistent peer IDs, which means that peer IDs do not change between sessions. This is not the case in the MDHT.

The crawler used by Stutzbach et al. is called *Cruiser* and first introduced in [SR05a]. It features a modular design and was first used only for the unstructured P2P network *Gnutella* but was later extended to cover KAD as well [SR06b]. Like Blizzard, Cruiser uses a graph exploration approach. In [SR06a], the authors state that the crawler can capture 1000 peers in 3-4 minutes and 250 peers in around one minute. The authors also discuss common pitfalls that can cause biased samples [SR06b]. Later, a new crawler called *Montra* was developed, partly by the same authors [MRGS09]. Montra targets the KAD network as well but uses a passive traffic monitoring approach rather than crawling peers actively. Montra is efficient enough to monitor up to 32,000 KAD peers or 37,000 Azureus peers using a moderately configured PC [MRGS12]. Other than the crawlers mentioned before, Montra focusses more on the analysis of P2P traffic rather than peers. It can thus not directly been compared to other crawlers.

In [FPJ+07], Falkner et al. use their own, unnamed crawler to crawl the Azureus DHT. The crawler uses instrumented DHT clients that were deployed on 250 machines of the PlanetLab platform. To our knowledge, development on the crawler has seized since the publication.

In [YN11], Yoshida et al. describe a measurement approach that allows crawl BitTorrent peers that are located behind a NAT-gateway or firewall more easily. The authors then compare different measurement methodologies and characterize session lengths and inter-arrival times. They find that peer-level measurement approaches, i.e., approaches in which the peers are directly contacted, are generally more accurate than approaches on tracker-level when assessing session lengths, but not when assessing inter-arrival times.

Another long-term measurement study targeting the MDHT was conducted by Wang and Kangasharju [WK13]. Inspired by Steiner et al.'s Blizzard, the crawler uses a graph exploration approach as well. However, the authors claim to have found a systematic error in all other crawlers (not just graph exploration based ones). The error would cause a considerable number of peers to be missed by the measurements. An plausible explanation of why this error would apply to all previous measurement approaches is not given. The authors introduce a number called *correction factor* to extrapolate from their estimations in order to account for missed peers.

8.6.2 DHT Measurement Studies

Jiminez et al. [JOK09] measured the ratio of MDHT peers that are located behind certain types of NAT gateways and firewalls by conducting a 24 hour measurement. In general, their results match the observations made in our own measurements very well, although we found slightly more fully accessible peers and less unresponsive peers. In a similar study [WCZJ04], Wang et al. found a ratio of 25-36% of guarded hosts in the file-sharing networks *eDonkey* and *Gnutella*.

Steiner et al. [SENB09, SENB07] analyzed session lengths of peers of the Kademlia-based KAD network. The authors found a mean of 670 minutes and a median of 155 minutes. However, these values can not be directly compared to our results as they were measured in a different network and a different time. The authors also find similar diurnal fluctuations of peer numbers as observed within the MDHT. The measurements they conducted did not last long enough to observe any weekly or seasonal fluctuations. The authors also reported on a high percentage of peers coming from China (>20%) during their measurements which were conducted in Summer 2006.

Stutzbach et al. [SR06a, SR05b] carefully analyzed session lengths, NAT gateways, and peer numbers in three large P2P networks, including the KAD DHT, which is similar but independent from the MDHT. Whereas most absolute numbers the authors report on are obsolete today, our work is influenced by some of their findings such as the session length distributions and the importance to model peer dynamics.

In 2013, Wang and Kangasharju [WK13] reported on their own measurements of the MDHT, in which they used similar metrics as ours. Contrary to our findings of 7-10 million peers presented in [JAH11], the authors estimate the number of participating peers to have been as high as 27 million in 2013. These numbers have been contradicted by the development team of the µtorrent client who stated in 2013 to beginning of 2014 in the BEP42 standard, which defines a new BitTorrent Security Extension [Nor14a]: "*The size of the DHT is approximately 8.4 million nodes. This is estimated by observing that a typical routing table typically has about 20 of its top routing table buckets full. That means the key space is dense enough to contain 8 nodes for every combination of the 20 top bits of node IDs.*" We suspect issues in Wang and Kangasharju's methodology to be the cause of the stark discrepancy of their measurement results to other studies.

8.6.3 BitTorrent Measurement Studies

Due to the widespread use of BitTorrent, many studies exist that focus on characterizing the BitTorrent ecosystem, e.g., [ZDWR11, NRZ+07, PGES05, GCX+05, IUKB+04]. Among others, they often try to assess peer metrics such as BitTorrent's popularity in certain countries or their session lengths. While some of these studies make use of the DHT for their measurements [SZFY12, NRZ+07], most rely on crawling BitTorrent's *swarms* and *trackers* (cmp. Section 7.2.1). Because most BitTorrent clients also include an MDHT client, BitTorrent peers typically act as MDHT peers as well. Statistics of BitTorrent peers can thus be compared to MDHT peers directly, as long as BitTorrent remains the dominant incentive to use the MDHT. This opens a new avenue to assess BitTorrent peers.

Whereas tracker-based crawling allows to analyze file-sharing specific metrics, such as the content shared in BitTorrent, it lacks the representativeness of a DHT-based analysis when it comes to characterizing the peer landscape [ZIP+10]. This is mainly due to the difficulty of choosing an appropriate set of trackers and the uncertainty of whether or not the monitored content is representative for the entirety of all BitTorrent users. In contrast, the peer samples we collect from the MDHT are created by picking peers at random from a uniform distribution (the ID space) and can thus be seen as representative for all peers. Parts of our results can thus be used to complement studies targeting the BitTorrent ecosystem.

In 2011, Zhang et al. published one of the most comprehensive studies of the BitTorrent ecosystem [ZDWR11]. In their paper, the authors study BitTorrent's tracker, peer, and content landscape. The necessary data was mined by crawling a number of public trackers for nine months. To our knowledge, the measurements are not ongoing any more but have been stopped. Among others, the authors find that during their measurements most trackers reside in Northern Europe, while most peers were coming from the US (≈ 0.9 millions), followed by the UK (≈ 0.3 millions). While our historical data from 2011 matches the peer numbers of these two countries very well, Russian peers were at least as common in 2011 as American peers, according to our measurements. Chinese peers should have also been more prevalent than peers from the UK. Neither of these countries are shown in the studies graph, probably because the authors focused on trackers targeting the western (English-speaking) world. The authors also find that peers from Singapore and the United Arab Emirates are most overrepresented when compared to their countries number of Internet users. We also found that peers from these countries are more common than their their number of Internet users would make you assume (factor of around 2), but are way *less* common than peers from most Eastern-European countries (factors of 3 to 15). We find that care should be taken when making general assumptions that are based on these results only, as large parts of the world are not included in this study and the results are getting older every year. We feel that our measurement solution could be used to resolve these issues to a large extent.

In [SZFY12], Su et al. study short- and long-term swarm evolution in BitTorrent by a hybrid measurement system that combines crawls of trackers and swarms with information gathered from the MDHT. The authors find that users' interest in a specific torrent shows a strong diurnal periodicity that strongly affects swarm evolution. We suspect this periodicity to be a symptom of the diurnal fluctuations we found in our peer number measurements. In this case, Su et al.'s study would provide a valuable example of how an application's quality of service (in this case the health of a torrent's swarm) is affected by peer behavior.

8.7 Conclusion

In this chapter, we presented an ongoing large-scale measurement study on the MDHT. Our objectives are not only to provide a valuable service for MDHT-based applications that rely on certain DHT characteristics but also to support other researchers and developers with understanding user behavior and making informed choices. We monitor the MDHT continuously since August 2010 and assess different key DHT properties. The backbone of our analysis is a series of representative sets of peer samples. Every day, 53 of such samples each consisting of tens of thousands of peers are collected. This makes our study the to our knowledge longest and most complete measurement study of a publicly deployed DHT ever run.

First, we explained the architecture of our monitoring framework BitMON. In particular, we illustrated a novel peer sampling approach that leverages lookups to retrieve peers and differs from typical crawlers, which use raw FIND_NODE requests in a graph exploration fashion. The main advantage of our approach is that it is more resilient to biases in collected samples.

We then analyzed our collected data in detail. Among others, we analyzed the global number of participating peers, the composition of the DHT with respect to the peers' countries of origin, the lengths of the peers' sessions, and the prevalence of guarded hosts. Some of our most important findings include:

- The MDHT indeed evolves over time in terms of size, peer composition, and other properties. For instance, the ratio of Russian peers has more than doubled from below 9% in October 2010 to over 18% in June 2014.
- The MDHT is also subject to sudden, drastic changes. On multiple occasions, we noticed events that massively affected the MDHT: the unavailability of a bootstrapping server lead to around 25% less peers in the network, a bug in an update of a popular BitTorrent client lead to around ten million additional (artificial) peers, and the number of Chinese peers dropped to 50% in just two months.
- Otherwise, the MDHT is remarkably stable and its popularity around the world seems unbroken. With the recent advent of more and more commercial DHT-based applications such as Tribler or BitTorrent Sync, we do not expect public interest in the MDHT to vanish soon.

We draw two main conclusions from these observations. First, we expect the MDHT to continue getting more attractive as a platform for decentralized applications. With BitTorrent Sync and Tribler, economic use-cases besides file-sharing reach our for customers. The ongoing improvement of lookups performance in µtorrent and recent additions of security related and other features [Nor14a] show the growing significance of the MDHT, which is only of lesser importance for traditional file-sharing clients.

Second, we see that the DHT can not yet achieve the reliability of classic centralized architectures. In particular, DHT-based applications have to be able to cope with short- and long-term changes in key properties of the DHT. In order to establish DHTs as a viable competitor to centralized platforms, the research community should focus on how to provide a constant quality of service.

In Chapter 10, we therefore present an approach that allows DHT clients to adapt to MDHT changes dynamically in order to optimize lookup performance.

9
DHT Modeling

In 1987, George E. P. Box wrote in his book "Empirical model-building and response surfaces" [BD87]: "*Essentially, all models are wrong, but some are useful.*" This is especially true for models of public P2P networks as these systems are strongly influenced by the behavior of the participating users and the only "perfect" model is the P2P-network itself. For this reason, today no model of a public DHT exists that would allow to assess lookup performance accurately, although various P2P simulators exist. Available simulation models typically abstract from at least some key DHT characteristics that have a strong impact on lookup performance.

In this chapter, we present *KadSim*, a model of the MDHT that aims at allowing users to assess the performance of lookup algorithms in the MDHT. KadSim was implemented for the Java-based simulator PeerSim [MJ09]. The purpose of our model is to provide a means to assess the performance of lookup algorithms in public DHTs at the example of the MDHT. A typical use-case for such a model is the optimization of the client, either to test how a client that demonstrated high performance in a private DHT would cope with a more dynamic environment or to assess how well a lookup algorithm would be able to adapt to changes in the public DHT it is currently deployed in. For example, the user might want to know how lookup performance develops in case that the number of participating peers doubles, halves, or session lengths decrease.

Hence, the model should support the following tasks:

- Predict performance of a client implementation when deployed in a public DHT.
- Predict impact of DHT changes on lookup performance.

In particular, KadSim should allow to simulate a large-scale public DHT such as the MDHT in its entirety. It thus should be possible to simulate DHTs consisting of millions of peers.

In order to build a suitable model, we first provide an in-depth requirement analysis in Section 9.2 in which we identify key properties that affect lookup performance.

In Section 9.2, each property (for instance, the peers' session lengths) is then modeled based on our own real-world measurements and other studies conducted on the MDHT. Tradeoffs between simulation accuracy and simulation performance are discussed and options on how to improve accuracy or performance, respectively, are presented.

In Section 9.4, the model is then validated by testing commonly proposed lookup optimizations in our simulation as well as in the real-world. For this task, we use the JKad client as it is able to mimic common lookup optimizations.

Section 9.5 discusses limitations of our model and proposes optimizations to further improve the model's accuracy in the future.

Section 9.6 concludes this chapter.

9.1 Related Work

In the following, P2P simulators and models will be introduced. As the measurement studies that our model is based upon have already been presented and discussed in Chapter 8, they will be omitted in this section.

In surveys such as [NLB+07, ZCY09], the authors evaluate commonly used P2P simulators. They conclude that most simulators (among others OverSim [BHK07] and PlanetSim [AL08]) are incapable of simulating P2P networks consisting of millions of peers, with the exception of PeerSim, which is stated to be scalable to up to 1 million peers [NLB+07]. PeerSim[1] [MJ09] is a Java-based P2P simulator that supports discrete event-based simulations. PeerSim is today one of the most commonly used P2P simulator. Main reasons for its wide employment are its good scalability as well as the fact that it is comparatively easy to understand and modify. PeerSim abstracts from the complete network layer, which is rarely modeled in P2P simulations.

With HiFiP2P [SLG+09], Shi et al. published a scalable, Java-based P2P simulator that includes a realistic model of the network layer (underlay). HiFiP2P supports parallel and distributed simulation, a fact that can help when simulating millions of peers. In their study, the authors simulated a Chord-based [SMK+01] DHT that was formed by 1 million peers and compare simulation performance to a combination of the PlanetSim [AL08] and J-Sim[2] simulators. However, no comparison with PeerSim is given.

We chose to build our model for PeerSim because of the simulator's good scalability. In this chapter, we show that PeerSim is indeed capable of simulating up to 9 million peers (and probably more) in a realistic scenario.

Hildebrandt et al. [HBH07] proposed RealPeer, an approach for simulation-based development of P2P systems. Among others, their approach proposes to share the source-code between simulation and real-world implementations of P2P protocols, an idea we also follow. To evaluate their approach, the authors created and simulated

[1]http://peersim.sourceforge.net, [last visited in October 2014]

[2]http://www.j-sim.org/, [last visited in October 2014]

a Gnutella P2P network consisting of 1000 peers. Unfortunately, the used model is simplistic and is not build upon detailed real-world observations.

9.2 Requirement Analysis

Widely deployed public DHTs are far too complex to be ever understood completely. Besides the complexity introduced by the high number of components and the dynamic creation and termination of links, the main cause is that components are controlled by individual persons, rather than by deterministic algorithms. Human behavior is thus an inherent part of a public DHT. Examples for human behavior in public DHT's include that the users choose which client implementations they want to use, how often and how long they let their client run, how much stress they put on their internet connection while running a DHT client, or how they configure their NAT gateway, if present.

As it is hence impossible to distinctly derive an adequate level of abstraction from a complete description of the system, an empiric strategy is required that helps us to decide which DHT properties have to be modeled in order to predict lookup performance with reasonable predictive accuracy.

Our strategy is based on our lookup algorithm definition (Definition 9 on page 93) and its notion of elementary *Lookup Events*. By analyzing by which DHT properties each type of event is effected the most, we derive a set of DHT properties that have to be included by our model. This strategy is feasible because any lookup can be described as a concatenation of lookup events, no matter which individual lookup algorithm was used, as was already illustrated in Section 7.5. Any DHT property that affects a lookup's performance thus has to influence at least on lookup event the affected lookup consists of. Our strategy hence allows us to analyze lookup algorithms in general rather than focusing on a specific implementation. For this reason, lookup events constitute a good basis for analyzing the impact that DHT properties have on lookup performance.

In the following, each of the three kinds of lookup events will be analyzed. Then it will be deduced which DHT properties affect instances of the respective event type the most.

9.2.1 Request Transmission

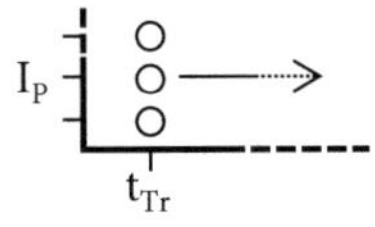

Figure 9.1:]

Request Transmission event as introduced in Section 7.5 on page 94. At t_{Tr} ms a request is sent to the peer using the ID I_P.

At any moment during a lookup, the lookup algorithm can decide to query another peer and create a Request Transmission event. For convenience, Figure 9.1 illustrates again how this type of event is visualized in our graphical notation. The lookup algorithm has to decide *when* a new peer should be queried and *which* peer should be queried, as the source peer "knows" only a limited number of peers at any point in time. A peer is known, if it is either contained in the source peer's routing table or if it was returned by previous requests started during the lookup. Both decisions depend on the lookup algorithm and the source peer's internal state only, i.e., its routing table and data structures used by the lookup algorithm. In particular, the decision making process is *not* influenced directly by the DHT's current state. That means that a client that is run in a simulation environment will decide to query the same peers as another client, which is not run in a simulation environment, as long as two conditions are met: both clients use the same lookup algorithm and both clients' internal states are identical.

While it is comparatively easy to copy a given lookup algorithm for inclusion in a specific simulator, it is harder to assess which DHT properties affect a client's state. A client's internal state typically consists of two data structures: (i) the routing table and (ii) data structures stored by the lookup algorithm for the lookup's lifespan, which typically includes a list of peers that were returned by previous FIND_NODE requests.

We regard the influence that the source peer's routing table has on the transmission of new requests as less important. The reason for this is that the source peer's routing table is typically only accessed to retrieve the first peers to query during a lookup, as with each request, peers are received that are closer to the target ID than the closest known peers so far.

The lookup algorithm can only store information that was collected from previous queries, as by definition this is the only means for a lookup algorithm to communicate. This information is modeled by the other two types of lookup events and thus not covered at this place.

We thus conclude that in order to reproduce request transmission events in sufficient detail, it is enough to ensure that the implementation of the lookup algorithm used in the simulation environment closely resembles the real world implementation.

9.2.2 Request Timeout

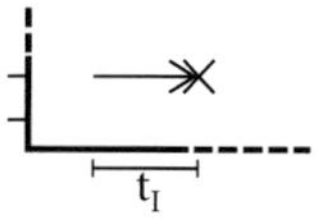

Figure 9.2: Request Timeout as introduced in Section 7.5 on page 94. At t_I ms after the request was sent, the lookup algorithm triggers a timeout.

Any request started during a lookup might remain unanswered, resulting in a timeout event (compare Figure 9.2). With 35 to 70% of all sent requests resulting in a timeout, timeouts occur frequently in the MDHT. As timeouts seriously impair lookup performance, it is important to model the probability for a timeout to occur as realistically as possible.

Unfortunately, this probability is affected by a wide range of factors. Among the most important ones are the following (*Guarded Hosts*, *Session Length*, and *Network Latency* have already been introduced in Section 7.6.2):

- **Guarded hosts**: Due to their commonness [3], guarded hosts are one of the most important reasons for the high ratio of observed timeouts.
- **Session length**: When a peer tries to contact another peer that has meanwhile gone offline, a timeout occurs after a timeout threshold expires. If session lengths are small, this happens more frequently as peers are getting offline more quickly.

  The session length of a given peer depends on two factors: the behavior of the peer's user (i.e., after what time she shuts down the client) and technical constraints such as regular 24 hour disconnects that are carried out by some ISPs.
- **Lookup algorithm** and **Network Latency**: The lookup algorithm has to define after which duration an unanswered request is considered to have timed out. If this duration is chosen too small, requests might falsely be detected as having timed out.
- **Routing table**: To reduce the number of timeouts occurring during lookups, Kademlia clients regularly refresh their routing tables by pinging their entries and replacing unresponsive ones. The thoroughness with which a peer refreshes its routing table influences the number of stale entries found within its routing table. Stale entries might later be propagated to other peers. Thus, the mechanism a peer uses to refresh its own routing table does not only affect the performance of the peer's own lookups but those started by other peers as well.

9.2.3 Response Reception

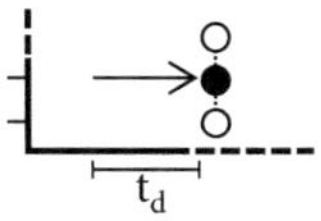

Figure 9.3: Response Reception as introduced in Section 7.5 on page 94. At t_d ms after the request was sent, a response is received containing eight peers. In our graphical representation, only previously unknown peers are shown (two in this example).

Response reception events describe the successful reception of an incoming response to a FIND_NODE request (see Figure 9.3). This event type is described by the time interval t_d after which the response was received (i.e., the round trip time between both peers) and the returned peers.

The returned peers constitute candidates to be queried in the future. As further Request Transmission, Request Timeout, and Request Reception events might be triggered by this, it is important to model the returned peers with respect to the properties that are important for these types of events. These are all properties that

[3] In multiple studies the total ratio of guarded hosts has been estimated to lie between 50% and 70% [JAH11, JOK09, WCZJ04].

have previously been identified, i.e., the peer's *session length*, *guarded hosts*, *network latency*, and the *routing table implementation*.

All returned peers originate from the queried peer's routing table. It is hence important to model how a routing table is filled. In order to do so, not only the routing table's maintenance routines need to be modeled, but also the composition of the DHT, as all routing table entries are eventually drawn from this population. In conclusion, the following properties have to be modeled:

- **Network Latency**: The network latency between peers affects lookup performance as it dictates the duration of successful FIND_NODE requests.

- **Routing Table**: The structure and maintenance routines used by the peers within the DHT have to be modeled, as the peers returned by any FIND_NODE request are drawn from these routing tables. It should be noted that in heterogeneous DHTs, multiple kinds of routing table implementations can be used at the same time.

- **DHT Composition**: The composition of the DHT has to be modeled with respect to the peer's *session length*, *guarded hosts*, *network latency*, and employed *routing table implementation*. The absolute number of peers found within the DHT has also be defined as it affects the numbers of hops that are required by a lookup algorithm to reach an arbitrary target ID.

9.3 KadSim-Model

In the previously presented analysis, key DHT properties have been identified that need to be included in a our DHT model. In the following, we will explain in detail how each property is modeled in KadSim and justify our design decisions. Where necessary, we also describe the model's implementation. In Section 9.5, limitations of the model are discussed and a number of possible improvements are presented. Table 9.1 summarizes the relation between the foundation of our analysis, i.e., the lookup events, and the properties of our model.

DHT Property	Tr.	TO.	Rcp.	Modeled in
DHT Composition			×	Peer Population Model, Section 9.3.1
Lookup Algorithm	×	×		Peer Model, Section 9.3.2
Routing Table		×	×	
Session Length		×		Behavior Model, Section 9.3.3
Network Latency		×	×	Internet Model, Section 9.3.4
Guarded Hosts		×		

Table 9.1: Relation between DHT properties and Lookup Events. It is listed which types of Lookup Events are affected the most by any particular DHT property, as analyzed in Section 9.2. *Tr.* stands for Request Transmission, *TO.* for Request Timeout, and *Rcp.* for Response Reception.

9.3.1 Peer Population Model

Public DHTs like the MDHT consist of a highly diverse set of autonomic peers. In practice, it is impossible to accurately model the full level of diversity of a public DHT, as every peer behaves at least a little bit different from any other, solely because it is operated by a different user. Thus, peer diversity has to be reduced in the model.

In order to simulate different scenarios, sometimes a more accurate model might be required while sometimes a less accurate model could be sufficient. For this reason, we chose to provide a tool with which a user is able to choose an appropriate level of accuracy himself. This tool is the concept of peer *populations*. A population is a group of an arbitrary number of peers that share specific properties with each other. For example, peers originating from China might use a different client implementation than peers coming from the US whereas peers being controlled by users of a specific age group might share similar session lengths. Depending on the desired level of abstraction, DHTs can be modeled as a set of few or many populations.

As some lookup algorithms might wish to exploit correlation of peers within certain populations – for instance to filter high latency peers – while others do not, our model supports arbitrary numbers of peer populations. Users can thus adjust the model to the required level of detail, easing scenario configuration in cases that do not require a very diverse model while still allowing for a higher precision in more complex scenarios. Although using multiple populations demands a higher effort from the user for configuring the model, it does not increase KadSim's computational complexity or memory consumption significantly, as long as a reasonable number of populations is used (n <1000). Depending on the complexity of the configured stochastic distributions, a single population instance typically occupies far less than 1 kB of memory.

In our model, every peer belongs to exactly one population. Populations can consist of up to thousands or millions of peers. Populations possess *properties* that describe how *session lengths*, the *guarded host* state, the *client implementation*, and *network latencies* are modeled for this population. These properties will be explained more thoroughly in their corresponding sections.

In case peer specific information has to be stored to model a property, a property can store a *state* on a specific peers. A property state may contain any kind of data that the corresponding property has to store. For example, the guarded host property has to store for each peer whether or not the peer is located behind a NAT gateway.

9.3.2 Peer Model

The *Peer Model* is the part of our model that describes the implementation of the client(s) used in the DHT. The model can be divided in two parts: (i) the clients' lookup algorithm and (ii) the routing table implementation, which includes the routing table's structure, its maintenance routines, and its bootstrapping mechanism. Our model is based on the design decision that the routing table implementation most commonly used in the DHT should be modeled as accurately as possible while it is far less important to model the lookup algorithms used by other peers. However, the lookup algorithm whose performance should be tested obviously has to be modeled in detail.

Our reasoning behind this decision is as follows: The routing table implementation used by most peers in a DHT has a large impact on the lookup performance experienced by other peers, as it determines which peers are returned when a request is received. The quality of the maintenance and filtering routines used by the routing table thus not only determines the probability with which stale peers are returned but also the distance of the returned peers to the target ID. These characteristics strongly affect the lookup's convergence speed and the number of timeouts encountered. It is hence important to model the routing table implementation most commonly used in a public DHT.

Compared to the routing table, the lookup algorithm used by a specific client has a far lesser effect on the lookup performance of other peers. This is mainly because iterative rather than recursive lookups are used in all large public DHTs and thus a lookup is controlled by the source peer alone. While the lookup algorithm also slightly affects the freshness of the routing table's content by indirectly "checking" each peer that is contacted during a lookup, we expect alternative lookup algorithms deployed in the wild to differ only slightly in this regard. It is hence sufficient to accurately model the algorithm to be tested in the simulation environment. If, however, a "pathological" lookup algorithm was to be deployed that focused on updating the routing tables of remote peers rather than on completing the lookup, it might be necessary to model this algorithm in detail.

In the following it is explained how both lookup algorithms and routing tables are implemented in KadSim.

Lookup Algorithm

In order to simulate the performance of a lookup algorithm in KadSim, the lookup algorithm has to be implemented for KadSim. This is a comparatively easy task, as the internal data structures used by simulated peers are very similar to real Kademlia clients. The core algorithm remains largely untouched. Typically, only the transmission and reception of requests has to be modified because the simulation environment has to schedule events instead of sending real packets.

For our validation, we implemented JKad's lookup algorithm as it follows the BEP5 specification but is also able to mimic the behavior of common lookup algorithm variants, for instance by sending only a limited number of requests in parallel. The algorithm has already been described in Section 7.3.3. This way, different configurations can be tested and directly validated against the JKad client. As furthermore both JKad and PeerSim are implemented in Java, parts of the algorithm's implementation could directly be reused.

Routing Table

Modeling the routing table implementations used in a DHT is much easier if the DHT to simulate is *homogeneous*, i.e., only one type of client is used, instead of being *heterogeneous*, i.e., multiple types of clients are used.

For instance, if the user wants to use KadSim to assess the performance of freshly created DHT that is formed only by peers that use the user's novel client implementation, she can simply translate her implementation to the simulation environment. It is, however, a more difficult task to predict the performance of a new client when brought into an already existing, heterogeneous DHT, as various clients would have to be modeled.

This problem is especially apparent for the MDHT. As we already mentioned in Section 7.3, the MDHT is composed of a multitude of different client implementations. While µtorrent seems to be the most popular client, multiple different versions of the client exist and it is unknown which share of peers uses which version. Although we possess a rough specification of optimizations employed by newer versions of the µtorrent client (compare Section 7.3.4), we have neither access to the client's source code as it is not publicly available, nor do we know in which version each optimizations was first introduced. This makes it very hard to reproduce how the "average" peer builds its routing table.

For these reasons, our peer model is based on the official BEP5 recommendations that were already presented in Section 7.1.

9.3.3 Behavior Model

The *Behavior Model* is the part of our model that defines the behavior of the peers' users. It thus describes human factors rather than characteristics of technical components.

Session Length

In our model, the session length is defined as the time interval between a peer's creation and its destruction (i.e., when the peer goes offline). A peer's session length is drawn from a stochastic distribution configured for the peer's population. While many authors found session lengths to follow heavy tailed distributions [SENB09, SW04], Stutzbach et al. showed that the Weibull distribution is a good fit [SR06b]. Our own long-term measurements confirm these findings. For our validation, we thus used a fitted Weibull distribution with scale $\lambda = 183.4min$ and shape $k = 0.594$. Figure 8.14 on page 118 compares this distribution to real-world session lengths.

Population Size and Churn

Little's Law [LG08] connects the size of a peer population to the peers' session lengths and the peers' *inter-arrival time*, which we define as the average difference in time between two consecutive peer arrivals: if on average every t_I seconds a new peer joins the DHT and stays online for t_S seconds, the number of concurrently participating peers n converges against $n = t_S/t_I$.

When aiming at creating a population of a specific size, the according number of peers should not just be created at the beginning of the simulation, because this would interfere with how peers fill their routing tables over time. Instead, peers should be added gradually to the network at a rate reflecting peer inter-arrival times. For a specific DHT size n the necessary inter-arrival time can be calculated by $t_I = t_S/n$.

The previous chapter already established that in reality the size of a population changes during the day. However, it is typically not desirable to model these fluctuations in a simulation environment, as these fluctuations make it much harder to study lookup performance. A better approach is to conduct multiple simulations that use different but stable population sizes as sensitivity study. For our validation, we thus chose a DHT size of 8 million peers which represents the DHT size of an average weekday around 12 pm CET. Together with the session length distribution presented above, this leads to an average inter-arrival time of $t_I = t_S/n = 16,775.2s/8,000,000 = 2.10ms$.

9.3.4 Internet Model

The *Internet Model* is the part of the our model that specifies the environment the peers are deployed in. In particular, this includes the technical infrastructure of the user and the Internet, which is used to communicate with other peers.

Guarded Hosts

Guarded hosts are peers that are either located behind a firewall or a NAT gateway. Peers hidden behind a firewall that is not properly configured to forward packets will not be able to receive any incoming Kademlia packets, but might still be able to send requests. As these peers will thus never answer requests, they are filtered out from routing tables with relative ease. They will thus typically not be present in other peers' routing tables for long. In our measurements, 11.8% of all tested peers[4] showed this behavior. As we hence do not expect peers that are located behind a firewall to play an important role in the DHT, we chose not to include them into our model.

It is important, however, to model the behavior of peers that are located behind NAT gateways. While every type of NAT gateway allows the guarded peer to send packets, the decision about whether or not any incoming packets are forwarded depends on the current state of the gateway's *connection table*. Through this table, gateways track any outgoing connections by adding a new entry whenever a new host is contacted. When an incoming packet is received, the gateway searches for a matching entry (depending on the gateway's type either by the host's IP address, its port number, or both). Only if a matching entry is found, the packet is forwarded, else it is discarded. Entries typically last for 2 minutes only [JOK09, RWHM03].

Introducing connection tables for simulated peers can significantly increase the simulation's memory footprint, especially if one wants to simulate the MDHT in its original size. We thus used a more abstract model that does not use connection tables. In this model, we assume that responses are only sent in reply to a request and are sent in timely manner, i.e., with a delay of less than 2 minutes. This allows us to decide whether the gateway would forward an individual packet without the help of a connection table. The model behaves as follows:

- *Responses* are never blocked. The reason for this is that in order for a response to be sent a request must have already been received – an entry must thus have recently been added to the source peer's connection table anyway. The destination peer's NAT gateway on the other hand would never block outgoing packets.

- *Requests* are blocked if the recipient is located behind a NAT gateway. While outgoing requests will not be blocked at the source peer's NAT gateway, they

[4] Note that this is *not* equal to the ratio of "firewalled" peers peers found among all routing table entries – we expect this number to be much lower.

will be blocked by the recipient's (if existent), if no matching entry exists in the connection table. At this point, we assume that no such entry exists, as most requests are sent to peers that were received from other peers' routing tables. That means that most of the time, source and destination peers do not know each other. It is thus unlikely that a matching entry exists in the connection table .

In reality packets might also be forwarded if the connection table stores an entry that shares the same IP address with the sender of the received packet and a *restricted cone NAT* [RWHM03] is used. We did not model this behavior because we not only deem it a rare event, but also this type of NAT gateway is very uncommon (Jiminez et al. find that less than 5.5% of all tested peers use this NAT types [JOK09]).

In our model, a ratio of a population of peers can be configured to use NAT gateways. On creation of an individual peer, this ratio is interpreted as the probability that the newly created peer uses a NAT gateway. Any requests sent to such a peer are then blocked. Responses sent to the NAT-guarded peer are unaffected.

For our validation, we configured a global ratio of 39.6% NAT-guarded peers which closely reflects our empirical findings [JAH11, JOK09].

Network Latency

As already introduced in Section 7.6.2, the network latency between two peers can be described as the sum of three components: the delay introduced by the source peer's local IT infrastructure, the delay introduced on the packet's way through the Internet towards the destination peer, and the delay introduced by the destination peer's local IT infrastructure. A perfect model would perfectly describe each of these three components. While the latencies introduced on one peer's side can be assumed to affect all packets sent or received by this peer to the same degree, the delay introduced by the Internet depends on the communication partner as well, especially on its geographical location.

Our RTT model is based on the observation that it is more important to describe the probability for high RTTs to occur than it is to accurately describe low RTTs, as high RTTs are likely to cause timeouts. High timeouts are commonly caused within the sending or receiving peer's infrastructure due to overloaded NAT gateways or bandwidth constraints [DW09]. It is thus important to model the probability of these events to happen.

In order to monitor the likelihood of these events, we measured the RTTs of a high number of requests. In this experiment, 10,000 lookups were started for random target IDs. The RTTs of all successfully answered requests were measured. Figure 9.4 depicts the results as a histogram. In our model, RTTs are drawn from a distribution that was derived by fitting these results by a Mixture Normal distribution. A histogram of the resulting distribution $0.43 * Norm(52, 19^2)] + 0.25 * Norm(115, 13^2) + 0.05 * Norm(184, 13^2) + 0.27 * Norm(325, 100^2)$ is also shown in Figure 9.4.

As future work, an improved model could however incorporate models that aim at predicting Internet latencies accurately, such as *iPlane*, for instance [MKBA+09].

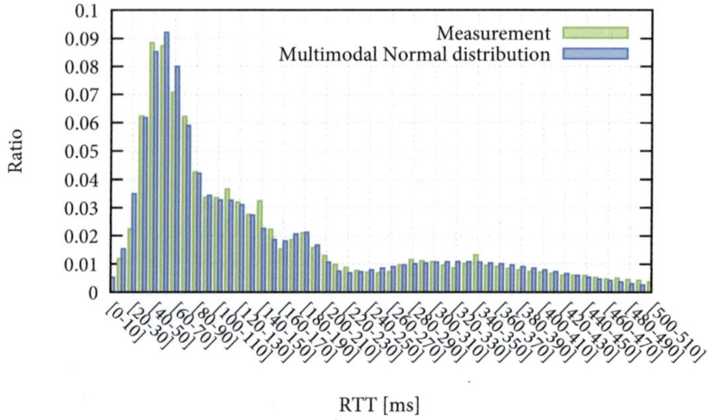

Figure 9.4: The distribution of measured RPC round trip times compared to our RTT model, depicted as histogram.

A reason for our decision not to include similar models is that they would require a more accurately model of the geographic position of each peer.

9.3.5 Condensed Overview

Table 9.2 provides a condensed view on our model by listing all presented properties. For each property, a brief summary of its model is given. In the last column, studies our model is based on are listed.

9.4 Model Validation and Simulation Performance

In order to validate our model, we compared the performance of typical lookup algorithm variants in simulation to their performance in the real-world MDHT. Each variant is represented by a different JKad variant (compare Section 7.3.3). Each variant used a different combination of parallelism degree l, broadcast threshold b, and timeout threshold t. Three different parallelism degrees were tested ($l \in \{2, 4, 8\}$). In these variants, the broadcast threshold b was set to 8, so broadcasting was essentially deactivated. Each parallelism degree was tested with with timeout thresholds of 200, 500, and 1000 ms. In another group of variants, we furthermore set the broadcasting threshold to b to 0, which means that JKad's covering or broadcasting phase started immediately. Again, we tested the timeout threshold mentioned before. In the following, we will refer to this variants as the variants being run in *broadcasting mode*. This setup led to 12 tested lookup variants ($\{l := 2, l := 4, l := 8, b := 0\} \times \{t := 200, t := 500, t := 1000\}$).

Property	Model and abstraction level	See also
Peer Population Model *(described in Section 9.3.1)*		
Peer Variation	Peer populations; validation based on single-population model.	[JAH11, SENB07]
Peer Model *(described in Section 9.3.2)*		
Lookup Algorithm	Emulation (not abstracted); Multiple BEP5 Variants implemented.	[FPJ+07, JOK11, SR06a]
Routing Table	According to BEP5 specifications.	[Loe08]
Behavior Model *(described in Section 9.3.3)*		
Churn Model	Peers join and leave dynamically.	[JAH11, SR06b]
DHT Size	Population size converges against 8 million peers; Validation started at ≈ 7.5 million peers.	[JAH11]
Session Length	Population-based Distribution derived from measurements: PDF: $Weibull(183.4\text{min}, 0.594)$	[SENB07, SR06b, JAH11]
Inter-arrival Time	Constant, derived from Session Length and DHT Size; Validation based on 2.10 ms.	[SR06b]
Internet Model *(described in Section 9.3.4)*		
Network Latency	One Distribution for each pair of Populations; Validation based on measured mixed Normal Distribution. PDF: $0.43 * Norm(52, 19^2)] + 0.25 * Norm(115, 13^2) + 0.05 * Norm(184, 13^2) + 0.27 * Norm(325, 100^2)$	
Guarded Hosts	Single model for 4 different NAT types; All NATs behave like simplified port-restricted cone NAT: only responses are received; 39.6% of all peers are behind NAT.	[RWHM03, JOK09, JAH11]

Table 9.2: The KadSim model.

9.4.1 Measurement Setup

For each lookup algorithm configuration to test, we started 10,000 lookups with JKad (V. 0.7.159). All experiments were run on a Linux machine (Intel T7200 Dual Core @ 2 GHz, 2GB RAM) that was directly connected to the Internet using a 2 GBit/s connection. It was not protected by any NAT- or Firewall-capable devices.

For each set of 10,000 lookups, a new JKad instance was started. To build its routing table, the client was started and left idle for 120 seconds. Then, a new lookup was started every second. For each lookup, a new target ID was chosen at random. After the last lookup had been started, the client was given 30 more seconds to wait for incoming responses before it was stopped. The traces of all performed lookups were stored on disk for later analysis. All measurements took place between 10 am and 2 pm CET during November 2013. Based on our MDHT monitoring results (compare Section 8.4.1), we estimate that the MDHT's size lay between around 8 and 10 millions peers during that time.

9.4.2 Simulation Setup

For our simulation we used the PeerSim simulator (V. 1.0.5) that was extended by KadSim. For each lookup algorithm configuration to test, 10,000 lookups were simulated in a single simulation run. Each run was initiated by creating an initial set of 5000 peers. Then, the DHT was allowed to grow for 24 hours of simulation time before the lookups were started. At that time around 7.5 millions of (simulated) peers were alive. All lookups were started from a single peer that was selected by picking peers at random until a peer was found that was not located behind a NAT gateway and scheduled to be alive for at least 11,000 more simulated seconds. Then, a new lookup was started from the source peer every second. As done during the real-world measurements, a new target ID was chosen at random for each lookup.

The simulations were run on the high performance cluster *InstitutsCluster II (IC2)*[5] and were assigned 64 GB of RAM and 16 CPU cores (2 Intel Xeon Octa-Core @ 2.6 GHz) each. A more detailed description of the simulations' performance is given in Section 9.4.4.

9.4.3 Results

Tables 9.3 and 9.4 compare the performance of the tested variants in simulation and real-world measurements by five different performance metrics. All metrics have already been introduced in Section 7.6.1 on page 96. For every combination of metric variant, a performance value was calculated for each of the 10,000 performed lookups. The values for each set of lookups were then averaged. The table shows the averages and 95% confidence intervals, with the exception of the result distances, which show the median. Furthermore, the deviation of the simulation results from the real-world measurements is shown. In the following, we will discuss each metric.

[5]http://www.scc.kit.edu/dienste/ic2.php, [last visited in October 2014]

- The results show that despite the vastly variable *lookup durations* shown by the algorithm variants, the simulation results in general closely reflect the measured lookup duration. The highest deviation was close to 20% but deviation typically stayed below 10%.
- Similarly, simulation was able to predict the number of *requests sent* per lookup well. The simulation results deviated typically by less than 10% from the measurement results and never by more than 17%.
- For the number of *responses received* per lookup, deviation was even smaller in most cases: for all but the variants using broadcast mode, deviation was below 9%.
- *Timeout block time* (TBT) varies strongly between algorithm variants, ranging from 300 ms to over 6 s. Unsurprisingly, high timeout thresholds greatly increase TBT, whereas high parallelism degrees greatly lower TBT. Even for the most efficient variants TBT makes up at least 25% of the lookup duration.

  Prediction quality was still reasonable for this metric, but worse than for most other metrics. While the TBT predicted in the simulations often deviated by 10% or less from the measured values, it could occasionally be as high as 40%.
- As the last evaluated metric, the *target distance* metric also showed similar results in both simulation and measurements. For half of the tested variants, deviation was below 10% while the highest deviation was 30%.

9.4.4 Simulation Performance

Simulating large DHTs is a both memory and CPU consuming task. The simulations performed during our validation were run on the high performance cluster *InstitutsCluster II (IC2)* and were assigned 64 GB of RAM and 16 CPU cores (2 Intel Xeon Octa-Core @ 2.6 GHz) each. Because our model makes use of one thread only, the additional cores were used to speed up the Java garbage collector only. The simulations took on average 4338 min (= 72 h, 18 min) to complete.

Most of the allocated memory is used for holding the peers' routing tables: on average, a peer's routing table stores 160 entries, organized in 20 buckets. Each bucket is represented by an Object (8 byte) that holds a timestamp determines when it was last modified (4 byte) and two arrays ($2 * 12 = 24$ byte). The first array stores the pointers ($8 * 8 = 64$ byte) to the linked peer, and the second the timestamps that hold the time when the entry was last modified ($8 * 4 = 32$ byte). Each routing table is also an object (8 byte) that stores its 20 buckets in another array ($12 + 20 * 8 = 172$ byte). This data alone thus accounts for $8 + 172 + 20 * (8 + 4 + 24 + 64 + 32) = 2820$ byte per peer or $\approx$ 25.4 GB for 9 million peers.

Parameters		Lookup Duration [ms]			Requests Sent			Responses Received		
l	t	Meas.	Sim.	**Dev.**	Meas.	Sim.	**Dev.**	Meas.	Sim.	**Dev.**
2	200	3583 ± 20	3461 ± 34	**-3%**	43.3 ± 0.2	44.3 ± 0.4	**2%**	15.7 ± 0.0	16.6 ± 0.1	**6%**
2	500	5654 ± 36	5099 ± 51	**-9%**	32.4 ± 0.2	36.5 ± 0.4	**12%**	15.4 ± 0.0	16.7 ± 0.1	**8%**
2	1000	8995 ± 65	10638 ± 122	**18%**	30.3 ± 0.1	35.5 ± 0.3	**17%**	15.4 ± 0.0	16.7 ± 0.1	**8%**
4	200	1872 ± 11	2199 ± 20	**17%**	47.6 ± 0.2	55.5 ± 0.4	**17%**	20.7 ± 0.1	20.8 ± 0.1	**0%**
4	500	3619 ± 24	3294 ± 29	**-8%**	39.7 ± 0.2	41.4 ± 0.3	**4%**	21.2 ± 0.1	22.2 ± 0.1	**4%**
4	1000	6050 ± 41	5796 ± 55	**-4%**	39.0 ± 0.2	41.9 ± 0.3	**7%**	21.5 ± 0.1	23.1 ± 0.1	**7%**
8	200	1402 ± 7	1295 ± 9	**-7%**	68.9 ± 0.3	67.9 ± 0.4	**-1%**	29.5 ± 0.1	31.2 ± 0.1	**5%**
8	500	2663 ± 16	2262 ± 17	**-15%**	59.5 ± 0.3	58.0 ± 0.3	**-2%**	33.8 ± 0.1	34.1 ± 0.1	**1%**
8	1000	4264 ± 28	3932 ± 32	**-7%**	60.9 ± 0.3	59.5 ± 0.3	**-2%**	37.7 ± 0.2	35.9 ± 0.2	**-4%**
br.	200	1178 ± 8	1342 ± 13	**13%**	83.6 ± 0.3	88.5 ± 0.4	**5%**	42.2 ± 0.2	31.6 ± 0.1	**-25%**
br.	500	2072 ± 18	1838 ± 15	**-11%**	81.7 ± 0.3	76.6 ± 0.3	**-6%**	52.4 ± 0.2	38.7 ± 0.1	**-26%**
br.	1000	3706 ± 32	3180 ± 32	**-14%**	82.0 ± 0.3	78.1 ± 0.3	**-4%**	51.9 ± 0.2	37.5 ± 0.1	**-27%**

Table 9.3: First part of the comparison of the performance metrics of simulated ("Sim." columns) and real-world lookups ("Meas." columns), including 95% confidence intervals. "Dev." denotes the proportionate deviation of the simulated values from the measured ones. The *l* column specifies parallelism degree (with "br." meaning *broadcast mode*) while the *t* column specifies the used timeout threshold in ms.

Parameters		Timeout Block Time [ms]			Result Distance		
l	t	Meas.	Sim.	**Dev.**	Meas.	Sim.	**Dev.**
2	200	2352 ± 18	2325 ± 31	**-1%**	$2^{140.7}$	$2^{140.4}$	**-22%**
2	500	3530 ± 32	3471 ± 47	**-1%**	$2^{139.9}$	$2^{139.8}$	**-11%**
2	1000	6670 ± 61	8622 ± 116	**29%**	$2^{139.7}$	$2^{139.9}$	**2%**
4	200	775 ± 8	1082 ± 16	**40%**	$2^{140.3}$	$2^{140.5}$	**16%**
4	500	1590 ± 18	1421 ± 23	**-10%**	$2^{139.8}$	$2^{139.8}$	**-2%**
4	1000	3194 ± 33	3532 ± 48	**10%**	$2^{139.7}$	$2^{139.8}$	**-3%**
8	200	302 ± 4	294 ± 5	**-2%**	$2^{140.3}$	$2^{140.3}$	**-2%**
8	500	552 ± 8	444 ± 8	**-19%**	$2^{139.8}$	$2^{139.7}$	**-2%**
8	1000	1304 ± 16	1611 ± 23	**23%**	$2^{139.7}$	$2^{139.8}$	**8%**
br.	200	626 ± 8	602 ± 11	**-3%**	$2^{140.3}$	$2^{140.5}$	**12%**
br.	500	1221 ± 17	883 ± 13	**-27%**	$2^{139.9}$	$2^{139.8}$	**-9%**
br.	1000	2525 ± 31	2077 ± 29	**-17%**	$2^{139.6}$	$2^{140.0}$	**30%**

Table 9.4: Second part of the comparison of the performance metrics of simulated ("Sim." columns) and real-world lookups ("Meas." columns), including 95% confidence intervals. "Dev." denotes the proportionate deviation of the simulated values from the measured ones. The *l* column specifies parallelism degree (with "br." meaning *broadcast mode*) while the *t* column specifies the used timeout threshold in ms.

9.5 Discussion and Future Improvements

Corresponding to George E. P. Box's motivational statement "*Essentially, all models are wrong, but some are useful.*" KadSim has proven to be a useful tool to predict lookup performance of DHT clients that are similar to the BEP5 implementation, such as JKad. However, KadSim is not yet able to model the effect that some more recently published optimizations have on lookup performance. In particular, the model's prediction quality decreases under the following conditions:

- *Low timeout probabilities*: Our model often assumes that timeouts are likely to occur. Based on this assumption, the model abstracts from effects that affect lookup performance to a lesser extent. If KadSim is used to model a DHT in which lookups are rather unlikely to occur (e.g., a private DHT), this assumption does not hold any longer.
- *Peer Favoring*: In its current state, KadSim is not able to accurately model peer favoring mechanisms employed by clients like µtorrent. Below, we will however propose a new latency model that remedies this issue.
- *Non Kademlia-based communication*: Modern BitTorrent clients typically include non-Kademlia based mechanisms to exchange BitTorrent peers. As most of these BitTorrent peers include a DHT implementation as well, they can be also added to the client's routing table. An example of such a technique is BitTorrent's *Peer Exchange* mechanisms (PEX) [WDH+10]. As of now, KadSim is unable to model such kinds of inter-peer communication that does not rely on the Kademlia protocol.

In the following, we will discuss in which areas the model could be improved in the future. We will also sketch how prospective extensions could be designed.

9.5.1 Routing Table Implementation

First and foremost, the challenge of including a more realistic model of the peers' routing table implementations (most importantly µtorrent's) remains. With the recent release of BitTorrent *Sync* and *Bleep* – both of which use µtorrent as a DHT client – we expect the ratio of peers using this client to rise in the future. As structure, maintenance routines, and bootstrapping routines differ between µtorrent and the BEP5 implementation used in KadSim, we expect our model to deviate from real-world behavior in some aspects.

In order to test this presumption, we conducted an experiment in which we analyzed the routing tables of 500 randomly chosen peers both in real world measurements and simulation and counted the number of unresponsive peers found per bucket. In our simulation, peers were picked at random and their routing tables were analyzed directly. For our measurement, peers were chosen by starting a lookup for a random target ID and choosing the closest returned peer. Then, multiple Find_Node requests were sent. The target ID of the ith request had the i highest-order bits in common with the queried peer's ID. The remaining bits were chosen at random. This way, BEP5 conform routing tables are completely crawled. For peers that use variable bucket sizes eight peers are returned that have the first j bits in common with the ID of the queried peer for every j. Each returned entry was then pinged to determine whether or not the peer responded.

Figure 9.5 depicts the ratio of unresponsive peers found in each depth of the routing table. Bucket index i represents the bucket that covers all peers that have the first i bits in common with the queried peers. In BEP5 conform routing tables, bucket 0 thus covers half the ID space while bucket 2 covers a quarter. It can be seen that in our simulation model, buckets with low indexes contained a far higher ratio of unresponsive peers than can be found in real world measurements. Furthermore, real world peers show way more unresponsive peers on very "deep" buckets.

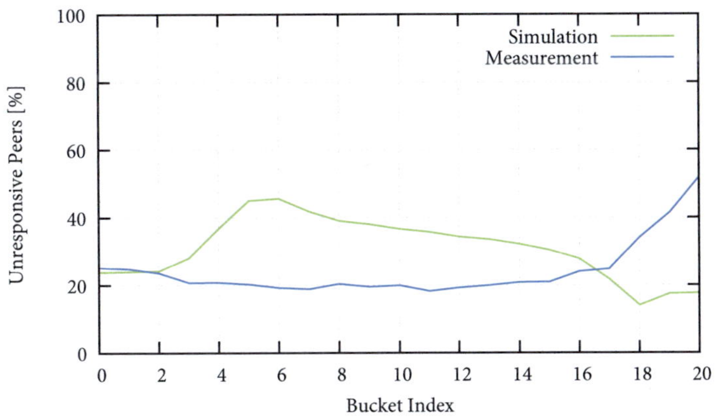

Figure 9.5: Ratio of unresponsive routing table entries per bucket, comparison between simulation and measurement.

We expect this behavior to be caused by different maintenance techniques used by µtorrent peers that more effectively filter unresponsive peers. As deeper buckets cover a smaller ID area, less incoming requests are received from peers that fit in deeper buckets, making routing table maintenance less effective on deeper bucket levels. Together, the over-representation of unresponsive peers on low bucket depths and their under-representation on high bucket depths could cancel each other out in our simulation.

In order to improve KadSim in this regard, µtorrent's behavior has to be analyzed in more detail. Besides the routing table's structure, µtorrent's maintenance and bootstrapping routines should be included in KadSim.

9.5.2 Guarded Hosts Ratio

All guarded host measurement studies we are aware of require peers that should be examined to contact a specific "probe" peer first. Hence, it cannot be assumed that the tested peers are a representative sample of the DHT's population. Instead, certain groups of peers are most certainly overrepresented, for instance peers that send more requests than others. It is thus unclear whether or not the modeled ratio of guarded hosts closely reflects the MDHT.

9.5.3 Network Latency

Clients such as µtorrent favor peers with low RTTs under the assumption of chronological correlation of packet latencies, i.e., peers that responded quickly to one query are more likely to respond quickly to a second query as well. It is thus advantageous to hold these peers in one's routing rather than other peers. This correlation is not yet modeled in KadSim. Optimizations that include peer favoring mechanisms can thus not accurately be simulated.

In order to improve our latency model, RTTs could in the future be drawn from peer-specific distributions rather than from a population specific one. The peer-specific distributions could then be parametrized by a mean and variance chosen from a population specific distribution.

In order to analyze how well real world RTTs can indeed be modeled by a population-specific and a number of peer-specific distributions, we conducted an experiment. In this experiment, we measured the RTTs of randomly chosen peers. The experiment was performed on a dual core Linux machine that was directly connected to the Internet via a 1 GBit/s connection. It was designed as follows:

1. A lookup was started for a random, uniformly chosen target ID. The returned peers were placed in a buffer.

2. For each peer in the buffer, the following steps were conducted:

   (a) The peer was Kademlia-pinged 40 times with a 50 ms break after each ping (first ping round).

   (b) The RTT of each successful ping was measured.

   (c) If a peer did reply to only 10 pings or fewer, it was discarded.

3. The process was repeated (beginning with step 1) until 10,000 peers had been tested.

4. After 10 and 60 minutes, each of the 10,000 peers was pinged again 40 times (second and third ping round).

Figure 9.6 depicts as a histogram of the average RTTs of the first round of pings for all tested peer. They match our previous model very well (compare Section 9.3.4). From this distribution, the mean values of a peer's specific RTT distribution could be drawn.

Figure 9.7 depicts a histogram of the standard deviations experienced by each peer during the first ping round. It can be seen, that the standard deviation was small for most peers (below 10 ms for almost 70% of all peers), i.e., RTTs deviated little from the peer's specific mean.

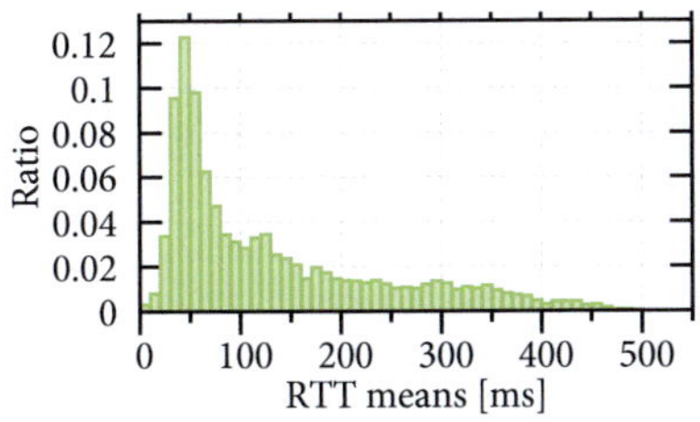

Figure 9.6: The means of the RTT distributions measured for 10,000 peers, depicted as a histogram, and a comparison to our model.

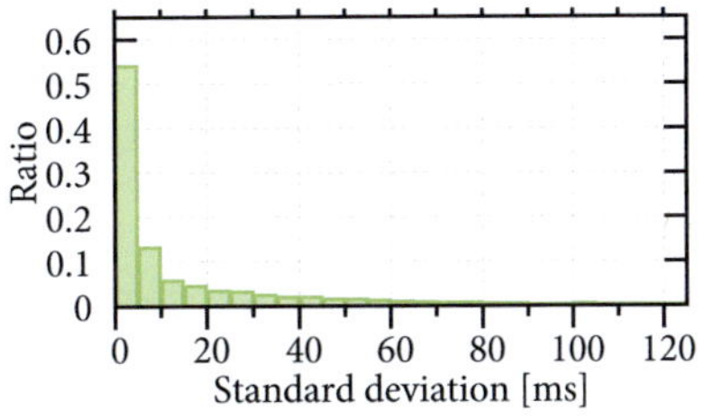

Figure 9.7: The standard deviation of the RTT distributions measured for 10,000 peers, depicted as a histogram, and a comparison to our model.

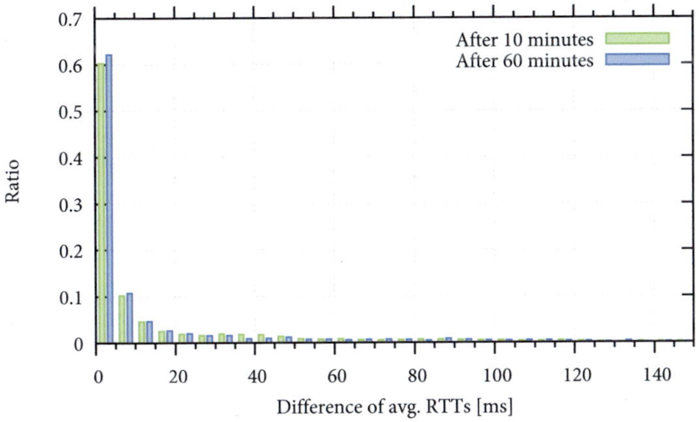

Figure 9.8: Variation of the mean of a peer's RTT distribution after 10 minutes.

Figure 9.8 illustrates to which extent RTTs fluctuated during longer time intervals. The figure depicts the differences of the average RTT measured during a peer's first ping round and the second, which was started after 10 minutes, respectively third, which was started after 60 minutes. Peers were only included in this diagram if they did not fail to respond to too many of our pings until the second and third ping rounds were complete. As a result, only 3240 peers were included. Again, the data is plotted as a histogram. The graph illustrates that the second and third ping rounds typically showed a mean RTT that was very similar to the first ping round: For almost 70% of all peers, the mean RTTs differed by at most 10 ms.

In summary, we conclude that RTTs can be assumed to be reasonably consistent for multiple queries sent to the same peer. Even after a break of one hour, mean RTTs differed typically by few milliseconds only. Peer-specific distributions constitute a good model of this behavior.

9.6 Conclusion

In this chapter, we presented KadSim, a simulation model of the Kademlia-based Mainline DHT (MDHT) for the PeerSim simulator. KadSim is designed to predict lookup performance within public DHTs consisting of multiple millions of peers. To our knowledge, KadSim is the first model that is capable of simulating large-scale public DHTs while still providing a high level of accuracy. It can be used to experiment with new lookup algorithms, to analyze the impact of changes within the current DHT such as growing peer numbers, changing session lengths, or declining use of NAT gateways. We parametrized KadSim to closely reflect the current state of the MDHT, the currently most widely used public DHT. For this purpose, we modeled key properties such as the MDHT's size, the peers' session lengths, the number of deployed NAT gateways, and expected packet latencies. The model is based on long-term measurement results presented in the last chapter and other studies. We validated KadSim against the MDHT by testing twelve alternative lookup algorithm variants in PeerSim and the real world and comparing key performance metrics. Our validation showed that the predicted lookup latency never differed by more than 18% from the real-world measurements and by less than 10% for 50% of the tested algorithm variants. The predicted number of sent packets deviated at most by 17% from the measurements and at most by 10% for 75% of the variants. While these results suggest a reasonable prediction quality, the validation also identified cases in which KadSim is unable to predict lookup performance reliably. To remedy these issues, future improvements to KadSim are proposed and discussed, among others including a more realistic model of inter-peer round trip times.

10 Self-Optimization of Lookup Algorithms

We already motivated in previous chapters that lookup performance is of utmost importance for many applications that need to access a DHT frequently. Low or unreliable lookup performance can be a serious inhibitor for the success of decentralized systems. For instance, Kreits et Niemelä – two of the developers of the popular music streaming service *Spotify* [1] – state that "the lookup time becomes a big issue, which is one of the reasons for Spotify not using a Distributed Hash Table (DHT) to find peers." [KN10]. Furthermore, many latency-sensitive application applications are also concerned with fluctuating performance values as they "treat lookup latency above a narrow threshold as failure." [JOK11].

If key DHT characteristics, such as its size or the popularity of NAT gateways among users, change, lookup performance is prone to degrade. In Chapter 8, we saw that public DHTs in fact *do* underlie both long-term and short-term changes. While some trends were relatively stable, we observed sudden and unpredicted events on multiple occasions that had massive effects on the MDHT as a whole, in addition to the gradually progressing evolution.

Current client implementations are unable to adapt optimally to these kind of fluctuations. In fact, clients are typically optimized for the DHT's state at implementation time, assuming a static and unchanging network. In this chapter, we show how a client can adapt its lookup algorithm to changing DHT conditions by modifying its parametrization dynamically. This is achieved by testing and comparing alternative configurations automatically at run-time. To reduce overhead, the client records requests that were sent during this optimization cycles and replays them, if the same peer is queried again. The approach is called *Simulation-based Runtime Adaptation (SRA)* and was published in [JH14]. This chapter is partly based on this publication.

[1] http://www.spotify.com/, [last visited in October 2014]

The main contributions presented in this chapter are:

- *Proof of Concept:* We show that SRA works and satisfies its goals by applying it to JKad. We provide a detailed description of the approach and present optimization results gathered within MDHT. The approach is generic and can be adapted to other algorithms or protocols.

- *Relevance Analysis:* "We show that self-adaptation is a useful feature for DHT clients. At the example of two possible scenarios of the MDHT's future state we show that the optimal combination of lookup parameters from today might not be optimal tomorrow. We illustrate that not adapting to changing DHT conditions can severely affect lookup performance. In one of our examples, the lookups of a client using static parameters were more than three times slower and had a 25% higher network overhead than those of a client using SRA." [JH14]

- *Overhead Evaluation:* "We show that SRA comes at almost no cost. As the approach is based on measuring lookup performance, it can adapt even to unforeseen changes in the DHT. Our evaluation also shows that the approach induces minimal overhead, as on average only 4 additional UDP packets are sent per second and the simulation is computationally inexpensive." [JH14]

Section 10.1 describes the main concept of the SRA approach, the automatic assessment of alternative lookup algorithm variants, conducted as an experiment in full-factorial experimental design. In Section 10.1.2, we explain how requests can be recorded for later reuse. In Section 10.1.3, we show how recorded requests can be replayed leveraging run-time simulation. Section 10.2 provides an in-depth evaluation of the SRA approach. Section 10.4 concludes this chapter.

10.1 Simulation-based Runtime Adaptation

As we already introduced in Chapter 7, lookup algorithms can typically be fine-tuned by various parameters. Two of themost common examples are the algorithm's *parallelism degree* l , i.e., the maximum number of requests pending at any time, and the *timeout threshold* t, i.e., the duration to wait for responses to a particular request. In general, a lower parallelism degree is to be preferred if the probability of requests to time out is low, while a high parallelism degree is advantageous if the probability is high. The reason for this is that the lookup algorithm in general wants to prevent being stuck in a state, in which all currently pending requests finally result in a timeout, as the waiting time would then essentially be wasted. On the other hand, the algorithm also does not want to send more requests than absolutely necessary, as each increases overhead. The timeout threshold should be set high enough to give most queried peers enough time to respond, but not much higher, as each additional millisecond is wasted on peers that do not respond. Inter-peer round trip times (RTT) and the probability for requests to timeout are only two MDHT properties that influence the timeout threshold's optimal value. In summary, it can be seen that to achieve optimal lookup performance, the algorithm has to be parametrized in dependence of the current state of the MDHT.

It should also be noted that most if not all changes to a lookup algorithms can be integrated in a way that allows to switch them on or off by a parameter. This way, even completely different algorithms can be combined. The SRA approach can then be used to select the best-suited algorithm on demand.

Self-optimization can either be is triggered periodically, for instance once a week, or on demand, for instance when lookup performance decreases. During these *optimization cycle*, an experiment is run at run-time in order to evaluate the lookup performance currently achieved by each individual combination of parameters. The experiment is conducted using a full-factorial experimental design [Jai91]. This also means that all possible parameter combinations are tested. The performance achieved by each parameter combination is compared and the optimal one is identified. Optimality is defined by a metric chosen by the developer or user – typically, the metric will try to balance the induced overhead with the lookup duration and other properties. The concrete criteria depend on the individual application. When a parameter combination is selected, the client is configured to use this set of values from now on and the optimization cycle is complete.

The full-factorial experimental design would normally introduce considerable strain on the client, as many parameter combinations need to be tested and multiple lookups need to be run for each one of them to achieve statistical significance. Thus, a massive number of requests would have to be sent normally. To avoid this, requests are recorded by saving the request's response and its delay. This *RPC record* can later be reused instead of sending a physical packet, in case the same peer is queried again. We will introduce this process in greater detail in Section 10.1.2.

To allow to replay RPC records, the whole experiment must be run in a simulation environment. "The lookup algorithm is separated from the engine by an interface and is in fact agnostic of it being run in this manner. Whenever the algorithm tries to query a peer, the simulator checks whether the request has to be physically executed or a matching RPC record exists that can be replayed. In the first case, the simulation is paused and a new RPC record is recorded just-in-time." [JH14] In Section 10.1.3, we explain how RPC records are replayed during simulation.

10.1.1 Experimental Design

For being able to use a full-factorial experimental design, a finite number of valid *levels* have to be set for each parameter. It is the responsibility of the lookup algorithm's developer to pick a satisfying amount of levels. For JKad, we used 7 levels for the parallelism degree parameter l (1, 2, 4, 6, 8, 10, 12), 5 levels for the covering threshold b (1, 2, 4, 6, 8), and 5 levels for the timeout threshold t (100, 200, 500, 1000, 2000 ms) (cmp. Section 7.3.3 for a description of JKad's lookup algorithm). The elements of the Cartesian product of these levels constitute the parameter combinations to test. For JKad, $7 * 5 * 5 = 175$ parameter combinations thus need to be tested.

To assess a parameter combination, the lookup algorithm is configured accordingly and a high number of lookups are run. A different, random target ID is used for each lookup. As a variance reduction technique, the same set of target IDs is used for every parameter combination.

The lookup performance is then deducted by measuring key performance metrics, such as the number of packets sent, received, and the lookup duration. These properties are averaged over all repetitions. The performance results is compared between all parameter combinations with the help of a user-defined metric. Depending on the requirements of the application, the client is used for, the metric can combine one or multiple performance properties at will. One example would be to simply choose the smallest lookup duration, another would be to trade an increase in overhead for a decreased lookup duration. Consider for instance the metric $\min_i(d_i + 100 * p_i)$, where d_i is the average lookup duration of parameter set i, and p_i is the average number of packets sent per lookup. According to this metric, it would thus be worth to send another request if this reduces lookup duration by at least 100 ms. However, this metric just constitutes an example.

By choosing the full-factorial experiment design, we avoid the threat of running in local extrema during optimization. This allows us to reliably predict lookup performance without human supervision, even if the inter-dependencies between the algorithm's parameters, the MDHT's properties, and lookup performance are not fully understood. While several other designs require to perform a lower number of tests, those designs have to make assumptions about the relation between parameter levels. If, for instance, one assumed linear growth of performance between a parameter's levels, it would be sufficient to test only the lowest and highest level and interpolate the others. "Our approach however is based on the idea that no such assumptions can be made about any parameters, as it is designed to adapt to unforeseen changes within the DHT network." [JH14]

10.1.2 Recording Requests

A serious disadvantage of the chosen design is its high overhead. The high number of lookups that need to be run could not only lead to significant computational overhead but also to high bandwidth consumption. The SRA approach records requests to peers to reduce this overhead. If the same peer is queried multiple times, the previously recorded request will be replayed. As we will see in Section 10.2, this idea has a massive impact on the induced overhead: on average, only 4 requests had to be sent per second (or 1.26 per tested lookup) for comparing 175 parameter combinations.

Recorded requests are called *RPC records*. An RPC record is meant to replicate a particular request's course of action and thus contains all necessary information. In the client, RPC records are stored within a hash table and indexed by the ID of the peer the recorded request was sent to. Requests are recorded by measuring and storing the duration until a response was received. If no response is received after the timeout threshold is reached, this information is stored as well. In summary, an RPC record consists of the following fields [JH14]:

- The *recipient* of the original request.
- The *target ID* used.
- A *flag*, indicating whether a response was received or not.
- The *response*, in case one was returned.
- The *delay* until the response was received or a timeout occurred.

Whenever the lookup algorithm tries to start a new request and an RPC record exists that matches the queried peer's ID, the client can replay the record instead of sending a physical packet. To do so, the response is retrieved from the record and transferred to the lookup algorithm when the specified delay has passed. To the lookup algorithm, the response packet looks exactly like a regular response. However, a query can only be substituted by replaying an RPC record if the following three requirements are met:

1. *Same target ID:* The target ID used must be identical to the target ID stored in the RPC record that should be replayed. The reason for this is that it depends on the transmitted target ID which peers are returned in the response – using different IDs would thus mean that the returned peers would not match. This requirement forbids the sharing of RPC records between different repetitions of the experiment. However, RPC records *can* be shared between multiple lookups of the same repetition, even if the lookups use different parameter combinations.
2. *Same recipient:* "The queried peer must be identical to the recipient of the RPC record that should be replayed. That means, both the peer ID and the IP address must match. The reasoning behind this is that different peers would return completely different responses as their routing tables would be filled with different peers." [JH14]
3. *Freshness:* The RPC record must not be too old, as a peer's routing table changes over time, or the queried peer might become unavailable. Records that are up to one minute old are considered "fresh" by us.

10.1.3 Run-Time Simulation

We already mentioned that the lookup algorithm has to run in a simulation environment during optimization cycles in order to allow RPC records to be replayed. RPC records are converted to events that can be executed by the discrete event simulation engine. All lookups initiated during optimization are run by this engine. The simulator is connected to component called *RPC collector*, which is responsible for recording and managing RPC records. Requests are recorded just-in-time, i.e., when the lookup algorithm tries to query a peer for which no RPC record has been collected yet.

To ease sharing of RPC records between multiple lookups, all lookups that of the same repetition of the experiment are simulated in parallel. All of these lookups share the same target ID. Because of this, at most one physical packet is sent per peer and repetition. When all lookups of one repetition have terminated, the RPC collector clears its hash map from all previously collected RPC records as a new target ID will be used in the next repetition. For each simulated lookup, a dedicated, independent event queue is used. The concurrently simulated lookups thus do not influence each other, with the exception of the shared use of RPC records. The lookup algorithm uses the same source code during simulation and normal operation and is in fact agnostic of being simulated. All lookups are simulated by the same thread by cycling from one event queue to another after each executed event. This way, multiple lookups can simultaneously be blocked (e.g., because they have to wait for pending response) without halting the simulation completely.

Figure 10.1 depicts how requests are recorded and replayed. Multiple simulation instances can be seen on the left. Each represents one simulated lookup and its event queue. Whenever the lookup algorithm tries to query a peer, the RPC collector is contacted (1). It is then checked if an RPC record has already been collected for the recipient of the just initiated request (2).

If no matching record exists, the RPC collector sends a new physical request to the corresponding real-world peer *P* and records the request (3). The simulation instance that caused the query is paused until the record has been successfully recorded, either by receiving a response or by expiration of the timeout period. Paused simulation instances will not be scheduled for simulation until un-paused. Any other simulation that tries to query *P* before RPC collection is complete is paused as well. When the RPC record has been collected successfully, it is added to the RPC collectors hash table and all waiting simulation instances are un-paused (4).

The new RPC record is then handled exactly as if it had existed in the first place. The engine creates a new event from the record and inserts it into the event queue of the corresponding simulation instance or instances (5). The event stands either for the reception of a response packet or a timeout, in case that the record does not contain a response packet or the timeout threshold used by the simulated lookup algorithm is shorter than the record's response delay. To execute the event, the response packet is

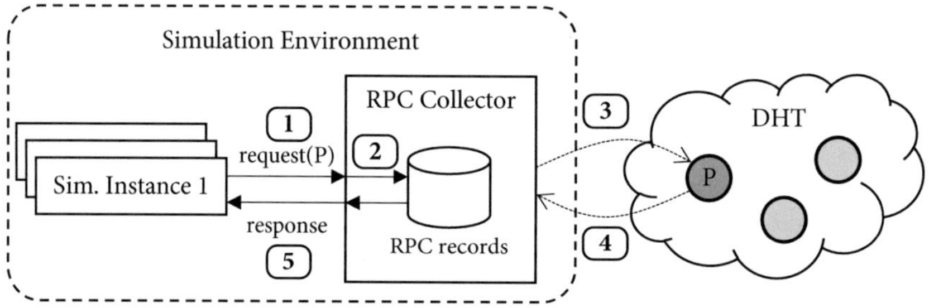

Figure 10.1: Simulation at run-time [JH14]. When a request is initiated during simulation (1), it is checked whether or not a matching RPC record already exists (2). If not, a new one is collected ((3) and (4)). Otherwise, simulation continues as usual (5).

forwarded to the lookup algorithm. This allows the algorithm to react to the response as usual, potentially by querying other peers.

10.2 Evaluation

In the following, we will evaluate the effect of the SRA approach on lookup performance its overhead. This section was taken directly from our publication [JH14] and slightly revised.

10.2.1 Impact on Lookup Performance

Our evaluation starts with an assessment of the impact the SRA approach has on lookup performance. In particular, we highlight three findings:

- In general, the achieved lookup performance differs significantly between parameter combinations.
- If DHT characteristics change, different parameter combinations than before might provide optimal performance.
- Using a static parameter combination might lead to significant performance reduction in case the DHT changes, even if the used combination was once optimal.

Our evaluation is based on testing the SRA approach within the MDHT under current and changing conditions and comparing the performance of alternative parameter combinations. As it is not feasible to wait for the MDHT to change in a drastic way, we created two hypothetical scenarios the MDHT could potentially evolve to. One represents a DHT in which request are *less* likely to time out, the other one in which requests are *more* likely to time out. These two scenarios are emulated by modifying the responses received by our client, for instance by dropping some packets or changing the returned peers.

Scenario A represents a DHT in which no peers are located behind NAT gateways. Hence, the probability for requests to time out is significantly decreased. If IPv6 reaches wide spread adoption, the real-world MDHT could evolve towards this scenario.

In scenario B we assume that requests are more likely to time out than today. One of multiple possible reasons for the MDHT to evolve into this direction is that users shut down their clients more quickly, which would lead to more stale routing table entries. For instance, greater legal pressure on file sharing users could potentially cause this kind of behavior. Another reason would be that even more users than today use NAT-capable gateways to connect to the internet, or that ISPs start to drop Kademlia packets on purpose.

To model scenario A, we modified our simulation approach. In this variant, RPC records are collected in advance to filter out any unresponsive peers that were returned. Whenever the lookup algorithm wants to query a peer, the simulation is halted and the simulator retrieves the RPC record matching the respective peer. The simulator now collects an RPC record for each of the peers found within the record's result packet (the request's *children*), if no record exists yet for the child. A timeout threshold is used that is higher than that of any tested parameter combination, e.g., 3 seconds in our evaluation. Any child that causes a timeout is then removed from the parent record's list of returned peers. After all unresponsive children have been removed, the simulation is unblocked and continues to create a new event from the RPC record as usual. As all unresponsive peers are removed from the received results, the lookup algorithm will never be able to send a request to any peer that would not respond eventually. However, if a short timeout threshold is used, the lookup algorithm will still experience timeouts.

To implement scenario B, we modified our approach in a different way. In this variant, a normal optimization round is run in which a certain percentage of successfully collected RPC records are dropped and registered as timeouts instead. For our evaluation, 75% of all successful requests were replaced by timeouts. As a result, timeout ratios increased from around 57% to 88% (cmp. Table 10.1).

For our analysis we ran the described scenarios on three weekdays (Mon., 24 Feb. to Wed., 26 Feb.), always starting around 9 am CET. At this time, around 7.5 million peers were online according to our measurements. We ran all experiments on the same Linux machine (Intel T7200 Dual Core @ 2 GHz, 2GB RAM) that was directly connected to the Internet using a 1 GBit/s connection. It was not located behind any NAT- or Firewall-capable devices. For each scenario we tested 175 different parameter combinations and ran 1000 lookup repetitions.

Table 10.1 shows how lookup performance varies within the three tested scenarios (real-world performance, scenario A, and scenario B). For each scenario the parameter combinations are given that led to the lowest lookup duration (labeled "fast") and to the lowest number of sent requests (labeled "eco"). Furthermore, both properties are combined by a metric that combines lookup duration und the number of sent packets (labeled "tradeoff"). We defined the metric as $f(d,s) = d + 100 * s$ with d representing the lookup duration in ms and s denoting the number of requests sent per lookup. To get optimal results according to this metric it is thus worth sending another request if this reduces lookup duration by at least 100 ms. Note that this simply constitutes an example for a reasonable combined metric as it depends on the specific use-case which tradeoffs are most desirable.

Table 10.1 also shows that similar parameter combinations lead to lookups with the shortest lookup duration or the lowest number of sent packets, if one just wants to optimize for one metric ("fast lookups at any costs"): unsurprisingly, the lookup algorithms run fastest with high parallelism degrees and short timeout thresholds, while for bandwidth-efficient lookup algorithms the opposite is true. However, different parameters are chosen in all three scenarios when optimizing for the "tradeoff" metric. In this case, lower parallelism degrees are chosen in scenarios with a low probability for timeouts to occur while higher degrees are preferred in scenarios in which requests time out frequently. It can furthermore be seen that lookup performance differs significantly, not only between the three scenarios but also between parameter combinations.

Parameter comb. Name	l	b	t	Duration [ms]	Sent Requests	Received Responses
fast	12	4	100	766 ± 13	93.9 ± 1.3	32.8 ± 0.4
eco	1	8	1000	15886 ± 394	27.0 ± 0.4	13.3 ± 0.1
tradeoff	4	2	200	1841 ± 34	44.1 ± 0.6	18.9 ± 0.2

(a) Real World Scenario.

Parameter comb. Name	l	b	t	Duration [ms]	Sent Requests	Received Responses
fast	12	4	100	478 ± 7	70.9 ± 0.9	40.3 ± 0.4
eco	1	6	500	2099 ± 63	14.9 ± 0.2	14.0 ± 0.2
tradeoff	2	4	1000	1381 ± 40	17.7 ± 0.2	17.4 ± 0.2

(b) Scenario A (all peers respond).

Parameter comb. Name	l	b	t	Duration [ms]	Sent Requests	Received Responses
fast	12	8	100	552 ± 26	64.3 ± 3.4	8.2 ± 0.5
eco	1	6	100	4563 ± 175	52.8 ± 2.2	6.6 ± 0.3
tradeoff	8	2	100	806 ± 39	57.0 ± 2.5	7.2 ± 0.4

(c) Scenario B (75% more unresponsive peers).

Table 10.1: Lookup performance in three different scenarios, including 95% confidence intervals.

In scenario A, fewer packets are sent than in the real world scenario, while the lookup duration is shorter. This is because failed requests would usually force the lookup algorithm to send a new request to the next available peer. In this scenario the lookup algorithm rarely has to do this, as the probability for requests to time out is very low. Also, increasing the timeout threshold is not as punishing as it would be in other scenarios, as every peer will respond eventually. Hence, increasing timeout threshold leads to fewer timeouts in this scenario.

In scenario B, way more packets than in the real world scenario have to be sent. However, far fewer responses are received, which might be surprising as one could assume that a constant number of requests is required to reach the target ID. However, because of the fact that many peers are unresponsive in this scenario, the DHT effectively consists of fewer peers. Hence, a lower number of responses are required to find the closest peers to a hash.

Table 10.2 illustrates the potential loss in performance, if one optimized the lookup algorithm in a specific scenario and the state of the DHT changes afterward. Each of the table's rows represents one of the parameter combinations that proved optimal in the three scenarios with respect to the "tradeoff" metric. For each parameter combination the lookup performance in each of the three scenarios is given, when using the respective parameters. Performance values are printed bold, if the corresponding parameter combination is optimal in this scenario. The values then represent the

Parameter comb.				Real world				
Name	l	b	t	Dur.	Sent	Rcv.	Metric	*Dev.*
tradeoff (RW)	4	2	200	**1841**	**44.1**	**18.9**	**6240**	
tradeoff (A)	2	4	1000	8057	29.1	15.0	10967	*+75.8%*
tradeoff (B)	8	2	100	992	71.7	25.3	8162	*+30.8%*

(a) Real World Scenario.

Parameter comb.				Scenario A (all peers respond)				
Name	l	b	t	Dur.	Sent	Rcv.	Metric	*Dev.*
tradeoff (RW)	4	2	200	798	29.7	22.6	3768	*+19.6%*
tradeoff (A)	2	4	1000	**1381**	**17.7**	**17.4**	**3151**	
tradeoff (B)	8	2	100	547	51.5	29.5	5697	*+80.8%*

(b) Scenario A (all peers respond).

Parameter comb.				Scenario B (75% unresponsive)				
Name	l	b	t	Dur.	Sent	Rcv.	Metric	*Dev.*
tradeoff (RW)	4	2	200	3038	71.7	10.8	10208	*+56.9%*
tradeoff (A)	2	4	1000	26861	74.4	13.3	34301	*+427.2%*
tradeoff (B)	8	2	100	**806**	**57.0**	**7.2**	**6506**	

(c) Scenario B (75% more unresponsive peers).

Table 10.2: Benefits of dynamic parametrization. Lookup performance decreases when using parameter combinations under conditions, the parameters were not optimized for. The "Dev." columns show the deviation of a specific parameter combination compared to the scenario's optimal combination. l is the parallelism degree, b the covering threshold, t the timeout threshold.

benchmark we compare the other parameter combinations against. For convenience, the *Metric* columns show the result of the metric function ($f(d,s) = d + 100 * s$). The *Dev.* columns show by which percentage these values deviate from the scenario's benchmark. A deviation of +100% would thus mean that the result of the metric function is twice as high as the benchmark.

The table shows that lookup performance can decrease when parameter combinations are used in scenarios the parameters were not chosen for. For instance, if one used in the real world scenario the parameter combination that is optimal in low-timeout scenario A, lookup performance is almost 80% off the possible optimum, with lookup duration being more than four times as high. The effect is similar if one used in scenario A the parameter combination optimal in scenario B. In scenario B, using a sub-optimal parameter combination can be even more costly, increasing lookup duration by a factor of 33 and the number of packets sent by 17 packets per lookup. It should also be noted that in the real-world and in the "toughest" scenario (Scenario B) lookups still have the potential of achieving similar performance, if the optimal parameter combination is used.

Although two of the considered scenarios are hypothetical, these results show that if the lookup algorithm does not adapt to changing network conditions, one risks significant deterioration of lookup performance.

10.2.2 Network Overhead

In the following, we will show that the reuse of collected RPC records drastically reduces the overhead of additional sent and received packets. While the exact savings depend on the specific lookup algorithms and parameters that are to be tested, our algorithm constitutes a good estimator for other popular implementations.

Table 10.3 depicts the number of requests that were sent during an exemplary optimization run. On average 239 requests were sent per minute (4.0 per second). On average, only 1.26 RPC records had to be collected per simulated lookup (without the use of RPC records, 52.9 packets would have been sent per lookup). This leads to a bandwidth consumption of 3.9 kBit/s of outgoing traffic, as the IPv4 frame of a FIND_NODE request is 122 Bytes long. As requests will often not be answered, the incoming traffic is even smaller. On average, 146.6 responses were received each minute in addition to the normal traffic generated by the DHT client, resulting in an additional bandwidth consumption of 2.6 kBit/s for response packets of 135 Bytes each. Without RPC records, 4921.8 packets would have been received per minute.

This overhead is only significant in settings that suffer from severe bandwidth constraints and hardly affects modern broadband connections. The number of packets sent per second is low enough to not overload usual NAT gateways employed by consumers, as these devices can typically cope with packets sent to up to 40 to 50 different peers per second [DW09].

10.2.3 Computational Overhead

In the following we will show that the simulation of lookups induces low computational overhead for reasonable numbers of parameters and levels.

Simulating a lookup introduces the overhead of scheduling and executing events. However, for each request sent by the lookup algorithm only one event needs to be scheduled, which represents either a timeout or the reception of a response. Thus, the number of events necessary to simulate a single lookup is limited, although exact numbers depend on the specific lookup algorithm used. During our evaluation an average number of 53.4 events were necessary to simulate a lookup (compare Table 10.3). The overhead for scheduling and handling such low numbers of events is small, even when compared to the processing required for normal lookup execution.

As simulations are frequently paused due to RPC collection, simulations are not CPU-bound. In our measurements, simulating one lookup for each of the 175 tested parameter combinations took on average 55.5 seconds. Each second, an average number of 138.3 events were processed.

We also monitored the CPU consumption of the client during our evaluation using the Linux-tool *top*. The client process never exceeded 20% CPU load and usually stayed below 10%. On average, the process induced 4% CPU load.

In summary, our evaluation shows that lookup simulation does not cause high computational overhead. The overhead can even be considered marginal for most modern consumer computers. It should also be noted that in most use cases self-optimization does not need to be triggered very frequently but only once a day or week. As the optimization could for instance furthermore be configured to only start when the system is experiencing low load (e.g. at night), the approach might even be feasible in CPU-constrained environments.

10.3 Discussion

In the last sections we have shown that our approach has the potential to improve lookup performance in a constantly evolving environment. We will now further discuss the benefit, applicability and limitations of our approach. With the exception of Subsection 10.3.3, this section is taken directly from our paper [JH14].

10.3.1 Benefit

In the last sections, we showed how lookup algorithms can be automatically optimized at run-time at the cost of a moderately increased bandwidth consumption during simulation. Our approach is not only generic, i.e. it can be applied to other DHT protocols as well, but also ensures through its combination of simulation and measurement that conclusions drawn from simulation are valid. As thus optimization will not accidentally degrade lookup performance, adoption of this approach comes at no risk.

Lookup optimization can provide a "free" increase of lookup performance or reduction of overhead, as well as the ability to react to the evolution of the DHT network. The approach could furthermore ease peer management by compensating some degree of fluctuation within the DHT network and making manual configuration unnecessary. Self-optimization also allows groups of peers, that experience different DHT conditions than others, to use an individual configuration. For instance, during European daytime the MDHT consists mostly of European peers, which could potentially result in different session lengths. Moreover, the automatic collection of RPC records and evaluation of the algorithm's performance potential could constitute a valuable tool for monitoring and improving a DHTs structure and performance.

10.3.2 Applicability

While we applied the SRA approach to the Kademlia-based BitTorrent Mainline DHT, it can be used in other DHTs as well. To be a good candidate, a DHT should have the following properties.

- Property 1: Differently parametrized lookups often query the same peers and use the same parameters for the request.
- Property 2: Repeated requests return the same result.
- Property 3: An iterative rather than recursive lookup implementation is used.

Metric	Value
Time / repetition	55.5 s
Events / Lookup	53.4
Events / s	138.3
CPU load	4%

(a) Computational Overhead

Metric	Value
Packets sent / min	239.0
Packets sent / s	4.0
Packets sent / Lookup	1.26
kBit / s (out)	3.9
Packets rcv. / min	146.6
Packets rcv. / s	2.44
kBit / s (in)	2.6
Packets rcv. / Lookup	0.78

(b) Network overhead.

Table 10.3: Overhead induced by optimization. All shown values are averages over a run in the real world scenario with 175 parameter combinations and 1000 repetitions.

Besides the MDHT, both other major public DHTs – the Vuze DHT (also known as Azureus DHT) and KAD – satisfy these requirements. Iterative implementations of the protocols Chord [SMK+01], Pastry [RD01a], and Tapestry [ZHS+04] are suitable as well.

If any requirements are not met, requests can either not be recorded (in the case of recursive lookups) or they cannot be replayed very often. However, if requests cannot be reused multiple times the full-factorial experiment design employed by the SRA approach is a poor choice, as it will lead to significant computational overhead and bandwidth consumption.

10.3.3 Limitations

The performance of lookup algorithms can not only be improved by optimizing the lookup algorithm itself but also by improving other aspects of the client, for example the routing table and its maintenance routines (compare Section 7.3.2). A limitation of our approach is that it cannot be applied to optimizations that alter the client's persistent state, most notably the quality of the routing table's entries. Examples for such optimizations include the favoring of low-latency-peers, or checking for stale peers more commonly. While popular clients like µtorrent make use of such optimizations, they typically also include techniques that do not alter the clients state. Our approach can hence still improve the lookup performance of these clients.

10.4 Conclusion

In this chapter, we presented a novel approach that enables DHT clients to adapt dynamically to constantly changing conditions within the DHT. In order to do so, the combination of parameters of the client's lookup algorithm is identified that currently leads to optimal performance. Optimality is defined by a metric chosen by the client developer or user. Typically, the metric will weigh the lookup's latency against the number of packets to send. The approach allows the client to efficiently, reliably, and automatically utilize its full performance potential, even if the DHT changes unpredictably.

Our evaluation compared possible scenarios of the MDHT's future state to its current state. In the first scenario, we assumed that IPv6 reaches wide spread adoption which would result in peers being more likely to answer queries, whereas in the second scenario we assumed them to be less likely to do so. Our results showed that a lookup algorithm that is optimally parametrized today would provide poor performance in both scenarios, contradicting the self-organization principle of P2P networks. Using fixed parameters has the potential to severely affect lookup performance, as in our evaluation lookup latency were up to three times higher while sending 25% more packets compared to the lookup algorithm's potential.

The study does not only prove that it is possible to dynamically adapt to unpredicted DHT conditions, but also that the costs for doing so are very low. By measuring lookup performance directly during normal operation at run-time and with high statistical significance, parameter combinations can be compared reliably and with virtually no risk of misjudging current trends or shifts regarding the DHT's composition. With user-defined metrics, lookup algorithms can be optimized for speed, efficiency, accuracy, or any tradeoff. The approach furthermore induces minimal overhead as only 4 additional UDP packets are sent per second and CPU load is marginal.

11 Conclusion

In the networked world of today, many, if not most large-scale systems are built by composing separately managed computers, services and resources. The increasing importance of the role that these *Multi-Party Systems (MPS)* play in today's world motivated this thesis to focus on how to cope with key challenges of these systems, namely the (partial) lack of *control* and *trust*. Often, the elimination of these challenges is a prerequisite for leveraging the inherent strengths of Multi-Party Systems which include good scalability, manageability, elasticity, and the reduction of costs. This thesis provided insights and approaches for coping with two classes of Multi-Party Systems: data outsourcing solutions following the *Database-as-a-Service (DaaS)* paradigm and public *Distributed Hash Tables (DHTs)*.

The first part of this thesis covered the DaaS scenario. In this scenario, a database containing sensitive information is outsourced to an only partially trusted external storage provider. The storage provider is assumed to be *honest-but-curious*, i.e., it does not tamper with the outsourced data but still tries to extract information for personal gain. The goal is to protect data confidentiality while still allowing the storage provider to evaluate queries received from the user.

In order to tackle this problem, we presented *Securus*, a confidential DaaS approach that allows to satisfy hard confidentiality requirements when outsourcing databases containing sensitive information. This is achieved by letting the user define *access* and *confidentiality requirements*, which are then used to generate a custom-tailored software adapter called *mediator* that acts as a gateway between user and storage provider. The mediator transforms queries by applying popular *Confidentiality Preserving Indexing* techniques (CPIs) and by fragmenting records. Securus' key challenge is to compute which set of CPIs and fragmentation approaches fits the user's needs.

In particular, Securus provides the following scientific contributions:

1. **Separation of security and domain knowledge:** Securus calculates how certain confidentiality requirements can be satisfied without requiring the user to understand any of the eventually employed security techniques or encryption schemes. Instead, she just has to possess domain knowledge about the outsourced data, i.e., understand its structure and semantics. Securus hence externalizes security knowledge and makes it applicable by domain rather than security experts. This not only simplifies the data outsourcing process but also makes the application of security mechanisms less error-prone.

2. **Meta model for access and confidentiality requirements:** For the definition of access and confidentiality requirements, a meta model is presented that does not require the user to possess any expert knowledge about security concepts but is nonetheless specific enough to allow Securus to compute an appropriate combination of security techniques. With the help of the domain specific language *Securus-Latin*, models that comply to this meta model can easily be defined by the user. Both the language and the meta model were designed for simplicity in order to allow quick user adoption.

3. **Extensible transformation approach:** Securus' transformation algorithm is designed as an analytical optimization problem that describes interdependencies between multiple dimensions of a scenario: the kinds of queries that need to be supported, the protection level of the stored data, and the attacker's capabilities. Each dimension is divided into multiple levels. The interdependencies are then modeled as an ILP problem that is solved by a generic ILP solver. As Securus does not use any heuristics, the generated solution is guaranteed to be optimal. This concept does not only allow to define Securus' core optimization routine concisely by a set of analytical constraints, but also simplifies its future extension. In particular, it is possible to introduce additional levels to one or more dimensions in order to permit an even more nuanced distinction of CPIs. This makes Securus a very sustainable approach.

The second part of this thesis covered public DHTs. Public DHTs are public P2P networks that allow to store and retrieve key/value pairs. Recently, more and more commercial DHT-based applications have been published. Several of them use the BitTorrent Mainline DHT (MDHT), which today is the most widely used public DHT consisting of multiple millions of concurrently participating peers. We thus chose the MDHT as our main object under study.

As a highly distributed Multi-Party System, the MDHT's performance is strongly affected by the lack of control over individual peers as peers join and leave the network unpredictably, may be deployed on constrained hardware, and exhibit unreliable behavior in general. Today, the community still lacks the understanding and the tools to assess how these issues influence the reliability and performance of large-scale public DHTs. The goal of the second part of this thesis was to analyze this interaction and to propose approaches that allow to cope better with the lack of control in public DHTs.

In particular, the following scientific contributions were provided in this part of the thesis:

1. **In-depth characterization of the MDHT**: This thesis presented an in-depth characterization of the MDHT. For this purpose, a detailed analysis of the behavior and performance of the key operation of a DHT – the *lookup* – was provided. In this analysis, a unifying definition of lookup algorithms was provided, commonly proposed optimizations were surveyed, and key performance inhibitors of lookups in public DHTs were identified. Furthermore, a long-term measurement study conducted on the MDHT was presented. With our ongoing study covering a period of more than four years (started in August 2010), it is the longest and most comprehensive study ever conducted on a public DHT. Among other properties, the study characterizes the MDHT with respect to the number of participating peers, their origin, session lengths, and the prevalence of NAT gateways. Besides this characterization, the following key conclusions were drawn:

   (a) The MDHT evolves over time with respect to its size, peer composition, and other properties. For instance, the ratio of Russian peers has more than doubled from below 9% in October 2010 to over 18% in June 2014 while the ratio of peers from the US has remained stable.

   (b) The MDHT is subject to sudden, drastic shifts. These shifts can be triggered by seemingly insignificant problems: the unavailability of a bootstrapping server led to around 25% less peers in the network while a bug in an update of a popular client lead to around ten million additional (artificial) peers.

   (c) Otherwise, the MDHT is remarkably stable and its popularity around the world seems unbroken. Our measurements did not show any evidence that would hint a beginning decline of global participation.

2. **Simulation-based model**: In order to better analyze the impact of changing DHT characteristics on lookup performance, we presented KadSim, a simulation model of the MDHT. To our knowledge, KadSim is the first model that is capable of simulating a large-scale public DHT in its entirety while still providing a high level of predictive accuracy. KadSim was parametrized to closely reflect the current state of the MDHT on the foundation of our measurement results and other studies. KadSim was validated against the MDHT by running twelve alternative lookup algorithms in the simulator and the real world and comparing their performance. Our validation showed reasonable prediction quality as lookup latencies never differed by more than 18% while the predicted number of sent packets deviated at most by 17% from the measurement results. However, the validation also identified cases in which KadSim was unable to predict lookup performance reliably. To remedy these issues, future improvements to KadSim were proposed and discussed.

3. **Self-Optimization of lookup algorithms**: We furthermore presented an approach that allows lookup algorithms to better adapt to unpredictably changing

conditions within the DHT. The Simulation-based Runtime Adaptation (SRA) approach identifies at runtime which configuration of the lookup algorithm would currently lead to optimal lookup performance with respect to a user-defined optimality metric. In order to be able to cope even with unpredicted changes, the approach measures the performance of each possible configuration but "replays" repeatedly initiated requests to reduce overhead by running them in a simulation engine. Our evaluation shows that the approach is not only very effective at optimizing lookup performance but also comes at low costs. By measuring lookup performance with high statistical confidence, the optimization is furthermore reliable enough to be run automatically and unsupervised.

In this thesis, we could demonstrate that it is indeed possible to deal with the lack of trust and control in Multi-Party Systems. However, a requirement is that the system must be well-understood, in particular with respect to the relation and interdependencies between the involved components. In the DaaS scenario, a core aspect that commonly was understood poorly both by domain and security experts is the conflict area of a scenario's confidentiality requirements, access requirements, and attacker capabilities. As we showed with Securus, it is possible to resolve this problem and generate an adequate solution by separating the knowledge about the specific scenario's requirements (*domain knowledge*) from the requirements' interdependencies (*security knowledge*). This separation does not only allow the user to specify individual scenarios on her own, but also makes it possible to "ship" security concepts as an integrated solution.

In the area of public DHTs, this thesis showed that public DHTs cannot be generally expected to be reliable and robust to external influences, despite being renowned for these properties: unforeseen and seemingly insignificant events can severely change the DHT's composition and behavior. Therefore, stakeholders such as developers of DHT-based applications need to *manage* the DHT. However, as public DHTs are (mostly) devoid of centralized components, they require their own special form of management. In particular, the inherent strengths of public P2P networks, such as self-organization and scalability, must not be constrained. Essential ingredients of this form of management are monitoring, simulation, and dynamic adaptation. For most of these activities the decentralized system itself does not have to be changed. Instead, developers of a DHT-based application can, for instance, monitor the DHT with the help of a dedicated "management component" that is separated from the DHT but allows them to quickly react to unforeseen incidents. The appropriate actions to take could then be determined with the help of simulation. Additionally, automatic adaptation of DHT clients at run-time allows to further increase the system's resilience to such events, as we also showed in this thesis. Together, these measures allow decentralized systems to establish a second, highly competitive option to centrally managed systems.

From this thesis, one can proceed into multiple different research directions. Out of these, we find the following two to be particularly promising. First, the ongoing market penetration of Multi-Party-Systems and the increasing security awareness in the enterprise world, especially in recent years, demands for integrated, ready-to-deploy security solutions. While today many solutions exists that target single security aspects, they are often hard to combine or even completely incompatible with one another. We regard it as one of the most important next steps to design approaches that cover and coordinate multiple security aspects at the same time. In particular, data confidentiality, integrity, service availability, access control, and anonymity have to be addressed. Many research questions remain to be solved in order to accomplish this goal, for instance with respect to understanding, formalizing, and coping with interdependencies between security mechanisms. However, if these challenges can be overcome, "secure DaaS" could become an integrated product that is easy to distribute and deploy.

Second, we consider it an important topic to recognize the management of a public DHT as an integral service that is a direct requirement for DHTs to become an attractive and sustainable platform for decentralized applications. Hence, publicly deployed DHTs should support application developers actively at monitoring and simulating the DHT's behavior. In particular, it should be easy to quickly analyze the DHT's current state. This could either be achieved by extending the DHT protocol, enabling clients to provide the required information directly, or by letting researchers design suitable frameworks and tools. One of the hardest questions on the way towards this goal include the task of designing an approach that allows to derive a comprehensive and accurate model of the DHT's current state automatically. This model could then be used to allow decentralized applications to adapt appropriately.

A
Peer Sightings per Country (June 2014)

In the following, we provide a full list of the peer participation in the MDHT per country during June 2014. Our results are based on *peer sightings*, which are defined as occurrences of peers in representative samples collected from the MDHT. Section 8.4.2 on page 111 further defines and explained the measurement and analysis procedure.

Table A.1 lists our results. For convenience, the number of inhabitants [1] and the estimated number of Internet users [2] (both in millions) are listed for each country. Then, the number of peer sightings and its share of all sightings is listed. The countries are ordered by their share. Lastly, it is stated by which factor a country is overrepresented when its number of peer sightings is compared to its inhabitants or its number of Internet users. If, for instance, only 2% of the world's Internet users but 4% of all peer sightings originate from a specific country, the country is overrepresented by a factor of 2. To filter outliers, only those countries were only included in our list that had at least 1 million inhabitants, 500,000 estimated Internet users, and at least 10,000 peer sightings.

For our analysis, 1,522 representative peer samples collected in June 2014 were processed. Together, 95,455,593 peer sightings were contained. Our analysis furthermore assumes a world population of 6,868,879,426 people and estimates 2,457,160,587 Internet users to exist over the world.

Rank	Name	Cont.	Pop. M	I.net Users M	Sightings k	Share [%]	Overrepr. per Inhab.	Overrepr. per I.net User
1	Russia	EU	140.7	61.5	17910.5	18.8	9.2	7.5
2	United States	NA	310.2	277.2	10545.7	11.1	2.4	1.0
3	Ukraine	EU	45.4	15.3	5074.6	5.3	8.0	8.5

[1] http://www.geonames.org/countries/, [last visited in October 2014]

[2] http://www.internetworldstats.com/list2.htm, [last visited in October 2014]

4	France	EU	64.8	50.3	4603.3	4.8	5.1	2.4
5	United Kingdom	EU	62.3	52.7	4093.0	4.3	4.7	2.0
6	Canada	NA	33.7	28.5	3975.8	4.2	8.5	3.6
7	Brazil	SA	201.1	81.8	3122.2	3.3	1.1	1.0
8	Australia	OC	21.5	19.6	2895.7	3.0	9.7	3.8
9	Hungary	EU	10.0	6.5	2677.6	2.8	19.3	10.6
10	India	AS	1173.1	121.0	2165.9	2.3	0.1	0.5
11	South Korea	AS	48.4	40.3	2159.9	2.3	3.2	1.4
12	Bulgaria	EU	7.1	3.6	2113.5	2.2	21.3	15.2
13	Romania	EU	22.0	8.6	2087.9	2.2	6.8	6.3
14	Spain	EU	46.5	30.7	1994.2	2.1	3.1	1.7
15	Sweden	EU	9.6	8.4	1700.7	1.8	12.8	5.2
16	China	AS	1330.0	617.6	1377.1	1.4	0.1	0.1
17	Netherlands	EU	16.6	15.1	1212.9	1.3	5.2	2.1
18	Japan	AS	127.3	101.2	1209.8	1.3	0.7	0.3
19	Greece	EU	11.0	5.0	1088.8	1.1	7.1	5.6
20	Italy	EU	60.3	35.8	1078.8	1.1	1.3	0.8
21	Israel	AS	7.4	5.3	1061.0	1.1	10.4	5.2
22	Kazakhstan	AS	15.3	5.4	882.4	0.9	4.1	4.2
23	Portugal	EU	10.7	5.5	765.3	0.8	5.2	3.6
24	Turkey	AS	77.8	36.5	761.7	0.8	0.7	0.5
25	Belarus	EU	9.7	4.4	744.8	0.8	5.5	4.3
26	Belgium	EU	10.4	8.5	724.0	0.8	5.0	2.2
27	Argentina	SA	41.3	28.0	710.0	0.7	1.2	0.7
28	Poland	EU	38.5	23.9	682.9	0.7	1.3	0.7
29	Norway	EU	5.0	4.6	620.4	0.7	8.9	3.5
30	Lithuania	EU	3.6	2.1	615.8	0.7	12.4	7.5
31	Serbia	EU	7.3	4.1	607.7	0.6	6.0	3.8
32	Denmark	EU	5.5	5.0	581.4	0.6	7.6	3.0
33	Thailand	AS	67.1	18.3	579.2	0.6	0.6	0.8
34	Slovenia	EU	2.0	1.4	573.8	0.6	20.6	10.4
35	UAE	AS	5.0	5.9	548.1	0.6	7.9	2.4
36	Mexico	NA	112.5	51.2	535.4	0.6	0.3	0.3
37	Moldova	EU	4.3	1.4	533.7	0.6	8.9	9.6
38	Latvia	EU	2.2	1.5	524.7	0.6	17.0	8.8
39	Malaysia	AS	28.3	17.7	516.2	0.5	1.3	0.7
40	Pakistan	AS	184.4	29.1	485.3	0.5	0.2	0.4
41	Saudi Arabia	AS	25.7	13.0	473.3	0.5	1.3	0.9
42	Philippines	AS	99.9	33.6	469.7	0.5	0.3	0.4
43	Taiwan	AS	22.9	16.1	459.5	0.5	1.4	0.7
44	South Africa	AF	49.0	6.8	440.1	0.5	0.6	1.7
45	Algeria	AF	34.6	5.2	437.4	0.5	0.9	2.2
46	Germany	EU	81.8	67.4	408.0	0.4	0.4	0.2
47	Chile	SA	16.7	10.0	334.1	0.3	1.4	0.9
48	Indonesia	AS	243.0	55.0	329.1	0.3	0.1	0.2
49	Vietnam	AS	89.6	30.9	276.9	0.3	0.2	0.2
50	Egypt	AF	80.5	29.8	274.1	0.3	0.2	0.2
51	Singapore	AS	4.7	3.7	272.7	0.3	4.2	1.9
52	Hong Kong	AS	6.9	4.9	269.8	0.3	2.8	1.4
53	Finland	EU	5.2	4.7	267.6	0.3	3.7	1.5
54	New Zealand	OC	4.3	3.3	234.7	0.2	4.0	1.8
55	Venezuela	SA	27.2	11.0	227.9	0.2	0.6	0.5
56	Colombia	SA	44.2	28.5	227.8	0.2	0.4	0.2

57	Switzerland	EU	7.6	6.4	206.7	0.2	2.0	0.8
58	Croatia	EU	4.5	3.2	183.0	0.2	2.9	1.5
59	Ireland	EU	4.6	3.1	154.8	0.2	2.4	1.3
60	Slovakia	EU	5.5	4.3	145.8	0.1	1.9	0.9
61	Czechia	EU	10.5	7.4	145.6	0.1	1.0	0.5
62	Morocco	AF	31.6	15.7	141.8	0.1	0.3	0.2
63	Bosnia and Herz.	EU	4.6	2.0	140.7	0.1	2.2	1.9
64	Armenia	AS	3.0	1.8	129.7	0.1	3.1	1.9
65	Azerbaijan	AS	8.3	4.7	120.8	0.1	1.0	0.7
66	Estonia	EU	1.3	1.0	113.5	0.1	6.3	2.9
67	Georgia	AS	4.6	1.3	101.4	0.1	1.6	2.0
68	Uruguay	SA	3.5	1.9	85.7	0.1	1.8	1.2
69	Macedonia	EU	2.1	1.1	84.4	0.1	2.9	2.0
70	Peru	SA	29.9	10.0	83.7	0.1	0.2	0.2
71	Tunisia	AF	10.6	3.9	79.4	0.1	0.5	0.5
72	Austria	EU	8.2	6.6	77.0	0.1	0.7	0.3
73	Iran	AS	76.9	36.5	77.0	0.1	0.1	0.1
74	Kyrgyzstan	AS	5.5	2.2	66.9	0.1	0.9	0.8
75	Ecuador	SA	14.8	11.6	56.8	0.1	0.3	0.1
76	Kuwait	AS	2.8	1.1	55.2	0.1	1.4	1.3
77	Cyprus	EU	1.1	0.7	54.1	0.1	3.5	2.1
78	Dominican Rep.	NA	9.8	4.6	53.4	0.1	0.4	0.3
79	Puerto Rico	NA	3.9	1.7	52.1	0.1	1.0	0.8
80	Bangladesh	AS	156.1	8.1	51.0	0.1	0.0	0.2
81	Jamaica	NA	2.8	1.6	50.9	0.1	1.3	0.8
82	Trin. and Tobago	NA	1.2	0.7	45.3	0.1	2.7	1.8
83	Uzbekistan	AS	27.9	8.6	42.0	0.0	0.1	0.1
84	Nepal	AS	29.0	2.0	40.3	0.0	0.1	0.5
85	Albania	EU	3.0	1.5	39.4	0.0	0.9	0.7
86	Sri Lanka	AS	21.5	2.5	39.2	0.0	0.1	0.4
87	Iraq	AS	29.7	1.3	32.9	0.0	0.1	0.6
88	Syria	AS	22.2	5.1	28.7	0.0	0.1	0.1
89	Ghana	AF	24.3	2.1	27.4	0.0	0.1	0.3
90	Ethiopia	AF	88.0	1.0	24.0	0.0	0.0	0.6
91	Jordan	AS	6.4	2.0	22.5	0.0	0.3	0.3
92	Costa Rica	NA	4.5	2.0	22.2	0.0	0.4	0.3
93	Oman	AS	3.0	1.7	22.1	0.0	0.5	0.3
94	Palestine	AS	3.8	1.5	19.4	0.0	0.4	0.3
95	Senegal	AF	12.3	2.0	18.3	0.0	0.1	0.2
96	Kenya	AF	40.0	21.3	16.5	0.0	0.0	0.0
97	Nigeria	AF	154.0	45.0	16.0	0.0	0.0	0.0
98	Paraguay	SA	6.4	1.5	16.0	0.0	0.2	0.3
99	El Salvador	NA	6.1	1.5	15.6	0.0	0.2	0.3
100	Panama	NA	3.4	1.5	14.7	0.0	0.3	0.3
101	Guatemala	NA	13.6	2.3	14.3	0.0	0.1	0.2
102	Angola	AF	13.1	3.0	13.1	0.0	0.1	0.1
103	Lebanon	AS	4.1	1.4	13.0	0.0	0.2	0.2
104	Bolivia	SA	9.9	2.0	10.9	0.0	0.1	0.1

Table A.1: MDHT Participation per Country (June 2014).

Bibliography

[ABG+05] Gagan Aggarwal, Mayank Bawa, Prasanna Ganesan, Hector Garcia-Molina, Krishnaram Kenthapadi, Rajeev Motwani, Utkarsh Srivastava, Dilys Thomas, and Ying Xu. Two can keep a secret: A distributed architecture for secure database services. In *Proceedings of CIDR*, 2005.

[AFG+10] Michael Armbrust, Armando Fox, Rean Griffith, Anthony D. Joseph, Randy Katz, Andy Konwinski, Gunho Lee, David Patterson, Ariel Rabkin, Ion Stoica, and Matei Zaharia. A view of cloud computing. *Commun. ACM*, 53(4):50–58, April 2010.

[AGH11] Dirk Achenbach, Matthias Gabel, and Matthias Huber. Mimosecco: A middleware for secure cloud storage. In Daniel D. Frey, Shuichi Fukuda, and Georg Rock, editors, *Improving Complex Systems Today*, Advanced Concurrent Engineering, pages 175–181. Springer London, 2011.

[AKSX04] Rakesh Agrawal, Jerry Kiernan, Ramakrishnan Srikant, and Yirong Xu. Order preserving encryption for numeric data. In *Proceedings of the 2004 ACM SIGMOD International Conference on Management of Data*, SIGMOD '04, pages 563–574, New York, NY, USA, 2004. ACM.

[AL08] Jordi Pujol Ahulló and Pedro García López. Planetsim: An extensible framework for overlay network and services simulations. In *Proceedings of the 1st International Conference on Simulation Tools and Techniques for Communications, Networks and Systems & Workshops*, Simutools '08, pages 45:1–45:1. ICST (Institute for Computer Sciences, Social-Informatics and Telecommunications Engineering), 2008.

[And04] David P. Anderson. Boinc: a system for public-resource computing and storage. In *Grid Computing, 2004. Proceedings. Fifth IEEE/ACM International Workshop on*, pages 4–10, Nov 2004.

[Bau08] Ingmar Baumgart. P2PNS: A Secure Distributed Name Service for P2PSIP. In *Proceedings of the 2008 Sixth Annual IEEE International Conference on Pervasive Computing and Communications*, pages 480–485, 2008.

[BBO07] Mihir Bellare, Alexandra Boldyreva, and Adam O'Neill. Deterministic and efficiently searchable encryption. In Alfred Menezes, editor, *Advances in Cryptology - CRYPTO 2007*, volume 4622 of *Lecture Notes in Computer Science*, pages 535–552. Springer Berlin Heidelberg, 2007.

[BCLO09] Alexandra Boldyreva, Nathan Chenette, Younho Lee, and Adam O'Neill. Order-preserving symmetric encryption. In Antoine Joux, editor, *Advances in Cryptology - EUROCRYPT 2009*, volume 5479 of *Lecture Notes in Computer Science*, pages 224–241. Springer Berlin Heidelberg, 2009.

[BD87] George EP Box and Norman R Draper. *Empirical model-building and response surfaces.*, page 424. John Wiley & Sons, 1987.

[BHK07] Ingmar Baumgart, Bernhard Heep, and Stephan Krause. Oversim: A flexible overlay network simulation framework. In *IEEE Global Internet Symposium, 2007*, pages 79–84, 2007.

[BL07] Andreas Binzenhöfer and Kenji Leibnitz. Estimating churn in structured p2p networks. In Lorne Mason, Tadeusz Drwiega, and James Yan, editors, *Managing Traffic Performance in Converged Networks*, volume 4516 of *Lecture Notes in Computer Science*, pages 630–641. Springer Berlin Heidelberg, 2007.

[BMR+06] Andrew Brampton, Andrew MacQuire, Idris A. Rai, Nicholas J. P. Race, and Laurent Mathy. Stealth Distributed Hash Table: a Robust and Flexible Super-Peered DHT. In *Proceedings of the 2006 ACM CoNEXT conference*, CoNEXT '06, pages 19:1–19:12, 2006.

[BQ04] Fabian E. Bustamante and Yi Qiao. Friendships that last: Peer lifespan and its role in p2p protocols. In Fred Douglis and BrianD. Davison, editors, *Web Content Caching and Distribution*, pages 233–246. Springer Netherlands, 2004.

[BS07] Andreas Binzenhöfer and Holger Schnabel. Improving the performance and robustness of kademlia-based overlay networks. In Torsten Braun, Georg Carle, and Burkhard Stiller, editors, *Kommunikation in Verteilten Systemen (KiVS)*, Informatik aktuell, pages 15–26. Springer Berlin Heidelberg, 2007.

[CDV+05] Alberto Ceselli, Ernesto Damiani, Sabrina De Capitani Di Vimercati, Sushil Jajodia, Stefano Paraboschi, and Pierangela Samarati. Modeling and assessing inference exposure in encrypted databases. *ACM Trans. Inf. Syst. Secur.*, 8(1):119–152, February 2005.

[CDVF+07] Valentina Ciriani, Sabrina De Capitani Di Vimercati, Sara Foresti, Sushil Jajodia, Stefano Paraboschi, and Pierangela Samarati. Fragmentation and encryption to enforce privacy in data storage. In *Computer Security–ESORICS 2007*, pages 171–186. Springer, 2007.

[Cha98] Surajit Chaudhuri. An overview of query optimization in relational systems. In *Proceedings of the Seventeenth ACM SIGACT-SIGMOD-SIGART Symposium on Principles of Database Systems*, PODS '98, pages 34–43, New York, NY, USA, 1998. ACM.

[Cho13] Kristina Chodorow. *MongoDB: the definitive guide*. O'Reilly Media, Inc., 2013.

[CJNP02] Jean-Sébastien Coron, Marc Joye, David Naccache, and Pascal Paillier. Universal padding schemes for rsa. In Moti Yung, editor, *Advances in Cryptology - CRYPTO 2002*, volume 2442 of *Lecture Notes in Computer Science*, pages 226–241. Springer Berlin Heidelberg, 2002.

[CKC+13] Rubén Cuevas, Michal Kryczka, Angel Cuevas, Sebastian Kaune, Carmen Guerrero, and Reza Rejaie. Unveiling the incentives for content publishing in popular bittorrent portals. *Networking, IEEE/ACM Transactions on*, 21(5):1421–1435, Oct 2013.

[CSM11] Damiano Carra, Moritz Steiner, and Pietro Michiardi. Adaptive load balancing in kad. In *Peer-to-Peer Computing (P2P), 2011 IEEE International Conference on*, pages 92–101. IEEE, 2011.

[CVF+09] Valentina Ciriani, Sabrina De Capitani di Vimercati, Sara Foresti, Sushil Jajodia, Stefano Paraboschi, and Pierangela Samarati. Fragmentation design for efficient query execution over sensitive distributed databases. In *Proceedings of the 2009 29th IEEE International Conference on Distributed Computing Systems*, ICDCS '09, pages 32–39, Washington, DC, USA, 2009. IEEE Computer Society.

[CVF+10] Valentina Ciriani, Sabrina De Capitani Di Vimercati, Sara Foresti, Sushil Jajodia, Stefano Paraboschi, and Pierangela Samarati. Combining fragmentation and encryption to protect privacy in data storage. *ACM Transactions on Information and System Security (TISSEC)*, 13(3):22:1–22:33, July 2010.

[CW07] Scott A. Crosby and Dan S. Wallach. An analysis of bittorrent's two kademlia-based dhts. Technical report, Technical Report TR07-04, Rice University, 2007.

[DCdVFJ+13] S. De Capitani di Vimercati, S. Foresti, S. Jajodia, S. Paraboschi, and P. Samarati. On information leakage by indexes over data fragments. In *Data Engineering Workshops (ICDEW), 2013 IEEE 29th International Conference on*, pages 94–98, April 2013.

[DH06] Jochen Dinger and Hannes Hartenstein. Defending the sybil attack in p2p networks: taxonomy, challenges, and a proposal for self-registration. In *Availability, Reliability and Security, 2006. ARES 2006. The First International Conference on*, pages 756–763, April 2006.

[DHJ+07] Giuseppe DeCandia, Deniz Hastorun, Madan Jampani, Gunavardhan Kakulapati, Avinash Lakshman, Alex Pilchin, Swaminathan Sivasubramanian, Peter Vosshall, and Werner Vogels. Dynamo: Amazon's highly available key-value store. In *Proceedings of Twenty-first ACM SIGOPS Symposium on Operating Systems Principles*, SOSP '07, pages 205–220, New York, NY, USA, 2007. ACM.

[DJWC08] Jochen Dinger, Konrad Jünemann, Oliver Waldhorst, and Michael Conrad. Autonome kommunikationsinfrastrukturen. eine praxisnahe betrachtung. *PIK-Praxis der Informationsverarbeitung und Kommunikation*, 31(2):69–75, 2008.

[DKK+01] Frank Dabek, M. Frans Kaashoek, David Karger, Robert Morris, and Ion Stoica. Wide-area cooperative storage with CFS. In *ACM SIGOPS Operating Systems Review*, volume 35, pages 202–215, 2001.

[DVJ+03] Ernesto Damiani, S. De Capitani Vimercati, Sushil Jajodia, Stefano Paraboschi, and Pierangela Samarati. Balancing confidentiality and efficiency in untrusted relational dbmss. In *Proceedings of the 10th ACM Conference on Computer and Communications Security*, CCS '03, pages 93–102, New York, NY, USA, 2003. ACM.

[DW09] Jochen Dinger and Oliver P. Waldhorst. Decentralized bootstrapping of p2p systems: A practical view. In Luigi Fratta, Henning Schulzrinne, Yutaka Takahashi, and Otto Spaniol, editors, *NETWORKING 2009*, volume 5550 of *Lecture Notes in Computer Science*, pages 703–715. Springer Berlin Heidelberg, 2009.

[FFM04] Michael J. Freedman, Eric Freudenthal, and David Mazières. Democratizing content publication with coral. In *Proc. of the 1st conf. on Symposium on Networked System Design and Impl. - Volume 1*, pages 18–18, 2004.

[FGK03] S. Frankel, R. Glenn, and S. Kelly. RFC3602 - The AES-CBC Cipher Algorithm and Its Use with IPsec. http://tools.ietf.org/html/rfc3602, September 2003.

[FLRS05] Michael J. Freedman, Karthik Lakshminarayanan, Sean Rhea, and Ion Stoica. Non-transitive connectivity and dhts. In *Proceedings of the 2Nd Conference on Real, Large Distributed Systems - Volume 2*, WORLDS'05, pages 55–60, Berkeley, CA, USA, 2005. USENIX Association.

[For10] Sara Foresti. *Preserving privacy in data outsourcing*, volume 99. Springer, 2010.

[FPJ+07] Jarret Falkner, Michael Piatek, John P. John, Arvind Krishnamurthy, and Thomas Anderson. Profiling a Million User DHT. In *Proc. of the 7th ACM SIGCOMM conference on Internet measurement*, IMC '07, pages 129–134, 2007.

[Fre10] Michael J. Freedman. Experiences with coralcdn: A five-year operational view. In *NSDI*, pages 95–110, 2010.

[FSK05] Bryan Ford, Pyda Srisuresh, and Dan Kegel. Peer-to-Peer Communication Across Network Address Translators. In *Proceedings of the Annual Conference on USENIX Annual Technical Conference*, pages 13–13, 2005.

[FSK14] Jason Farina, Mark Scanlon, and M-Tahar Kechadi. Bittorrent sync: First impressions and digital forensic implications. *Digital Investigation*, 11, Supplement 1(0):S77 – S86, 2014. Proceedings of the First Annual (DFRWS) Europe.

[GCX+05] Lei Guo, Songqing Chen, Zhen Xiao, Enhua Tan, Xiaoning Ding, and Xiaodong Zhang. Measurements, analysis, and modeling of bittorrent-like systems. In *Proceedings of the 5th ACM SIGCOMM Conference on Internet Measurement*, IMC '05, pages 4–4, Berkeley, CA, USA, 2005. USENIX Association.

[GH14] Matthias Gabel and Gerald Hübsch. Secure database outsourcing to the cloud using the mimosecco middleware. In Helmut Krcmar, Ralf Reussner, and Bernhard Rumpe, editors, *Trusted Cloud Computing*, pages 187–202. Springer International Publishing, 2014.

[GM84] Shafi Goldwasser and Silvio Micali. Probabilistic encryption. *Journal of Computer and System Sciences*, 28(2):270 – 299, 1984.

[GMR+12] Nelson Gonzalez, Charles Miers, Fernando Redígolo, Marcos Simplício, Tereza Carvalho, Mats Näslund, and Makan Pourzandi. A quantitative analysis of current security concerns and solutions for cloud computing. *Journal of Cloud Computing*, 1(1), 2012.

[GO14] Inc. Gurobi Optimization. Gurobi optimizer reference manual, 2014.

[Gon01] Li Gong. Jxta: a network programming environment. *Internet Computing, IEEE*, 5(3):88–95, May 2001.

[GTF+11] Vignesh Ganapathy, Dilys Thomas, Tomas Feder, Hector Garcia-Molina, and Rajeev Motwani. Distributing data for secure database services. In *Proceedings of the 4th International Workshop on Privacy and Anonymity in the Information Society*, PAIS '11, pages 8:1–8:10, New York, NY, USA, 2011. ACM.

[HBH07] Dieter Hildebrandt, Ludger Bischofs, and Wilhelm Hasselbring. Realpeer–a framework for simulation-based development of peer-to-peer systems. In *Parallel, Distributed and Network-Based Processing, 2007. PDP '07. 15th EUROMICRO International Conference on*, pages 490–497, 2007.

[HGSB13] Matthias Huber, Matthias Gabel, Marco Schulze, and Alexander Bieber. Cumulus4j: A provably secure database abstraction layer. In Alfredo Cuzzocrea, Christian Kittl, Dimitris E. Simos, Edgar Weippl, and Lida Xu, editors, *Security Engineering and Intelligence Informatics*, volume 8128 of *Lecture Notes in Computer Science*, pages 180–193. Springer Berlin Heidelberg, 2013.

[HHK+10] Christian Henrich, Matthias Huber, Carmen Kempka, Jörn Müller-Quade, and Ralf Reussner. Technical report: Secure cloud computing through a separation of duties, 2010.

[HILM02] Hakan Hacıgümüş, Bala Iyer, Chen Li, and Sharad Mehrotra. Executing SQL over Encrypted Data in the Database-Service-Provider Model. In *Proc. of SIGMOD*, 2002.

[HIM04] Hakan Hacıgümüş, Bala Iyer, and Sharad Mehrotra. Efficient execution of aggregation queries over encrypted relational databases. In *Database Systems for Advanced Applications*, pages 125–136. Springer, 2004.

[HM10] Terry Halpin and Tony Morgan. *Information modeling and relational databases.* Morgan Kaufmann, 2010.

[HMCK12] Bijit Hore, Sharad Mehrotra, Mustafa Canim, and Murat Kantarcioglu. Secure multidimensional range queries over outsourced data. *The VLDB Journal*, 21(3):333–358, June 2012.

[IUKB+04] Mikel Izal, Guillaume Urvoy-Keller, Ernst W Biersack, Pascal A Felber, Anwar Al Hamra, and Luis Garces-Erice. Dissecting bittorrent: Five months in a torrent's lifetime. In Chadi Barakat and Ian Pratt, editors, *Passive and Active Network Measurement*, volume 3015 of *Lecture Notes in Computer Science*, pages 1–11. Springer Berlin Heidelberg, 2004.

[JADH10] Konrad Jünemann, Philipp Andelfinger, Jochen Dinger, and Hannes Hartenstein. Bitmon: A tool for automated monitoring of the bittorrent dht. In *Peer-to-Peer Computing (P2P), 2010 IEEE Tenth International Conference on*, pages 1–2, Aug 2010.

[JAH11] Konrad Jünemann, Philipp Andelfinger, and Hannes Hartenstein. Towards a basic dht service: Analyzing network characteristics of a widely deployed dht. In *Computer Communications and Networks (ICCCN), 2011 Proceedings of 20th International Conference on*, pages 1–7, July 2011.

[Jai91] Raj K. Jain. *The Art of Computer Systems Performance Analysis: Techniques for Experimental Design, Measurement, Simulation, and Modeling*. Wiley, 1991.

[JH14] Konrad Jünemann and Hannes Hartenstein. Self-optimization of dht lookups through run-time performance analysis. In *High Performance Computing & Simulation (HPCS), 2014 International Conference on*, pages 407–415, July 2014.

[JKH12] Konrad Jünemann, Jens Köhler, and Hannes Hartenstein. Data outsourcing simplified: Generating data connectors from confidentiality and access policies. In *Cluster, Cloud and Grid Computing (CCGrid), 2012 12th IEEE/ACM International Symposium on*, pages 923–930, May 2012.

[JOK09] Raúl Jiménez, Flutra Osmani, and Björn Knutsson. Connectivity Properties of Mainline BitTorrent DHT nodes. In *IEEE Ninth International Conf. on Peer-to-Peer Computing, (P2P '09)*, pages 262–270, 2009.

[JOK11] Raúl Jiménez, Flutra Osmani, and Björn Knutsson. Sub-Second lookups on a Large-Scale Kademlia-Based overlay. In *11th IEEE International Conf. on Peer-to-Peer Computing 2011 (P2P'11)*, Kyoto, Japan, 2011.

[JWHL13] Konrad Jünemann, Andreas Wagner, Andreas Harth, and Michael Langhammer. iZEUS AP 530: Basisdienste. Arbeitspaketbericht, Projekt iZEUS, September 2013.

[KJ14] Jens Köhler and Konrad Jünemann. Securus: From confidentiality and access requirements to data outsourcing solutions. In Marit Hansen, Jaap-Henk Hoepman, Ronald Leenes, and Diane Whitehouse, editors, *Privacy and Identity Management for Emerging Services and Technologies*, volume 421 of *IFIP Advances in Information and Communication Technology*, pages 139–149. Springer Berlin Heidelberg, 2014.

[KJH14] Jens Köhler, Konrad Jünemann, and Hannes Hartenstein. Securus: Composition of confidentiality preserving indexing approaches for secure database-as-a-service. *PIK-Praxis der Informationsverarbeitung und Kommunikation*, 37(2):149–155, 2014.

[KL06] Jonathan Katz and Yehuda Lindell. *Introduction to modern cryptography: principles and protocols*. CRC Press, 2006.

[KLKP08] Sebastian Kaune, Tobias Lauinger, Aleksandra Kovacevic, and Konstantin Pussep. Embracing the peer next door: Proximity in kademlia. In *Peer-to-Peer Computing, 2008. P2P'08. Eighth International Conference on*, pages 343–350. IEEE, 2008.

[KN10] Gunnar Kreitz and Fredrik Niemelä. Spotify–large scale, low latency, p2p music-on-demand streaming. In *Peer-to-Peer Computing (P2P), 2010 IEEE Tenth International Conference on*, pages 1–10. IEEE, 2010.

[KPR12] Seny Kamara, Charalampos Papamanthou, and Tom Roeder. Dynamic searchable symmetric encryption. In *Proceedings of the 2012 ACM Conference on Computer and Communications Security*, CCS '12, pages 965–976, New York, NY, USA, 2012. ACM.

[KV08] Florian Kerschbaum and Julien Vayssière. Privacy-preserving data analytics as an outsourced service. In *Proceedings of the 2008 ACM Workshop on Secure Web Services*, SWS '08, pages 87–96, New York, NY, USA, 2008. ACM.

[LF03] Alexander Linden and Jackie Fenn. Understanding gartner's hype cycles. *Strategic Analysis Report Nº R-20-1971. Gartner, Inc*, 2003.

[LG08] John DC Little and Stephen C Graves. Little's law. In *Building Intuition*, pages 81–100. Springer, 2008.

[LM10] Avinash Lakshman and Prashant Malik. Cassandra: a decentralized structured storage system. *ACM SIGOPS Operating Systems Review*, 44(2):35–40, 2010.

[LO05] Jun Li and Edward R. Omiecinski. Efficiency and security trade-off in supporting range queries on encrypted databases. In Sushil Jajodia and Duminda Wijesekera, editors, *Data and Applications Security XIX*, volume 3654 of *Lecture Notes in Computer Science*, pages 69–83. Springer Berlin Heidelberg, 2005.

[Loe08] Andrew Loewenstern. BitTorrent Enhancement Proposal (BEP5): DHT Protocol. http://www.bittorrent.org/beps/bep_0005.html, 2008. last retrieved in August 2014.

[LSM+05] Jinyang Li, Jeremy Stribling, Robert Morris, M Frans Kaashoek, and Thomer M Gil. A performance vs. cost framework for evaluating dht design tradeoffs under churn. In *INFOCOM 2005. 24th Annual Joint Conference of the IEEE Computer and Communications Societies. Proceedings IEEE*, volume 1, pages 225–236. IEEE, 2005.

[LWZ+12] Bingshuang Liu, Tao Wei, Jianyu Zhang, Jun Li, Wei Zou, and Mo Zhou. Revisiting why kad lookup fails. In *Peer-to-Peer Computing (P2P), 2012 IEEE 12th International Conference on*, pages 37–42, Sept 2012.

[MCPCLG13] Adan G. Medrano-Chavez, Elizabeth Perez-Cortes, and Miguel Lopez-Guerrero. On the effect of peer online times on the lookup service of chord and kademlia p2p systems. In *Communications (LATINCOM), 2013 IEEE Latin-America Conference on*, pages 1–6, Nov 2013.

[MJ09] Alberto Montresor and Márk Jelasity. Peersim: A scalable p2p simulator. In *Peer-to-Peer Computing, 2009. P2P '09. IEEE Ninth International Conference on*, pages 99–100, 2009.

[MKBA+09] Harsha V. Madhyastha, Ethan Katz-Bassett, Thomas E. Anderson, Arvind Krishnamurthy, and Arun Venkataramani. iplane nano: Path prediction for peer-to-peer applications. In *Proceedings of USENIX NSDI*, volume 9, pages 137–152, 2009.

[MKGV07] Ashwin Machanavajjhala, Daniel Kifer, Johannes Gehrke, and Muthuramakrishnan Venkitasubramaniam. L-diversity: Privacy beyond k-anonymity. *ACM Transactions on Knowledge Discovery from Data (TKDD)*, 1(1), March 2007.

[MM02] Petar Maymounkov and David Mazières. Kademlia: A Peer-to-Peer Information System Based on the XOR Metric. In *P2P Systems*, pages 53–65, 2002.

[MPP05] Amihai Motro and Francesco Parisi-Presicce. Blind custodians: A database service architecture that supports privacy without encryption. In *Data and Applications Security XIX*, pages 338–352. Springer, 2005.

[MRGS09] Ghulam Memon, Reza Rejaie, Yang Guo, and Daniel Stutzbach. Large-scale monitoring of dht traffic. In *IPTPS*, volume 9, pages 1–11, 2009.

[MRGS12] Ghulam Memon, Reza Rejaie, Yang Guo, and Daniel Stutzbach. Montra: A large-scale dht traffic monitor. *Computer Networks*, 56(3):1080–1091, 2012.

[MT06] Einar Mykletun and Gene Tsudik. Aggregation queries in the database-as-a-service model. *Data and Applications Security XX*, pages 89–103, 2006.

[NLB+07] Stephen Naicken, Barnaby Livingston, Anirban Basu, Sethalat Rodhetbhai, Ian Wakeman, and Dan Chalmers. The state of peer-to-peer simulators and simulations. *SIGCOMM Comput. Commun. Rev.*, 37(2), March 2007.

[Nor14a] Arvid Norberg. BitTorrent DHT Security Extension, Version 1.0.0, Januar 2014. http://www.bittorrent.org/beps/bep_0042.html, 2014. last retrieved in August 2014.

[Nor14b] Arvid Norberg. Email: "DHT Implementation in uTorrent" - Publication Permission, personal communication, July 3, 2014.

[Nor14c] Arvid Norberg. Email: "DHT Implementation in uTorrent", personal communication, June 27, 2014.

[Nor14d] Arvid Norberg. Email: "Peers in Mainline DHT increases by 15 millions in 7 days - reasons?" – Part 1, personal communication, May 19, 2014.

[Nor14e] Arvid Norberg. Email: "Peers in Mainline DHT increases by 15 millions in 7 days - reasons?" – Part 2, personal communication, May 24, 2014.

[NRZ+07] Giovanni Neglia, Giuseppe Reina, Honggang Zhang, Donald F Towsley, Arun Venkataramani, and John S Danaher. Availability in bittorrent systems. In *INFOCOM 2007. 26th IEEE International Conference on Computer Communications. IEEE*, pages 2216–2224, May 2007.

[OGJK12] Flutra Osmani, Victor Grishchenko, Raul Jiménez, and Björn Knutsson. Swift: The missing link between peer-to-peer and information-centric networks. In *Proceedings of the First Workshop on P2P and Dependability*, P2P-Dep '12, pages 4:1–4:6, New York, NY, USA, 2012. ACM.

[OHKY10] Zhonghong Ou, Erkki Harjula, Otso Kassinen, and Mika Ylianttila. Performance evaluation of a Kademlia-based communication-oriented P2P system under churn. *Computer Networks*, 54(5):689–705, 2010.

[OU98] Tatsuaki Okamoto and Shigenori Uchiyama. A new public-key cryptosystem as secure as factoring. In Kaisa Nyberg, editor, *Advances in Cryptology – EUROCRYPT'98*, volume 1403 of *Lecture Notes in Computer Science*, pages 308–318. Springer Berlin Heidelberg, 1998.

[Pai99] Pascal Paillier. Public-key cryptosystems based on composite degree residuosity classes. In Jacques Stern, editor, *Advances in Cryptology - EUROCRYPT '99*, volume 1592 of *Lecture Notes in Computer Science*, pages 223–238. Springer Berlin Heidelberg, 1999.

[PGES05] Johan Pouwelse, PaweThl Garbacki, Dick Epema, and Henk Sips. The bittorrent p2p file-sharing system: Measurements and analysis. In *Peer-to-Peer Systems IV*, pages 205–216. Springer, 2005.

[Pre94] Bart Preneel. Cryptographic hash functions. *European Transactions on Telecommunications*, 5(4):431–448, 1994.

[PRZB11] Raluca Ada Popa, Catherine M. S. Redfield, Nickolai Zeldovich, and Hari Balakrishnan. Cryptdb: Protecting confidentiality with encrypted query processing. In *Proceedings of the Twenty-Third ACM Symposium on Operating Systems Principles*, SOSP '11, pages 85–100, New York, NY, USA, 2011. ACM.

[PZB11] Raluca Ada Popa, Nickolai Zeldovich, and Hari Balakrishnan. Cryptdb: A practical encrypted relational dbms. Technical report, MIT, 2011.

[RAD78] Ronald L Rivest, Len Adleman, and Michael L Dertouzos. On data banks and privacy homomorphisms. *Foundations of secure computation*, 4(11):169–180, 1978.

[RD01a] Antony Rowstron and Peter Druschel. Pastry: Scalable, decentralized object location, and routing for large-scale peer-to-peer systems. In *Middleware 2001*, pages 329–350. Springer, 2001.

[RD01b] Antony Rowstron and Peter Druschel. Storage management and caching in PAST, a large-scale, persistent peer-to-peer storage utility. In *ACM SIGOPS Operating Systems Review*, volume 35, pages 188–201, 2001.

[RFH+01] Sylvia Ratnasamy, Paul Francis, Mark Handley, Richard Karp, and Scott Shenker. *A scalable content-addressable network*, volume 31. ACM, 2001.

[RGK+05] Sean Rhea, Brighten Godfrey, Brad Karp, John Kubiatowicz, Sylvia Ratnasamy, Scott Shenker, Ion Stoica, and Harlan Yu. OpenDHT: a Public DHT Service and its Uses. In *Proceedings of the 2005 conference on Applications, technologies, architectures, and protocols for computer communications*, SIGCOMM '05, pages 73–84, 2005.

[RGRK04] Sean Rhea, Dennis Geels, Timothy Roscoe, and John Kubiatowicz. Handling churn in a dht. In *Proceedings of the USENIX Annual Technical Conference*, pages 127–140. Boston, MA, USA, 2004.

[RSKM09] Jedrzej Rybicki, Björn Scheuermann, Markus Koegel, and Martin Mauve. PeerTIS: a peer-to-peer traffic information system. In *Proc. of the 6th ACM intern. work. on Vehicular InterNETworking*, VANET '09, pages 23–32, 2009.

[RSS13] Stefanie Roos, Hani Salah, and Thorsten Strufe. Comprehending kademlia routing - a theoretical framework for the hop count distribution. Technical report, TU Darmstadt, 2013.

[RWHM03] J. Rosenberg, J. Weinberger, C. Huitema, and R. Mahy. RFC3489 - STUN - Simple Traversal of User Datagram Protocol (UDP) Through

Network Address Translators (NATs). http://tools.ietf.org/html/rfc3489, March 2003.

[SB08] Moritz Steiner and Ernst W. Biersack. Crawling azureus. *Institut Eurecom, France, Tech. Rep. EURECOM*, 2495(06), 2008.

[SBEN07] Moritz Steiner, Ernst W. Biersack, and Taoufik En-Najjary. Actively monitoring peers in kad. In *IPTPS*, volume 7, pages 26–27, 2007.

[SCB10] Moritz Steiner, Damiano Carra, and Ernst W. Biersack. Evaluating and improving the content access in kad. *Peer-to-peer networking and applications*, 3(2):115–128, 2010.

[SENB07] Moritz Steiner, Taoufik En-Najjary, and Ernst W. Biersack. A Global View of KAD. In *IMC '07: Proceedings of the 7th ACM SIGCOMM conference on Internet measurement*, pages 117–122, 2007.

[SENB09] Moritz Steiner, Taoufik En-Najjary, and Ernst W. Biersack. Long Term Study of Peer Behavior in the KAD DHT. *IEEE/ACM Transactions on Networking*, 17(5):1371–1384, 2009.

[SLG+09] Guangyu Shi, Youshui Long, Hao Gong, Changqing Wan, Chuanliang Yu, Xianqing Yang, Hongli Zhang, and Yunfei Zhang. Hifip2p: The simulator capable of massive nodes and measured underlay. In *Parallel, Distributed and Network-based Processing, 2009 17th Euromicro International Conference on*, 2009.

[SMK+01] Ion Stoica, Robert Morris, David Karger, M. Frans Kaashoek, and Hari Balakrishnan. Chord: A scalable peer-to-peer lookup service for internet applications. In *Proceedings of the 2001 Conference on Applications, Technologies, Architectures, and Protocols for Computer Communications*, SIGCOMM '01, pages 149–160, New York, NY, USA, 2001. ACM.

[SR05a] Daniel Stutzbach and Reza Rejaie. Capturing accurate snapshots of the gnutella network. In *INFOCOM 2005. 24th Annual Joint Conference of the IEEE Computer and Communications Societies. Proceedings IEEE*, volume 4, pages 2825–2830 vol. 4, March 2005.

[SR05b] Daniel Stutzbach and Reza Rejaie. Characterizing churn in peer-to-peer networks. *University of Oregon, Eugene, OR, Tech. Rep. CIS-TR-2005-03*, 2005.

[SR06a] Daniel Stutzbach and Reza Rejaie. Improving Lookup Performance Over a Widely-Deployed DHT. In *Proc. of the 25th IEEE International Conf. on Computer Communications (INFOCOM 2006).*, pages 1–12, 2006.

[SR06b] Daniel Stutzbach and Reza Rejaie. Understanding Churn in Peer-to-Peer Networks. In *Proceedings of the 6th ACM SIGCOMM conference on Internet measurement*, IMC '06, pages 189–202, 2006.

[SS13] Hani Salah and Thorsten Strufe. Capturing connectivity graphs of a large-scale p2p overlay network. In *Distributed Computing Systems Workshops (ICDCSW), 2013 IEEE 33rd International Conference on*, pages 172–177, July 2013.

[Sue02] Steve Suehring. *Mysql bible*. John Wiley & Sons, Inc., 2002.

[SW04] Subhabrata Sen and Jia Wang. Analyzing peer-to-peer traffic across large networks. *IEEE/ACM Trans. Netw.*, 12(2), April 2004.

[Swe02] Latanya Sweeney. k-anonymity: A model for protecting privacy. *International Journal of Uncertainty, Fuzziness and Knowledge-Based Systems*, 10(05):557–570, 2002.

[SWP00] Dawn Xiaoding Song, David Wagner, and Adrian Perrig. Practical techniques for searches on encrypted data. In *Security and Privacy, 2000. S P 2000. Proceedings. 2000 IEEE Symposium on*, pages 44–55, 2000.

[SZFY12] Majing Su, Hongli Zhang, Binxing Fang, and Ning Yan. A measurement study on swarm evolution of bittorrent. In *Cyber-Enabled Distributed Computing and Knowledge Discovery (CyberC), 2012 International Conference on*, pages 512–518, Oct 2012.

[TVS07] Andrew Tanenbaum and Maarten Van Steen. *Distributed systems*. Pearson Prentice Hall, 2007.

[WCZJ04] Wenjie Wang, Hyunseok Chang, A. Zeitoun, and S. Jamin. Characterizing Guarded Hosts in Peer-to-Peer File Sharing Systems. In *Global Telecommunications Conference. GLOBECOM '04*, volume 3, pages 1539–1543, 2004.

[WDH+10] Di Wu, Prithula Dhungel, Xiaojun Hei, Chao Zhang, and Keith W. Ross. Understanding peer exchange in bittorrent systems. In *Peer-to-Peer Computing (P2P), 2010 IEEE Tenth International Conference on*, pages 1–8, Aug 2010.

[Whi09] Tom White. *Hadoop: the definitive guide: the definitive guide*. O'Reilly Media, Inc., 2009.

[WJL+12] Andreas Wagner, Konrad Jünemann, Michael Langhammer, Jörg Henß, Steffen Stadtmüller, and Andreas Harth. iZEUS AP 520: Plattformkonzept E-Mobility Dienste. Arbeitspaketbericht, Projekt iZEUS, Oktober 2012.

[WK13] Liang Wang and Jussi Kangasharju. Measuring large-scale distributed systems: Case of bittorrent mainline dht. In *Peer-to-Peer Computing (P2P), 2013 IEEE 13th International Conference on*, 2013.

[WTN06] Di Wu, Ye Tian, and Kam-Wing Ng. Analytical study on improving dht lookup performance under churn. In *Peer-to-Peer Computing, 2006. P2P 2006. Sixth IEEE International Conference on*, pages 249–258, Sept 2006.

[www14a] Hazelcast Project Website. http://hazelcast.com, 2014. last visited in October 2014.

[www14b] Maidsafe Project Website. http://maidsafe.net/, 2014. last visited in October 2014.

[www14c] OpenChord Project Website. http://sourceforge.net/projects/open-chord/, 2014. last visited in October 2014.

[XGS11] Li Xiong, Slawomir Goryczka, and Vaidy Sunderam. Adaptive, secure, and scalable distributed data outsourcing: a vision paper. In *Proc. of 3DAPAS*, 2011.

[YLX+11] Jie Yu, Liming Lu, Peng Xiao, Zhoujun Li, and Yuan Zhou. Monitoring, analyzing and characterizing lookup traffic in a large-scale dht. *Computer Communications*, 34(13):1622–1629, 2011.

[YN11] Masahiro Yoshida and Akihiro Nakao. Measuring bittorrent swarms beyond reach. In *Peer-to-Peer Computing (P2P), 2011 IEEE International Conference on*, pages 220–229, Aug 2011.

[ZCBP11] Niels Zeilemaker, Mihai Capotă, Arno Bakker, and Johan Pouwelse. Tribler: P2p media search and sharing. In *Proceedings of the 19th ACM International Conference on Multimedia*, MM '11, pages 739–742, New York, NY, USA, 2011. ACM.

[ZCY09] Dengyi Zhang, Xuhui Chen, and Hongyun Yang. State of the art and challenges on peer-to-peer simulators. In *Wireless Communications, Networking and Mobile Computing, 2009. WiCom '09. 5th International Conf. on*, 2009.

[ZDWR11] Chao Zhang, Prithula Dhungel, Di Wu, and Keith W. Ross. Unraveling the bittorrent ecosystem. *Parallel and Distributed Systems, IEEE Transactions on*, 22(7):1164–1177, July 2011.

[ZHS+04] Ben Y Zhao, Ling Huang, Jeremy Stribling, Sean C Rhea, Anthony D Joseph, and John D Kubiatowicz. Tapestry: A resilient global-scale overlay for service deployment. *Selected Areas in Communications, IEEE Journal on*, 22(1):41–53, 2004.

[ZIP+10] Boxun Zhang, Alexandru Iosup, Johan Pouwelse, Dick Epema, and Henk Sips. Sampling bias in bittorrent measurements. In Pasqua D'Ambra, Mario Guarracino, and Domenico Talia, editors, *Euro-Par 2010 - Parallel Processing*, volume 6271 of *Lecture Notes in Computer Science*, pages 484–496. Springer Berlin Heidelberg, 2010.

[ZWXY13] Hao Zhang, Yonggang Wen, Haiyong Xie, and Nenghai Yu. *DHT Platforms*, pages 23–38. SpringerBriefs in Computer Science. Springer New York, 2013.